Betty Crocker's
Step-by-Step Cookbook

Prentice Hall Press

New York   London   Toronto   Sydney   Tokyo

Published by Prentice Hall Press
A Division of Simon & Schuster, Inc.
Gulf + Western Building
One Gulf + Western Plaza
New York, NY 10023

PRENTICE HALL PRESS and colophons are registered
trademarks of Simon & Schuster, Inc.

Betty Crocker is a registered trademark of
General Mills, Inc.

Library of Congress Cataloging-in-Publication Data

Crocker, Betty
    Betty Crocker's Step-by-step cookbook.—1st ed.
       p.   cm.
    Includes index.
    ISBN 0-13-074345-3 : $14.95
    1. Cookery.   I. Title.   II. Title: Step-by-step cookbook.
      III. Title: Step-by-step cookbook.
    [TX715.C9225 1988]   88-17890
    641.5—dc 19   CIP

Manufactured in the United States of America

10 9 8 7 6 5 4 3 2

Contents

Foreword

This collection of blue-ribbon recipes was selected from the Betty Crocker Step-by-Step Recipe Cards to bring you a happy mix of traditional and contemporary cooking. It's as old-fashioned as stuffed cabbage and as up-to-date as stir-frying. Given well over 1,000 recipes to choose from, we were able to hand-pick the very best — main dishes, sandwiches and soups, vegetables and salads, breads, desserts, appetizers and beverages. We included recipes with an international touch for variety, do-ahead and freezer fare for convenience and a host of party-time favorites for entertaining.

The hundreds of step-by-step and how-to photographs will help to streamline your time and effort in the kitchen — very little is left to chance. Preparation, cooking and baking techniques are clearly demonstrated. You'll <u>see</u> the difference between rigatoni and mostaccioli. You'll <u>see</u> how to bone a chicken breast. You'll <u>see</u> how to test a cake for doneness. For extra help, pointers on selecting meats and vegetables, special ingredient tips, shopping advice and time-saving hints are found throughout the book.

All of the recipes have been carefully updated, and each has the Betty Crocker "difference" — the assurance of success that comes from thorough testing in the Betty Crocker Kitchens.

Betty Crocker

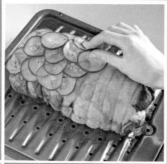

Meats

Make crosswise cuts ⅜ inch apart in each potato.

Place potatoes on rack in the roasting pan with beef.

Beef and Butter-Fan Potatoes

4½- to 5-pound high-quality beef rolled rump roast
½ teaspoon salt
⅛ teaspoon pepper
6 medium baking potatoes
3 tablespoons butter or margarine, melted
½ teaspoon seasoned salt
2 tablespoons fine dry bread crumbs
Paprika

Place beef rump roast fat side up on rack in shallow roasting pan. Sprinkle with salt and pepper. Insert meat thermometer so tip is in center of thickest part of beef and does not rest in fat. Roast uncovered in 325° oven until meat thermometer registers 150 to 170°, 2 to 2½ hours (see note).

About 2 hours before roast is done, pare potatoes. Make crosswise cuts ⅜ inch apart in each potato to within ½ inch of bottom. Heat 1 inch salted water (½ teaspoon salt to 1 cup water) to boiling. Add potatoes. Cover and heat to boiling; boil 10 minutes. Drain and cool slightly.

Brush each potato with butter, separating cuts slightly to resemble fan. Sprinkle with seasoned salt and bread crumbs. Place on rack with meat. Roast until potatoes are tender and golden, about 1½ hours. Sprinkle with paprika. Serve with beef juices. 6 SERVINGS—with beef for leftovers.

Note: Roasts are easier to carve if allowed to "set" 15 to 20 minutes after removing from oven. Since beef continues to cook after removal from oven, it should be removed when the meat thermometer registers 5° lower than the desired temperature.

Peppered Beef Flambé

3- to 3½-pound beef rolled rump or eye of
   round roast
1 tablespoon black peppercorns, cracked
   Watercress or parsley
   Tomato wedges
¼ cup Cognac
   Rye bread, sliced
   Horseradish Butter, Lemon Butter or
   Sesame Butter (below)

Heat oven to 325°. Roll beef roast in cracked pepper; press pepper into beef with heels of hands. Place beef on rack in shallow roasting pan. Insert meat thermometer in thickest part of beef. Roast uncovered to desired doneness, 150 to 170°, 25 to 30 minutes per pound.

Remove beef from oven. Garnish with watercress and tomato wedges. Heat Cognac in small saucepan just until warm. Ignite and pour flaming Cognac on beef. Slice and serve with rye bread and choice of butters.   12 TO 16 SERVINGS.

HORSERADISH BUTTER
Beat ½ cup butter or margarine, softened, and 2 to 3 tablespoons prepared horseradish.

LEMON BUTTER
Beat ½ cup butter or margarine, softened, ¼ cup snipped parsley, ½ teaspoon finely grated lemon peel and 1 teaspoon lemon juice.

SESAME BUTTER
Beat ½ cup butter or margarine, softened, 3 tablespoons toasted sesame seed and dash of red pepper sauce.

Place peppercorns in plastic bag and hit them with a mallet until coarsely cracked.

Roll beef roast in cracked pepper, then press pepper into beef with heels of hands.

Do-Ahead Boeuf en Gelée

Chill gelatin mixture quickly by placing in ice and water.

Brush small amount of the glaze on beef to coat surface.

Arrange the cherry tomatoes and snipped chives on beef.

Cut glaze into small squares and serve with beef slices.

4- to 4½-pound beef boneless chuck eye or
    rolled rump roast
1½ teaspoons salt
½ teaspoon pepper
1 envelope unflavored gelatin
2 tablespoons cold water
1 can (10½ ounces) condensed consommé
¾ cup dry red wine
    Cherry tomato halves
    Snipped chives or parsley

Heat oven to 350°. Trim excess fat from beef roast; wipe beef with damp cloth. Rub beef with salt and pepper; place on rack in shallow roasting pan. Place meat thermometer in thickest part of beef. Roast to desired doneness (140° for rare, 160° for medium), about 2 hours. Refrigerate about 6 hours.

■20 to 24 hours before serving, soften gelatin in water in saucepan; stir in consommé. Cook over low heat, stirring constantly, until gelatin is dissolved. Remove from heat; stir in wine. Place pan in bowl of ice and water; stir until mixture begins to thicken. Brush small amount of glaze on beef to coat entire surface; refrigerate until glaze is set, about 10 minutes.

Repeat 4 or 5 times with remaining glaze. (If glaze becomes too thick, heat over low heat.) Before pouring on final coat of glaze, dip cherry tomatoes in glaze; arrange tomatoes and chives on beef as pictured. Pour remaining glaze into loaf pan, 9x5x3 inches. Cover and refrigerate glaze and beef up to 24 hours.

■10 minutes before serving, cut beef into very thin slices. Cut glaze into small squares and serve with beef.
10 TO 12 SERVINGS.

Herbed Pot Roast

4- to 5-pound beef chuck pot roast
1 teaspoon salt
1 teaspoon dried basil leaves
½ teaspoon dried thyme leaves
¼ teaspoon pepper
1 clove garlic, finely chopped
½ cup water
3 medium carrots, cut diagonally into 1-inch
   slices (about 1½ cups)
½ pound small onions
1 package (9 ounces) frozen whole green
   beans

Trim excess fat from beef pot roast. Rub Dutch oven with
fat cut from beef; brown beef over medium heat. Sprinkle
with salt, basil, thyme, pepper and garlic; add water. Heat
to boiling; reduce heat. Cover and simmer 1½ hours.

Add carrots and onions. Rinse frozen beans under running
cold water to separate; place in Dutch oven. If necessary,
add small amount water. Heat to boiling; reduce heat.
Cover and simmer until beef and vegetables are tender, 30
to 40 minutes.   4 TO 6 SERVINGS—with beef for leftovers.

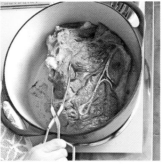
Brown the beef pot roast on
both sides in a Dutch oven.

Add carrot slices and onions to
pot roast in Dutch oven.

Blade pot roast, identified by the blade bone, and arm pot roast, identified by the arm bone, are two less-tender cuts of beef chuck that should be cooked by braising. Allow ½ to ¾ pound per serving when purchasing. Roasts can be stored in the refrigerator for 3 to 5 days or in the freezer for 8 to 12 months.

Hearty Roast and Vegetables

2½- to 3-pound beef chuck pot roast
1 teaspoon seasoned salt
½ teaspoon dried marjoram leaves
¼ teaspoon celery seed
¼ teaspoon pepper
1 clove garlic, finely chopped
½ cup water
1 package (10 ounces) frozen Brussels
  sprouts
4 medium carrots, cut into 3x½-inch strips
2 medium potatoes, cut into 1-inch slices
2 medium turnips, cut into eighths
1 medium onion, sliced
½ teaspoon salt

Trim excess fat from beef pot roast. Rub Dutch oven with fat cut from beef; brown beef in Dutch oven. Sprinkle with seasoned salt, marjoram, celery seed, pepper and garlic; add water. Heat to boiling; reduce heat. Cover and simmer 1½ hours.

Rinse frozen Brussels sprouts under running cold water to separate. Add vegetables to Dutch oven, placing Brussels sprouts on top; sprinkle with salt. If necessary, add ¼ cup water. Heat to boiling; reduce heat. Cover and simmer until beef and vegetables are tender, 30 to 40 minutes. Sprinkle with parsley.   4 TO 6 SERVINGS.

Pot Roast Italiano

3- to 3½-pound beef chuck pot roast
1 can (16 ounces) stewed tomatoes
1 can (2 ounces) mushroom stems and
   pieces
2 medium onions, cut into wedges
1 medium stalk celery, sliced (about ½ cup)
1 clove garlic, finely chopped
1 teaspoon salt
1 teaspoon Worcestershire sauce
¼ teaspoon pepper
   Gravy (below)
¼ cup sliced pimiento-stuffed olives
   Celery leaves

Trim excess fat from beef pot roast. Rub Dutch oven with fat trimmed from beef. Brown beef in Dutch oven over medium heat; drain. Add tomatoes, mushrooms (with liquid), onions, celery, garlic, salt, Worcestershire sauce and pepper. Heat to boiling; reduce heat. Cover and simmer until beef is tender, 1½ to 2 hours. Remove beef and vegetables to platter; keep warm. Prepare Gravy; serve with beef. Garnish beef with olives and celery leaves.
6 OR 7 SERVINGS.

GRAVY

1½ cups beef broth
⅓ cup cold water
2 tablespoons flour

Skim excess fat from beef broth. Measure broth; if necessary, add enough water to measure 1½ cups. Return broth to Dutch oven. Shake water and flour in covered container. Stir flour mixture slowly into broth. Heat to boiling, stirring constantly. Boil and stir 1 minute.

Remove vegetables from broth with a slotted spoon.

Skim any excess fat from the hot broth; measure broth.

For smooth gravy, add flour to water, not the reverse.

Add flour mixture slowly to broth, stirring constantly.

Place the cooked and cooled corned beef in a shallow roasting pan; spread apricot mixture over top. (Cooling the corned beef in the cooking liquid will result in more moist meat.) When slicing, cut thin diagonal slices across the grain. Corned beef is delicious used in salads, sandwiches and hash.

Apricot-Glazed Corned Beef

3- to 3½-pound corned beef brisket, well
   trimmed
1 tablespoon whole mixed pickling spices
1 medium onion, finely chopped (about ½
   cup)
½ cup apricot preserves
⅓ cup golden raisins
1 tablespoon lemon juice or vinegar
¼ teaspoon dry mustard or ground ginger
⅛ teaspoon salt

Place corned beef brisket in Dutch oven; cover with water. Add pickling spices. Heat to boiling; reduce heat. Cover and simmer until tender, 2¼ to 3½ hours.

Cool beef in broth at room temperature 1 hour. Place beef in shallow roasting pan. Mix remaining ingredients and spread over beef. Roast uncovered in 325° oven until hot and glazed, about 30 minutes. Cut beef across grain into thin slices.   6 SERVINGS—with beef for leftovers.

Corned Beef with Mustard Sauce: Omit apricot glaze and do not roast boiled beef. Mix ½ cup dairy sour cream, 1½ to 2 teaspoons prepared mustard, 1 teaspoon horseradish or steak sauce and ¼ teaspoon onion salt. Serve with boiled beef.

Freezer Stroganoff

2 pounds beef sirloin steak, ½ inch thick
½ pound fresh mushrooms, sliced
2 medium onions, sliced
1 clove garlic, finely chopped
¼ cup butter or margarine
1 cup water
2 teaspoons instant beef bouillon
1 teaspoon salt
1 teaspoon Worcestershire sauce
½ cup water
¼ cup all-purpose flour

Cut beef steak across grain into strips ½ inch wide and 1½ inches long. Cook and stir mushrooms, onions and garlic in butter in 10-inch skillet until onions are tender; remove vegetables. Brown beef in same skillet. Stir in 1 cup water, the instant bouillon, salt and Worcestershire sauce. Heat to boiling; reduce heat. Cover and simmer 15 minutes.

Stir ½ cup water into the flour; stir into beef mixture. Add vegetables. Heat to boiling, stirring constantly. Boil and stir 1 minute. Pour into two 1-quart freezer containers. Cool quickly. Cover and label; freeze up to 4 months.

■45 minutes before serving, dip containers into hot water to loosen. Place frozen stroganoff and ½ cup water in 10-inch skillet. Cover and heat over medium heat, turning occasionally, until meat is hot, about 30 minutes. Stir 1½ cups dairy sour cream into hot stroganoff and heat (do not boil). Garnish with parsley.   8 SERVINGS.

Stir the vegetables into the beef mixture in skillet.

Pour beef mixture into two 1-quart freezer containers.

Place frozen stroganoff and water in skillet to heat.

Stir dairy sour cream into hot stroganoff and heat.

Coat beef with flour; pound beef with mallet to tenderize.

Brown beef in skillet; push beef to side and add onion.

Pour the potato liquid mixture on beef and onion in skillet.

Rinse beans quickly under running cold water to separate.

Saucy Steak Skillet

1-pound beef boneless round steak, cut into
  serving pieces
¼ cup all-purpose flour
1 tablespoon vegetable oil
1 large onion, chopped (about 1 cup)
1 can (16 ounces) whole potatoes, drained
  (reserve liquid)
¼ cup catsup
1 tablespoon Worcestershire sauce
2 teaspoons bell pepper flakes
1 teaspoon instant beef bouillon
1 teaspoon salt
½ teaspoon dried marjoram leaves
¼ teaspoon pepper
1 package (9 ounces) frozen Italian green
  beans
1 jar (2 ounces) sliced pimiento, drained

Coat beef steak pieces with flour; pound into beef. Brown beef in oil in 10-inch skillet; push beef to side. Cook and stir onion in oil until tender; drain.

Add enough water to reserved potato liquid to measure 1 cup. Mix potato liquid, catsup, Worcestershire sauce, pepper flakes, instant bouillon, salt, marjoram and pepper; pour on beef and onion. Heat to boiling; reduce heat. Cover and simmer until beef is tender, 1¼ to 1½ hours.

Rinse frozen beans under running cold water to separate. Add potatoes, beans and pimiento to skillet. Heat to boiling; reduce heat. Cover and simmer until beans are tender, 10 to 15 minutes.   4 SERVINGS.

Beef-Eggplant Bake

1-pound beef round steak, ½ inch thick, cut into 1½ x ¼-inch strips
1 tablespoon vegetable oil
1 can (8 ounces) tomato sauce
1 can (6 ounces) tomato paste
½ cup water
1 medium onion, chopped (about ½ cup)
1 medium green pepper, chopped (about 1 cup)
1 teaspoon salt
1 teaspoon garlic salt
1 teaspoon dried oregano leaves
½ teaspoon dried basil leaves
1 package (9 ounces) frozen Italian green beans
1 medium eggplant, pared and cut into ¼-inch slices
1 cup shredded mozzarella cheese (about 4 ounces)
¼ cup grated Parmesan cheese

Brown beef round steak strips in oil in 10-inch skillet over medium heat. Stir in tomato sauce, tomato paste, water, onion, green pepper, salt, garlic salt, oregano and basil. Heat to boiling; reduce heat. Cover and simmer 30 minutes.

Heat oven to 350°. Rinse frozen beans under running cold water to separate. Layer half each of the eggplant slices, beans and beef mixture in ungreased 2-quart casserole; repeat. Cover and bake 50 minutes.

Sprinkle casserole with cheeses. Bake uncovered until cheese is melted and golden, about 5 minutes. Let stand 5 minutes before serving.   6 SERVINGS.

EGGPLANT, available year round, is most abundant in August and September. Look for a pear-shaped plant, 3 to 6 inches across, dark and glossy color with no blemishes. Eggplant contains minerals and vitamins as well as protein. It is delicious with meats, tomatoes, cheese, sour cream, yogurt and mushrooms.

Spread each beef cubed steak with stuffing mixture.

Roll up steaks and fasten with wooden picks.

Steak Roll-up Supper

 2 cups seasoned stuffing mix
⅔ cup hot water
 4 beef cubed steaks (4 ounces each)
 2 tablespoons vegetable oil
 1 can (15 ounces) tomato sauce
½ teaspoon salt
¼ teaspoon dried thyme leaves
¼ teaspoon dried rosemary leaves
¼ teaspoon poultry seasoning
 8 small white onions, peeled
 1 can (16 ounces) French-style green beans,
    drained

Combine stuffing mix and water. Spread each beef cubed steak with stuffing mixture. Roll and fasten with wooden picks. Brown beef rolls in oil in 10-inch skillet; drain. Mix tomato sauce, salt, thyme, rosemary and poultry seasoning. Add tomato sauce mixture and onions to skillet. Heat to boiling; reduce heat. Cover and simmer until beef is tender, about 1 hour.

Stir in beans. Cover and simmer until beans are hot, about 10 minutes.   4 SERVINGS.

Mushroom Steak and Potato Cakes

6 to 8 beef cubed steaks (about 2 pounds)
2 teaspoons salt
¼ teaspoon lemon pepper
2 cans (4 ounces each) sliced mushrooms
½ cup dry white or red wine
1 medium green pepper, chopped (½ cup)
1 small onion, chopped (about ¼ cup)
Potato Cakes (below)

Sprinkle steaks with salt and lemon pepper. Brown few steaks at a time in 10-inch skillet over medium heat, 5 to 10 minutes on each side. Stir in mushrooms (with liquid), wine, green pepper and onion. Heat over low heat until mushrooms are hot, about 5 minutes. Serve with Potato Cakes.   6 TO 8 SERVINGS.

POTATO CAKES

Mashed potato mix (enough for 4 servings)
⅓ cup shredded Cheddar cheese
¼ cup plus 2 tablespoons cracker crumbs
1 egg, slightly beaten
2 tablespoons snipped parsley
1 teaspoon finely chopped onion
½ teaspoon fines herbes (see note)
¼ teaspoon salt
1 tablespoon vegetable oil

Prepare potato mix as directed on package; cool. Mix potatoes, cheese, crumbs, egg, parsley, onion, fines herbes and salt. Heat oil in 10-inch skillet. Drop potato mixture by rounded tablespoonfuls into skillet. Flatten with spatula and fry over medium heat until light brown, about 3 minutes on each side; drain.

Note: Fines herbes is a mixture of the crushed dried leaves of thyme, oregano, sage, rosemary, marjoram and basil.

Flatten tablespoonfuls of potato mixture in the skillet; fry the cakes until light brown.

You can make cakes ahead of time and refrigerate. Then reheat in 350° oven 5 minutes.

Cut beef into 2-inch pieces.

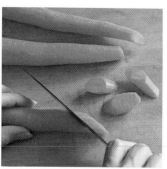
Cut carrots into ½-inch slices.

Savory Beef Ragout

1½ pounds beef chuck or bottom round, cut
　　into 2-inch pieces
　2 tablespoons vegetable oil
　¼ cup all-purpose flour
　2 cups water
　1 can (about 8½ ounces) stewed tomatoes
　3 sprigs parsley
　2 teaspoons salt
　½ teaspoon dried thyme leaves
　¼ teaspoon dried sage leaves
　¼ teaspoon pepper
　1 bay leaf
　1 clove garlic, finely chopped
　6 small onions
　3 large carrots, cut diagonally into ½-inch
　　slices (about 2 cups)
　1 package (10 ounces) frozen lima beans,
　　broken apart

Brown beef pieces in oil in Dutch oven; remove beef. Drain fat from Dutch oven, reserving 2 tablespoons. Return 2 tablespoons fat to Dutch oven. (If necessary, add enough oil to measure 2 tablespoons.)

Stir in flour. Cook and stir over low heat until smooth and bubbly; remove from heat. Add water. Heat to boiling, stirring constantly. Stir in beef, tomatoes, parsley, salt, thyme, sage, pepper, bay leaf and garlic. Heat to boiling; reduce heat. Cover and simmer 1 hour.

Add onions and carrots. Cover and simmer until beef and vegetables are tender, 40 to 50 minutes. Stir in frozen beans. Cover and simmer until beans are tender, about 10 minutes.　6 SERVINGS.

Beef and Sausage Stew

4 slices bacon
1 pound beef stew meat, cut into 1-inch
   pieces
1 large onion, sliced
2 cups water
1 can (12 ounces) beer
2 teaspoons instant beef bouillon
1 teaspoon salt
½ teaspoon dried thyme leaves
¼ teaspoon pepper
2 whole cloves
1 bay leaf
3 medium carrots, cut diagonally into ½-inch
   slices (about 1½ cups)
1 pound Polish sausage, cut into ½-inch
   slices
4 ounces uncooked noodles (about 2 cups)
½ medium head cabbage, coarsely shredded
   (about 2 cups)
2 medium apples, sliced

Fry bacon slices in Dutch oven over medium heat until crisp; remove bacon and drain on paper towels. Brown beef stew meat in bacon fat; push beef to side. Cook and stir onion in bacon fat until tender; drain. Stir in water, beer, instant bouillon, salt, thyme, pepper, cloves and bay leaf. Heat to boiling; reduce heat. Cover and simmer 1 hour.

Add carrots and sausage. Heat to boiling; reduce heat. Cover and simmer 30 minutes.

Crumble bacon; stir bacon, noodles, cabbage and apples into stew. Heat to boiling; reduce heat. Cover and simmer until noodles are tender, 10 to 15 minutes.   6 TO 8 SERVINGS.

Remove bacon with tongs; drain on paper towels.

Cut 1 pound Polish sausage into ½-inch slices.

Use a knife to shred cabbage coarsely and evenly.

Cut apples into fourths; core and then slice.

Cut the tomatoes into fourths with scissors.

Peel garlic clove; crush with garlic press.

Or chop peeled garlic clove on cutting board.

Brown flour-coated meat in vegetable oil.

Hearty Chili

1 medium green pepper, chopped (about 1 cup)
2 medium onions, chopped (about 1 cup)
1 clove garlic, crushed
1 tablespoon vegetable oil
1 pound beef stew meat, cut into ½-inch pieces
3 tablespoons flour
2 tablespoons vegetable oil
2 cans (28 ounces each) whole tomatoes, drained and cut into fourths (see note)
3 cans (16 ounces each) kidney beans
1 can (8 ounces) tomato sauce
1 to 2 tablespoons chili powder
2 teaspoons salt

Cook and stir green pepper, onions and garlic in 1 tablespoon oil in Dutch oven over medium heat until onions are tender, about 5 minutes; remove from Dutch oven. Coat beef stew meat with flour; brown in 2 tablespoons oil.

Stir in tomatoes, beans (with liquid), tomato sauce, chili powder, green pepper mixture and salt. Heat to boiling; reduce heat. Cover and simmer, stirring occasionally, until beef is tender, about 2 hours. Uncover and simmer, stirring occasionally, 30 minutes.   10 SERVINGS.

Note: If you like a thinner consistency, do not drain tomatoes.

Country Beef Dinner

1½ pounds beef stew meat, cut into 1-inch pieces
2 tablespoons vegetable oil
1 can (29 ounces) whole tomatoes
1 can (8 ounces) tomato sauce
3 cups water
1 large onion, chopped (about 1 cup)
2 teaspoons salt
½ teaspoon dried oregano leaves
½ teaspoon dried thyme leaves
4 ounces uncooked large macaroni (rigatoni, mostaccioli, shell or spiral)
1 package (10 ounces) frozen cut green beans
Grated Parmesan cheese

Rigatoni, spiral macaroni.

Mostaccioli, shell macaroni.

Brown beef stew meat in oil in Dutch oven; drain. Stir in tomatoes (with liquid), tomato sauce, water, onion, salt, oregano and thyme. Heat to boiling; reduce heat. Cover and simmer until beef is almost tender, 1½ to 2 hours.

Stir in macaroni. Heat to boiling; reduce heat. Cover and simmer, stirring occasionally, until macaroni is almost tender, about 20 minutes.

Rinse frozen beans under running cold water to separate. Stir beans into beef mixture; cook uncovered until beans are tender, 15 to 20 minutes. Sprinkle with cheese.
6 SERVINGS.

Short Ribs and Herb Dumplings

First cut rutabaga into ½-inch slices, then sticks.

Drop dough by spoonfuls onto ribs (not into liquid).

3 pounds beef short ribs
2 cups water
1 teaspoon salt
1 teaspoon instant beef bouillon
⅛ teaspoon pepper
1 bay leaf
1 medium rutabaga, cut into ½-inch sticks
2 medium onions, cut into fourths
½ teaspoon salt
Herb Dumplings (below)
1 package (10 ounces) frozen green peas

Trim excess fat from beef short ribs. Brown beef in 12-inch skillet or Dutch oven; drain. Add water, 1 teaspoon salt, the instant bouillon, pepper and bay leaf. Heat to boiling; reduce heat. Cover and simmer, stirring occasionally, 1 hour.

Skim fat from broth. Add rutabaga and onions; sprinkle with ½ teaspoon salt. Heat to boiling; reduce heat. Cover and simmer until rutabaga is almost tender, 30 to 40 minutes.

Prepare Herb Dumplings. Drop dumpling dough by spoonfuls onto beef as pictured. Cook uncovered over medium heat 10 minutes.

Rinse frozen peas under running cold water to separate. Sprinkle peas around dumplings. Cover and cook 10 minutes. Remove ribs, dumplings and peas with slotted spoon and arrange on serving platter. Serve with pan juices, skimming off fat if necessary.   4 SERVINGS.

HERB DUMPLINGS

Mix 1 cup biscuit baking mix, ⅓ cup milk and ¼ teaspoon poultry seasoning until a soft dough forms.

Savory Short Ribs

        3 pounds beef short ribs
    1½ cups water
        2 medium onions, sliced
        2 tablespoons vinegar or lemon juice
        2 teaspoons salt
    ¼ teaspoon pepper
        2 bay leaves
        1 package (10 ounces) frozen lima beans
        4 medium carrots, cut into 3x½-inch strips
        1 tablespoon packed brown sugar
    ¼ teaspoon ground ginger
        Gravy (below)

Trim any excess fat from the beef short ribs.

Brown ribs over medium heat, turning with tongs.

Trim excess fat from beef short ribs. Brown beef in 12-inch skillet; drain. Add water, onions, vinegar, salt, pepper and bay leaves. Heat to boiling; reduce heat. Cover and simmer 1 hour.

Add frozen beans, carrots, brown sugar and ginger. Heat to boiling; reduce heat. Cover and simmer until vegetables are tender, about 45 minutes. Remove beef and vegetables to platter; keep warm. Prepare Gravy; serve with short ribs.   4 SERVINGS.

GRAVY

    1½ cups beef broth
    ⅓ cup cold water
        3 tablespoons flour

Skim excess fat from beef broth. Measure broth; if necessary, add enough water to measure 1½ cups. Return broth to Dutch oven. Shake water and flour in covered container. Stir flour mixture slowly into broth. Heat to boiling, stirring constantly. Boil and stir 1 minute.

Beef Romano

Cut up enough of the leftover cooked beef to measure 2 cups.

Cook and stir beef and onion in oil until the onion is tender.

2 cups cut-up cooked beef
1 small onion, chopped (about ¼ cup)
1 tablespoon vegetable oil
1 package (10 ounces) frozen mixed vegetables
1 can (8 ounces) tomato sauce
½ cup water
½ teaspoon salt
¼ teaspoon dried oregano leaves
⅛ teaspoon garlic powder
Hot cooked spaghetti
¼ cup grated Parmesan cheese

Cook and stir beef and onion in oil in 10-inch skillet until onion is tender. Add remaining ingredients except spaghetti and cheese. Heat to boiling; reduce heat. Cover and simmer until vegetables are tender, about 3 minutes. Serve over hot cooked spaghetti and sprinkle with cheese.
4 SERVINGS.

A NOTE ON FREEZING

To freeze cooked meats, cut up and package in recipe-size quantities. Pack tightly, leaving as little air as possible. The recommended temperature for freezing and storing meat is 0° or lower. To retain the quality of the meat, use within 1 month. To thaw, place in refrigerator up to 24 hours or break apart with a fork and use immediately.

Beef and Bean Pie

1 package (10 ounces) frozen cut green
   beans
1 package (about 1 ounce) brown gravy mix
2 cups cut-up cooked beef
1 medium onion, chopped (about ½ cup)
½ teaspoon dill weed
½ teaspoon salt
   Mashed potato mix (enough for 8
   servings)
1 jar (5 ounces) pasteurized process sharp
   American cheese spread

Heat oven to 350°. Cook beans as directed on package; drain. Prepare gravy mix as directed on package. Stir beef, onion, dill and salt into gravy. Pour into ungreased 2-quart casserole. Top with beans.

Prepare potato mix as directed on package except—reduce water to 2¼ cups and omit butter. Stir in cheese spread. Mound mixture on casserole. Bake uncovered until topping is light brown, 45 to 50 minutes.   6 SERVINGS.

Add onion to beef mixture.

Add green beans to casserole.

Stir cheese into the potatoes.

Mound mixture on the beans.

Skillet Hash

2 cups cut-up cooked beef
1 can (16 ounces) stewed tomatoes
1⅓ cups water
¾ cup quick-cooking brown rice
1 medium onion, chopped (about ½ cup)
1 to 2 teaspoons chili powder
¾ teaspoon salt
   Pickled chili peppers

Mix all ingredients except peppers in 10-inch skillet. Heat to boiling; reduce heat. Cover and simmer until rice is tender, 15 minutes. Garnish with peppers.   4 SERVINGS.

Beef Plate

2 packages (3 ounces each) sliced smoked beef or sliced corned beef
1 can (8 ounces) whole new potatoes, cut into ¼-inch strips
1 can (4 ounces) mushroom stems and pieces, drained
1 medium green pepper, cut into ¼-inch strips
1 small onion, sliced (reserve 6 rings)
1 medium stalk celery, coarsely chopped
1 medium dill pickle, chopped
½ cup Italian salad dressing
Lettuce leaves
1 can (16 ounces) whole green beans, drained
¼ teaspoon dried thyme leaves
1 can (2 ounces) anchovies, drained
6 spiced peaches

Reserve 1 package beef. Snip remaining beef into small pieces. Mix beef pieces, potatoes, mushrooms, green pepper, onion slices, celery and pickle. Add dressing; toss. Refrigerate at least 6 hours.

Arrange lettuce on 6 plates. Spoon beef mixture onto lettuce; top with onion rings. Place reserved beef and the beans around lettuce. Sprinkle with thyme; top with anchovies. Garnish with peaches and parsley.   6 SERVINGS.

Corned Beef Salad with Onion Buns

1 package (10 ounces) frozen Brussels sprouts
¼ cup vinegar
¼ cup vegetable oil
1 teaspoon salt
½ teaspoon caraway seed
¼ teaspoon pepper
1 medium cucumber, sliced
10 cherry tomatoes, cut in half
4 lettuce cups
12 ounces corned beef, cut into thin slices
Onion Buns (below)

Cook Brussels sprouts as directed on package; drain. Shake vinegar, oil, salt, caraway seed and pepper in tightly covered container. Pour dressing on hot Brussels sprouts and cucumber, tossing to coat evenly. Cover and refrigerate at least 3 hours.

Just before serving, add tomatoes and toss. Spoon into lettuce cups; garnish with snipped parsley. Arrange corned beef slices beside lettuce cups. Serve with Onion Buns.
4 SERVINGS.

ONION BUNS

4 pumpernickel buns
Soft butter or margarine
1 large sweet onion, cut into 8 slices
½ cup mayonnaise or salad dressing
2 tablespoons grated Parmesan cheese

Cut buns in half and butter each half. Place onion slice on each half. Mix mayonnaise and cheese; spread over onions. Set oven control to broil and/or 550°. Broil 4 to 5 inches from heat until hot and bubbly, 2 to 3 minutes.

Creamy Dried Beef Mold

1 envelope unflavored gelatin
½ cup cold water
1 cup mayonnaise or salad dressing
1 teaspoon prepared mustard
⅔ cup skim milk
1 can (8½ ounces) lima beans, drained
1 jar (2½ ounces) dried beef, finely cut up
   (see note)
2 medium stalks celery, chopped (about 1
   cup)
¼ cup grated American cheese food
1 tablespoon lemon juice
2 teaspoons instant minced onion
   Celery leaves

Sprinkle gelatin on cold water in saucepan to soften; stir over low heat until gelatin is dissolved. Remove from heat. Mix mayonnaise and mustard in medium bowl; beat in gelatin mixture. Stir in milk. Cover and refrigerate until slightly thickened, 30 to 45 minutes.

Stir in beans, beef, celery, cheese, lemon juice and onion. Pour into 4-cup mold. Refrigerate until firm, about 3 hours. Unmold and garnish with celery leaves. 4 TO 6 SERVINGS.

Note: If dried beef is too salty, pour boiling water on it and drain.

If dried beef is too salty, pour boiling water on it.

Refrigerate gelatin mixture until slightly thickened.

Stir in beans, beef, celery, cheese, lemon juice, onion.

Pour into 4-cup mold. Refrigerate until firm, 3 hours.

Dip tomatoes into boiling water 1 minute, then into cold.

Use a sharp paring knife to peel off the skin easily.

Cut the tomatoes into eighths.

Spoon mixture into tomatoes.

Tongue Salad

6 medium tomatoes
½ teaspoon salt
½ cup mayonnaise or salad dressing
2 tablespoons chopped onion
½ teaspoon dried tarragon leaves
2 cups cut-up cooked tongue
6 slices bacon, crisply fried and crumbled
1 medium stalk celery, thinly sliced
6 lettuce cups

Peel tomatoes and cut into eighths, cutting to within 1 inch of bottoms as pictured. Spread sections carefully; sprinkle with salt. Mix mayonnaise, onion and tarragon. Toss with tongue, bacon and celery; spoon tongue mixture into tomatoes. Serve in lettuce cups.   6 SERVINGS.

Tongue Madeira

2 tablespoons butter or margarine
1 tablespoon flour
1 teaspoon instant beef bouillon
¼ teaspoon salt
⅛ teaspoon pepper
½ cup water
¼ cup Madeira
8 to 12 slices cooked tongue

Heat butter in skillet over low heat until melted. Stir in flour, instant bouillon, salt and pepper. Heat over low heat, stirring constantly, until mixture is smooth and bubbly; remove from heat. Stir in water and Madeira. Heat to boiling, stirring constantly. Boil and stir 1 minute. Add tongue slices and heat until tongue is hot, about 5 minutes. Garnish with snipped parsley.   4 SERVINGS.

Liver and Bacon Skillet

4 slices bacon
1 medium onion, chopped (about ½ cup)
1 tablespoon flour
1 tablespoon chili powder
1 pound beef liver, cut into ¼-inch strips
1 can (16 ounces) whole tomatoes
1 can (12 ounces) whole kernel corn with
   sweet peppers
1 teaspoon salt
   Dash of pepper

Fry bacon in 12-inch skillet or Dutch oven until crisp; drain on paper towels. Crumble bacon and reserve. Drain fat from skillet, reserving 2 tablespoons. Return 2 tablespoons fat to skillet. Cook and stir onion in fat until tender, about 2 minutes.

Mix flour and chili powder. Coat liver with flour mixture; add to onion in skillet. Cook and stir until liver is light brown. Stir in tomatoes (with liquid), corn (with liquid), salt and pepper. Heat to boiling; reduce heat. Simmer uncovered until liver is tender, about 5 minutes. Sprinkle with reserved bacon.   4 SERVINGS.

Cut liver while bacon fries.

Drain bacon; cook onion.

Coat liver strips with flour.

Stir in tomatoes and corn.

Ranch Stew with Cheese Rolls

Prepare stew; cook 15 minutes.

Start rolls while stew cooks.

1½ pounds ground beef
 1 medium onion, chopped (about ½ cup)
 2 cans (10½ ounces each) condensed
      vegetable soup
 1 can (16 ounces) pork and beans in tomato
      sauce
 3 cups water
 1 medium stalk celery, sliced (about ½ cup)
1¼ teaspoons salt
 ½ teaspoon Worcestershire sauce
 ¼ teaspoon dried thyme leaves
 ⅛ teaspoon instant minced garlic
 ⅛ teaspoon ground cumin
     Cheese Rolls (below)

Cook and stir ground beef and onion in Dutch oven over medium heat until beef is light brown; drain. Stir in remaining ingredients except Cheese Rolls. Heat to boiling; reduce heat. Cover and simmer 15 minutes. Serve with Cheese Rolls.   6 SERVINGS.

CHEESE ROLLS

Heat oven to 425°. Mix 1 cup shredded Cheddar cheese (about 4 ounces) and ¼ cup butter or margarine, softened. Split rolls from 1 package (11 ounces) brown and serve rolls horizontally in half. Spread each half with about 1 tablespoon cheese-butter mixture; replace tops. Heat on ungreased baking sheet until cheese is melted and rolls are golden brown, 8 to 10 minutes.

Hamburger Chop Suey

1 pound ground beef
1 medium onion, sliced
2 large stalks celery, sliced (about 1½ cups)
1 tablespoon instant beef bouillon
2 cups hot water
¼ cup cold water
3 tablespoons soy sauce
2 tablespoons cornstarch
¼ teaspoon monosodium glutamate
1 can (16 ounces) bean sprouts, drained
1 can (8 ounces) water chestnuts, drained
    and sliced
4 cups hot cooked rice
½ cup slivered almonds or chopped cocktail
    peanuts, toasted (see note)
1 jar (2 ounces) sliced pimiento, drained

To save time, slice several celery stalks together.

Toast nuts in 350° oven until golden, 10 to 15 minutes.

Cook and stir ground beef over medium heat in 10-inch skillet until light brown; drain. Stir in onion, celery, instant bouillon and hot water. Heat to boiling; reduce heat.

Shake cold water, soy sauce, cornstarch and monosodium glutamate in tightly covered container. Stir into beef mixture. Heat to boiling, stirring constantly. Boil and stir 1 minute. Stir in bean sprouts and water chestnuts; heat until water chestnuts are hot. Serve over rice. Garnish with toasted almonds and pimiento.   6 SERVINGS.

Note: To toast almonds, spread on ungreased baking sheet and bake in 350° oven, stirring occasionally, until golden, 10 to 15 minutes.

1 small onion equals ¼ cup chopped onion or 1 tablespoon (or more) instant minced.

For recipes low in liquid, soak instant minced onion in equal amount of water 3 minutes.

Beef-Spaghetti Casserole

1 pound ground beef
1 medium green pepper
2 cups hot cooked spaghetti (about 4 ounces uncooked)
1 can (16 ounces) Chinese vegetables, drained
1 can (10¾ ounces) condensed cream of shrimp soup
1 can (8 ounces) water chestnuts, drained and sliced
1 can (4 ounces) mushroom stems and pieces, drained
½ cup water
1 small onion, finely chopped (about ¼ cup)
1 teaspoon salt
¾ cup shredded sharp cheese (about 3 ounces)

Heat oven to 375°. Cook and stir ground beef until light brown, 15 to 20 minutes; drain. Slice 3 rings from green pepper; reserve rings for garnish. Chop remaining green pepper.

Stir chopped green pepper and remaining ingredients except cheese into meat. Pour into ungreased 2-quart casserole; sprinkle with cheese. Bake uncovered 30 minutes. Top with green pepper rings; bake 5 minutes.   6 SERVINGS.

Cornmeal Casserole Pie

1 cup yellow cornmeal
1 cup cold water
2 cups boiling water
1 tablespoon butter or margarine
1 teaspoon salt
1 pound ground beef
2 small onions, sliced
½ medium green pepper, chopped (about
    ½ cup)
3 tablespoons yellow cornmeal
1 can (16 ounces) whole tomatoes
1 can (15 ounces) kidney beans, drained
1 to 2 teaspoons chili powder
1 teaspoon salt
½ teaspoon crushed dried chilies
¼ teaspoon garlic salt
½ cup shredded taco-flavored or Cheddar
    cheese (about 2 ounces)
    Shredded lettuce

Heat oven to 350°. Mix 1 cup cornmeal and the cold water in 2-quart saucepan. Stir in boiling water, butter and 1 teaspoon salt. Cook over medium heat, stirring constantly, until mixture thickens and bubbles; reduce heat. Cover and simmer 5 minutes, stirring occasionally. Spread evenly over bottom and side of greased 3-quart casserole. Bake uncovered 15 minutes.

While cornmeal crust is baking, prepare filling. Cook and stir ground beef over medium heat until light brown; drain. Stir in onions, green pepper, 3 tablespoons cornmeal, the tomatoes (with liquid), beans, chili powder, 1 teaspoon salt, the chilies and garlic salt. Pour into crust; sprinkle with cheese. Bake uncovered until bubbly, about 35 minutes. Serve on lettuce in bowls.   8 SERVINGS.

Cook cornmeal until thick; cover and simmer 5 minutes.

Spread cornmeal over bottom and side of casserole.

Stir vegetables, cornmeal and seasonings into ground beef.

Pour hot filling into baked crust; bake until bubbly.

You can remove the fat from ground beef with baster.

Or skim fat from ground beef with large spoon.

Or remove ground beef with slotted spoon and pour off fat.

Or use slotted cover to hold beef while you pour off fat.

Deep Dish Hamburger Pie

1 pound ground beef
2 teaspoons instant minced onion
2 teaspoons chili powder
1 teaspoon dried oregano leaves
1 can (10¾ ounces) condensed tomato soup
1 can (16 ounces) sliced carrots, drained
1 can (12 ounces) vacuum-pack whole kernel
  corn
Sesame Topping (below)

Heat oven to 400°. Cook and stir ground beef over medium heat until light brown; drain. Place beef in ungreased baking dish, 11¾x7½x1¾ inches. Stir in onion, chili powder, oregano, soup, carrots and corn.

Drop Sesame Topping by teaspoonfuls around edges of baking dish. Bake uncovered until topping is golden brown, about 15 minutes.   6 SERVINGS.

SESAME TOPPING
 1 cup biscuit baking mix
¼ cup butter or margarine, softened
 3 tablespoons boiling water
 2 tablespoons sesame seed

Mix all ingredients until a soft dough forms.

Taco Burgers

1 package (12 ounces) corn chips
1½ pounds ground beef
1 package (1¼ ounces) taco seasoning mix
1 package (3 ounces) cream cheese, cut into
    12 strips about ⅛ inch thick
    Paprika

Crush enough of the corn chips (about ⅔ cup) to measure ⅓ cup. Mix ground beef, crushed chips and seasoning mix. Shape mixture into 6 patties about 4 inches in diameter.

Set oven control to broil and/or 550°. Broil patties with tops 4 to 5 inches from heat 5 minutes; turn and broil 3 minutes. Crisscross 2 strips cheese on each patty and sprinkle with paprika. Broil until cheese is puffed and golden, 2 minutes. Serve with remaining corn chips.   6 SERVINGS.

Add crushed corn chips and seasoning mix to ground beef.

Crisscross 2 strips of cream cheese on each beef patty.

Beanburgers

1 pound ground beef
½ teaspoon salt
¼ teaspoon pepper
4 slices process American cheese
1 can (16 ounces) cut green beans, drained
1 can (11 ounces) condensed Cheddar
    cheese soup
1 tablespoon chili sauce
1 teaspoon prepared mustard

Shape ground beef into 8 thin patties about 3½ inches in diameter. Brown patties in 10-inch skillet and cook to desired doneness; drain. Sprinkle with salt and pepper. Top each of 4 patties with 1 cheese slice; cover with a remaining patty. Mix beans, soup, chili sauce and mustard; pour on patties. Heat to boiling; reduce heat. Cover and simmer until beans are hot, about 10 minutes.   4 SERVINGS.

Lemon-Cabbage Rolls

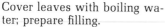
Cover leaves with boiling water; prepare filling.

Mound filling at stem end of each cabbage leaf.

Roll leaves, folding in sides; fasten with picks.

Place rolls in ungreased baking dish. Add water; bake.

6 cabbage leaves
1 pound ground beef
1 small onion, chopped (about ¼ cup)
1 clove garlic, finely chopped
½ cup uncooked regular rice
2 tablespoons snipped parsley
1½ teaspoons salt
¼ teaspoon lemon pepper
¼ teaspoon ground cinnamon
¼ teaspoon dried oregano leaves
1½ cups water
½ cup crumbled feta or shredded Swiss
     cheese (about 2 ounces)
¼ teaspoon salt
1 cup water
     Lemon Sauce (below)

Cover cabbage leaves with boiling water. Cook and stir ground beef, onion and garlic over medium heat until beef is light brown; drain.

Stir rice, parsley, 1½ teaspoons salt, the lemon pepper, cinnamon, oregano, 1½ cups water and cheese into beef. Heat to boiling; reduce heat. Cover and simmer, stirring occasionally, until water is absorbed, about 15 minutes.

Heat oven to 350°. Dry cabbage leaves; sprinkle with ¼ teaspoon salt. Mound ½ cup filling at stem end of each cabbage leaf. Roll, folding in sides; fasten with wooden picks. Place in ungreased baking dish, 11¾x7½x1¾ inches. Pour 1 cup water over cabbage rolls. Cover and bake 30 minutes; drain. Spoon hot Lemon Sauce over cabbage rolls; garnish with parsley.   6 SERVINGS.

LEMON SAUCE

Mix 1 package (about 1 ounce) chicken gravy mix, ¾ cup water and 1 to 2 teaspoons lemon juice. Heat to boiling, stirring occasionally.

Taco Tossed Salad

1 pound ground beef
½ cup taco sauce
1 small head lettuce, torn into bite-size pieces
1 medium green pepper, cut into strips
1 medium tomato, cut into 8 wedges
½ cup pitted ripe olives, drained
2 cups shredded Cheddar cheese (about 8 ounces)
1 package (1¼ ounces) taco-flavored tortilla chips, crumbled (about 1 cup)
½ cup Thousand Island salad dressing

Cook and stir ground beef over medium heat until light brown; drain. Stir in taco sauce and heat. Toss lettuce, green pepper, tomato wedges, olives, cheese and chips. Spoon hot beef mixture and salad dressing over lettuce mixture; toss. Serve immediately.   8 SERVINGS.

Remove the seeds and membranes; cut pepper into strips.

Spoon hot beef mixture and dressing onto lettuce and toss.

FREEZING CHEESE

Hard cheeses like Cheddar, Edam, Gouda and Swiss freeze well in small packages of about ½ pound each. To freeze, wrap cheese tightly to prevent drying and crumbling and remember to label. Thaw cheese slowly in the refrigerator—the mottled color, the result of frozen moisture on the surface, will disappear and the normal color will return as it thaws.

Swedish Dilled Meatballs

Mix meatball ingredients; re-frigerate for 2 hours.

Brown the meatballs. Remove from skillet and drain.

Stir the flour and seasonings into 1 tablespoon fat.

Add water; heat to boiling. Cook and stir 1 minute.

1 pound ground beef
½ pound ground pork
¾ cup dark rye bread crumbs
1 egg
1 medium onion, finely chopped (about
    ½ cup)
½ cup milk
2 teaspoons dried dill weed
2 teaspoons salt
1 teaspoon Worcestershire sauce
⅛ teaspoon pepper
¼ cup all-purpose flour
1 teaspoon paprika
½ teaspoon salt
⅛ teaspoon pepper
2 cups water
¾ cup dairy sour cream

Mix ground beef, ground pork, bread crumbs, egg, onion, milk, dill, 2 teaspoons salt, the Worcestershire sauce and ⅛ teaspoon pepper. Cover and refrigerate 2 hours.

Shape ground beef mixture by rounded tablespoonfuls into balls. Brown meatballs in 12-inch skillet over medium heat about 20 minutes; remove meatballs. Drain fat from skillet, reserving 1 tablespoon. Return 1 tablespoon fat to skillet. (If necessary, add enough shortening to fat to measure 1 tablespoon.)

Stir flour, paprika, ½ teaspoon salt and ⅛ teaspoon pepper into fat in skillet. Stir in water; heat to boiling, stirring constantly. Boil and stir 1 minute. Add meatballs; heat until meatballs are hot. Stir in sour cream until gravy is smooth.   6 TO 8 SERVINGS.

Beef Balls Provençale

1 pound ground beef
1 egg
1 small onion, chopped (about ¼ cup)
⅓ cup dry bread crumbs
¼ cup milk
1 teaspoon salt
1 teaspoon Worcestershire sauce
⅛ teaspoon pepper
1 tablespoon vegetable oil
Vegetables Provençale (below)
Grated Parmesan or Romano cheese

Mix all ingredients except oil, Vegetables Provençale and cheese. Shape mixture by tablespoonfuls into 1½-inch balls. (For ease in shaping meatballs, wet hands with cold water occasionally.) Cook meatballs in oil in 12-inch skillet over medium heat until light brown on all sides; remove from skillet. Drain fat from skillet.

Prepare Vegetables Provençale. Top with meatballs. Heat to boiling; reduce heat. Cover and simmer until vegetables are crisp-tender, 10 to 15 minutes. Sprinkle with cheese. 4 SERVINGS.

VEGETABLES PROVENCALE
4 small zucchini, cut into ½-inch slices
1 small eggplant, pared and cut into ½-inch pieces (about 2½ cups)
1 medium onion, sliced
2 cloves garlic, finely chopped
1 can (16 ounces) stewed tomatoes
1 teaspoon salt
½ teaspoon dried oregano leaves

Mix all ingredients in 12-inch skillet.

Cut the eggplant into ½-inch slices; pare and cut into pieces.

Prepare the vegetables and mix with seasonings in skillet.

Cut red pepper pieces while the meatballs brown.

Remove meatballs from skillet; drain on paper towels.

Meatballs on Crisp Noodles

1 pound ground beef
2 tablespoons soy sauce
½ teaspoon ground ginger
1½ cups water
2 tablespoons cornstarch
2 packages (6 ounces each) frozen pea
   pods
1 small red pepper, cut into 1x¼-inch
   pieces (about ½ cup)
1 teaspoon instant beef bouillon
¾ teaspoon salt
   Chow mein noodles

Mix ground beef, soy sauce and ginger. Shape by rounded tablespoonfuls into balls. Cook and stir meatballs in 10-inch skillet over medium heat until brown, about 15 minutes; drain.

Mix water and cornstarch. Rinse frozen pea pods under running cold water to separate; drain. Stir cornstarch mixture, pea pods, red pepper, instant bouillon and salt into meatballs. Heat to boiling; boil and stir 1 minute. Serve over chow mein noodles.   4 SERVINGS.

Meat Loaf and Dilled Limas

2 pounds ground beef
2 eggs, slightly beaten
1 cup dairy sour cream
¾ cup dry bread crumbs
¾ cup catsup
1 envelope (about 1½ ounces) onion soup
   mix
1 teaspoon prepared mustard
   Dilled Limas (below)

Heat oven to 350°. Mix ground beef, eggs, sour cream, bread crumbs, ¼ cup of the catsup, the soup mix and mustard. Press mixture firmly in ungreased 6½-cup ring mold. Loosen edges with spatula and unmold in ungreased jelly roll pan, 15½x10½x1 inch, by tapping mold on bottom of pan. Bake uncovered until done, 45 to 50 minutes. Fill center with Dilled Limas. Brush Meat Loaf with remaining ½ cup catsup.   6 TO 8 SERVINGS.

DILLED LIMAS

1 package (10 ounces) frozen lima beans
1 package (10 ounces) frozen green peas
2 tablespoons water
½ teaspoon salt
2 tablespoons butter or margarine
¼ teaspoon dried dill weed

Heat oven to 350°. Rinse frozen beans and peas under running cold water to separate; drain. Place in ungreased 1-quart casserole. Sprinkle with water and salt; dot with butter. Cover and bake until vegetables are tender, about 50 minutes. Stir dill into vegetables.

To unmold, first loosen edges of meat mixture with spatula.

Tap inverted mold sharply on the bottom of a jelly roll pan.

Tasty Pork Roast

Overlap cabbage leaves on foil; place roast on leaves.

Place onion slices and spinach leaves between 12 cuts.

Wrap the pork roast securely in the aluminum foil.

Place in baking pan; insert meat thermometer.

10 large cabbage leaves
5-pound pork boneless loin roast
2 tablespoons Kosher salt or coarse
  Hawaiian salt
1 teaspoon liquid smoke
1 teaspoon garlic powder
1 medium onion, sliced
2 packages (10 ounces each) frozen spinach
  leaves, thawed
½ medium onion, sliced and separated into
  rings
¼ cup grated Parmesan cheese (optional)

Heat oven to 325°. Overlap cabbage leaves on piece of aluminum foil large enough to wrap securely around pork roast, about 36x18 inches. Place roast on cabbage leaves. Make about 12 vertical cuts almost to bottom of roast (do not cut through). Rub all surfaces of roast with salt, liquid smoke and garlic powder. Place onion slices and spinach leaves between cuts.

Tie roast lengthwise with string to hold it together if necessary. Wrap roast securely in foil. Place in shallow baking pan; insert meat thermometer.

Roast until meat thermometer registers 185°, about 3 hours. Garnish with onion rings and sprinkle with cheese.
13 SERVINGS.

Brandied Pork

4-pound pork center loin roast
1 can (6 ounces) frozen pineapple-orange
   juice concentrate
1 small onion, chopped (about ¼ cup)
1 clove garlic, finely chopped
1 teaspoon crushed gingerroot*
½ teaspoon salt
¼ cup brandy

Place pork loin roast fat side up on rack in shallow roasting pan. Make vertical cuts between bones, cutting almost to bottom of roast. Insert meat thermometer so tip is in center of thickest part of pork and does not touch bone or rest in fat. Roast in 325° oven until thermometer registers 170°, about 2 hours.

Heat frozen concentrate, onion, garlic, gingerroot and salt just to boiling over medium heat; remove from heat. During last hour of roasting, stir brandy into juice mixture and brush over pork every 15 minutes. Serve remaining sauce with pork. 8 SERVINGS—with pork for leftovers.

*½ teaspoon ground ginger can be substituted for the gingerroot.

Party Pork with Peanuts

1 pound pork tenderloin, cut into ¾-inch
   pieces
1 tablespoon vegetable oil
1 teaspoon soy sauce
¼ teaspoon salt
¼ teaspoon monosodium glutamate
   Sweet-Sour Sauce (below)
1 tablespoon cornstarch
2 tablespoons water
   Reserved pineapple chunks from
   Sweet-Sour Sauce
1 medium green pepper, cut into ¼-inch
   strips
12 cherry tomatoes
¾ cup salted peanuts, chopped
3 cups hot cooked rice or noodles

Cook and stir pork pieces in oil in skillet over medium heat until brown, at least 15 minutes. Sprinkle with soy sauce, salt and monosodium glutamate. Prepare Sweet-Sour Sauce; pour on pork in skillet. Heat to boiling; reduce heat. Cover and simmer 15 minutes.

Mix cornstarch and water; stir into pork mixture. Cook, stirring constantly, until mixture thickens and boils. Boil and stir 1 minute. Stir in reserved pineapple chunks, the green pepper and tomatoes; heat until pineapple and tomatoes are hot. Stir ½ cup of the peanuts into hot rice. Serve pork mixture over rice; top with remaining peanuts. 6 SERVINGS.

SWEET-SOUR SAUCE
Drain syrup from 1 can (15½ ounces) pineapple chunks into measuring cup. Reserve pineapple chunks. Mix ⅓ cup of the syrup, ½ cup each sugar, water, vinegar and catsup, 2 teaspoons Worcestershire sauce and ⅛ teaspoon red pepper sauce.

Flatten pork tenderloin pieces to ½-inch thickness by pounding them with a mallet.

Wrap 1 slice of bacon around each tenderloin piece, then fasten with a wooden pick.

Place large mushroom cap on each tenderloin piece. (Use mushroom stems in gravy.)

Pour mixture of beef broth and crushed garlic on tenderloin pieces in baking pan.

Tenderloin Rounds

12 slices bacon
 2 pounds pork tenderloin
12 large mushrooms (caps removed)
 1 can (10½ ounces) condensed beef broth
 1 clove garlic, crushed
 ¼ cup water
 2 tablespoons flour

Heat oven to 350°. Fry bacon until limp; drain. Cut pork tenderloin into 12 pieces; flatten to ½-inch thickness. Wrap 1 slice bacon around each pork piece; fasten as pictured. Place pork pieces in ungreased jelly roll pan, 15½x10½x1 inch. Place 1 mushroom cap on each pork piece. Chop stems; reserve. Mix broth and garlic; pour on pork. Bake uncovered 45 minutes, spooning broth mixture onto pork every 15 minutes.

Shake water and flour in covered container; pour into 1-quart saucepan. Add enough water to broth to measure 1 cup; stir into flour mixture. Heat over low heat, stirring constantly, until smooth and bubbly. Stir in reserved mushrooms; heat. Serve with pork.   6 SERVINGS.

Pork Paprika

1 can (16 ounces) sauerkraut, drained
3 medium potatoes, shredded
½ cup milk
½ teaspoon salt
⅛ teaspoon pepper
1 pound bacon, crisply fried and crumbled
1 medium onion, thinly sliced
1 pound smoked pork shoulder roll, thinly
    sliced (see note)
1½ cups dry white wine
1 tablespoon paprika
2 tablespoons snipped parsley

Heat oven to 400°. Mix sauerkraut, potatoes, milk, salt and pepper. Spread half of the mixture in ungreased baking dish, 13½x8¾x1¾ inches. Reserve ⅓ cup of the bacon. Layer remaining bacon, the onion and pork slices on sauerkraut mixture in baking dish. Top with remaining sauerkraut mixture.

Pour wine on sauerkraut mixture; sprinkle with reserved bacon and the paprika. Cover and bake 1 hour. Let stand 10 minutes before serving. Sprinkle with parsley.
8 SERVINGS.

Note: Packaged smoked pork shoulder roll usually comes in 2-pound size or larger. Remaining pork can be thinly sliced and broiled or panfried, or simmered whole in water until light brown (40 minutes per pound).

One pound pork shoulder roll serves eight in this recipe.

Spread half of the sauerkraut mixture in the baking dish.

Add all but ⅓ cup bacon, then the onion and pork slices.

Add the remaining sauerkraut, wine, bacon and paprika.

Pork and Sauerkraut Stew

    4 slices bacon
    2 pounds pork boneless Boston shoulder
    1 tablespoon paprika
    2 to 3 teaspoons caraway seed
    1 teaspoon salt
    1 clove garlic, finely chopped
    1 can (16 ounces) sauerkraut, drained
 1½ cups water
    4 medium onions, sliced
   10 small new potatoes (about 1 pound)
  ½ teaspoon salt
    Snipped parsley
  ¾ cup dairy sour cream

Fry bacon slices in Dutch oven over medium heat until crisp; remove bacon and drain on paper towels. Trim excess fat from pork shoulder; cut pork into 1-inch pieces. Brown pork pieces in bacon fat; drain. Sprinkle pork with paprika, caraway seed, 1 teaspoon salt and the garlic. Stir in sauerkraut, water, onions and potatoes. Sprinkle with ½ teaspoon salt. Heat to boiling; reduce heat. Cover and simmer until pork is tender, about 1 hour.

Crumble bacon; sprinkle bacon and parsley over pork mixture. Serve with sour cream.   6 SERVINGS.

Pork Chop Succotash

    6 pork chops, ½ to ¾ inch thick
    1 can (16 ounces) whole tomatoes
 1½ teaspoons salt
  ½ teaspoon dried marjoram leaves
  ¼ teaspoon pepper
    1 package (10 ounces) frozen baby lima
      beans
 1½ cups ½-inch slices fresh okra*
    1 can (12 ounces) vacuum-pack whole
      kernel corn

Brown pork chops in 12-inch skillet or Dutch oven; drain. Mix tomatoes (with liquid), salt, marjoram and pepper; pour on chops. Heat to boiling; reduce heat. Cover and simmer 30 minutes.

Remove chops from skillet. Rinse frozen lima beans under running cold water to separate. Add lima beans, okra and corn to skillet; top with chops. Heat to boiling; reduce heat. Cover and simmer until vegetables are tender, 10 to 15 minutes.   6 SERVINGS.

*1 package (10 ounces) frozen okra can be substituted for the fresh okra.

Canadian Bacon Succotash: Substitute 1½ pounds Canadian-style bacon, cut into ½-inch slices, for the pork chops. Prepare as directed except—decrease salt to 1 teaspoon. Cover and simmer bacon mixture 15 minutes before adding vegetables.

Pork Chop Scallop

6 to 8 pork chops, ½ to ¾ inch thick
1 teaspoon salt
2 cups water
2 medium carrots, thinly sliced (about 1 cup)
1 package (9 ounces) frozen Italian green
   beans
2 tablespoons butter or margarine
1 package (5.25 ounces) scalloped potato mix
1 can (10¾ ounces) condensed cream of
   celery soup
⅔ cup milk
½ teaspoon dried basil leaves
½ teaspoon Worcestershire sauce

Heat oven to 350°. Trim excess fat from pork chops. Rub skillet with fat trimmed from pork. Brown pork in skillet; sprinkle with salt. Heat water to boiling in 3-quart saucepan. Add carrots and frozen beans; heat to boiling. Stir in butter and potato slices and Sauce Mix from scalloped potato package.

Mix soup, milk, basil and Worcestershire sauce; stir into vegetable mixture. Pour into ungreased baking dish, 13½x8¾x1¾ inches. Place pork on top. Cover and bake 45 minutes.

Uncover and bake until pork is tender, 10 to 15 minutes. Let stand 5 minutes before serving.   6 TO 8 SERVINGS.

Stir soup mixture into vegetable mixture in saucepan.

Place pork chops on top in baking dish; cover and bake.

Pork Steak Dinner in a Dish

Brown the pork steaks, two at a time, in skillet.

Pour soup mixture on pork, potatoes and onion.

4 pork blade or arm steaks, about ½ inch
  thick
10 small new potatoes (about 1 pound)
 1 small onion, chopped (about ¼ cup)
 1 can (10¾ ounces) condensed cream of
  chicken soup
 1 can (2 ounces) mushroom stems and
  pieces
 2 tablespoons dry sherry (optional)
 ½ teaspoon garlic salt
 ½ teaspoon Worcestershire sauce
 ¼ teaspoon dried thyme leaves
 1 package (10 ounces) frozen green peas and
  carrots

Brown pork steaks in 10-inch skillet; drain. Add potatoes and onion. Mix soup, mushrooms (with liquid), sherry, garlic salt, Worcestershire sauce and thyme. Pour on pork, potatoes and onion. Heat to boiling; reduce heat. Cover and simmer until tender, 50 to 60 minutes.

Rinse frozen peas and carrots under running cold water to separate; add to pork and vegetables. Cover and simmer until peas and carrots are tender, 10 to 15 minutes.
4 SERVINGS.

Pork and Potato Stacks

1¾ cups hot water
1 package (6 ounces) hash brown
  potato mix with onions
6 pork cubed steaks (about 1½ pounds)
2 tablespoons shortening
½ teaspoon salt
1 cup shredded Cheddar cheese (about
  4 ounces)
1 carton (8 ounces) dairy sour cream
¼ cup milk
1 teaspoon salt
¼ teaspoon pepper
¼ teaspoon dried dill weed

Pour water on potatoes; let stand 10 minutes. Brown pork cubed steaks in shortening in two 10-inch skillets, about 7 minutes on each side. Sprinkle with ½ teaspoon salt; place on ungreased baking sheet.

Heat cheese in 2-quart saucepan over medium heat, stirring constantly, until melted. Stir in sour cream, milk, 1 teaspoon salt, the pepper and dill. Drain potatoes; stir into cheese mixture.

Set oven control to broil and/or 550°. Top each steak with ½ cup of the potato mixture. Broil with tops 3 inches from heat until potatoes are light brown, 3 to 4 minutes.
6 SERVINGS.

Brown steaks in two skillets.

Stir potatoes into the cheese.

Measure the potato mixture.

Invert mixture on hot steaks.

Do-Ahead Glazed Pork Ribs

Place ribs meaty sides up on rack in a foil-lined pan.

Bake ribs 45 to 60 minutes, brushing with the sauce.

Carefully mold aluminum foil to inside of the Dutch oven.

Arrange ribs in Dutch oven; pour remaining sauce on top.

4 to 4½ pounds pork ribs (spareribs, back
   ribs or country-style ribs), cut into serving
   pieces
1 bottle (12 ounces) chili sauce (about 1 cup)
1 jar (10 ounces) plum jelly
3 to 4 teaspoons hot sauce or ¼ cup soy
   sauce

Place pork ribs meaty sides up on rack in aluminum foil-lined shallow roasting pan. Bake uncovered in 350° oven 45 minutes.

Heat chili sauce, jelly and hot sauce to boiling in 1-quart saucepan, stirring constantly. Brush pork with about ½ cup of the sauce; bake until tender, 45 to 60 minutes. While baking, brush 2 or 3 times with ¾ cup of the sauce. Crisscross 2 pieces heavy-duty aluminum foil in Dutch oven; carefully mold as pictured. Pour remaining sauce on pork in foil-lined Dutch oven. Cool quickly. Wrap pork securely in foil; remove from Dutch oven and label. Freeze up to 4 months.

■**40 minutes before serving,** remove from freezer and un-wrap. Place ⅓ cup water and frozen ribs in Dutch oven. Cover and heat over medium heat, turning occasionally, until pork is hot, about 30 minutes.   5 OR 6 SERVINGS.

Mandarin Pork Curry

1 medium onion, sliced
1 medium stalk celery, sliced (about ½ cup)
2 tablespoons vegetable oil
2 cups cut-up cooked pork
1¼ cups water
1 teaspoon instant chicken bouillon
1 to 2 teaspoons curry powder
½ teaspoon salt
2 tablespoons flour
¼ cup water
1 can (11 ounces) mandarin orange segments, drained
Hot cooked rice

Cook and stir onion and celery in oil in 10-inch skillet until onion is tender. Add pork, 1¼ cups water, the instant bouillon, curry powder and salt. Heat to boiling; remove from heat.

Blend flour and ¼ cup water; stir gradually into pork mixture. Heat to boiling, stirring constantly. Boil and stir 1 minute. Add orange segments and heat until oranges are hot. Serve over hot rice.   4 TO 6 SERVINGS.

Pork and Apple Curry: Substitute 1 medium apple, cut up, for the mandarin orange segments. Cook and stir with the onion and celery.

Add cut-up pork to the onion and celery in skillet.

Stir the flour-water mixture into the pork mixture.

Pork-Stuffed Eggplant

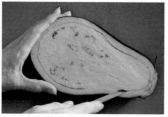

A grapefruit knife works well for cutting side of eggplant.

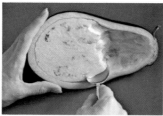

Scoop enough eggplant from the shells to measure 3 cups.

Heat pork mixture to boiling.

Spoon the mixture into shells.

2 small eggplants (about 1 pound each)
1 medium green pepper, chopped (about ½ cup)
1 small onion, chopped (about ¼ cup)
3 tablespoons vegetable oil
2 cups cut-up cooked pork
1½ cups cooked rice
1 can (16 ounces) whole tomatoes
1 clove garlic, crushed
1 teaspoon salt
½ teaspoon dried basil leaves
¼ teaspoon lemon pepper
4 tablespoons grated Parmesan cheese

Cut eggplants in half. Cut enough eggplant from shells to measure 3 cups; reserve shells. Cook and stir eggplant, green pepper and onion in oil over medium heat, 5 minutes.

Heat oven to 350°. Add pork, rice, tomatoes (with liquid), garlic, salt, basil and lemon pepper to eggplant mixture; break up tomatoes with fork. Heat to boiling; reduce heat. Cover and simmer 10 minutes.

Place eggplant shells in ungreased shallow baking pan; spoon pork mixture into shells. Sprinkle 1 tablespoon cheese over each shell. Bake uncovered until eggplant is tender, 30 to 40 minutes.   4 SERVINGS.

Pizzaghetti

1 pound mild Italian bulk sausage
1 tablespoon vegetable oil
1 can (16 ounces) stewed tomatoes
1 can (8 ounces) tomato sauce
½ teaspoon dried basil leaves, crushed
½ teaspoon salt
¼ teaspoon garlic powder
¼ teaspoon pepper
7 ounces uncooked spaghetti
1 can (12 ounces) whole kernel corn with
    sweet peppers
⅓ cup sliced pimiento-stuffed olives
5 thin slices mozzarella or Monterey Jack
    cheese

Cook and stir Italian bulk sausage in oil in 10-inch skillet over medium heat until light brown, about 6 minutes; drain. Stir in tomatoes, tomato sauce, basil, salt, garlic powder and pepper. Heat to boiling; reduce heat. Simmer uncovered, stirring occasionally, 10 minutes.

Cook spaghetti as directed on package; drain. Stir corn (with liquid) and olives into sausage mixture. Simmer uncovered 5 minutes. Serve over spaghetti; top each serving with a cheese slice.   5 SERVINGS.

Cook the spaghetti while the sauce simmers.

Stir the corn and sliced olives into the sauce.

Sausage and Succotash

Slice celery and chop onion while sausage browns.

Sprinkle each serving with corn chips and cheese.

1 pound pork bulk sausage
2 medium stalks celery, sliced (about 1 cup)
1 medium onion, chopped (about ½ cup)
1 teaspoon salt
⅛ teaspoon instant minced garlic
1 can (16 ounces) pork and beans in tomato sauce
1 can (16 ounces) succotash
1 can (6 ounces) tomato paste
⅓ cup pitted ripe olives, cut in half
1 cup corn chips, crushed
1 cup shredded sharp Cheddar cheese (about 4 ounces)

Cook and stir pork bulk sausage in 10-inch skillet over medium heat until light brown; drain. Stir in celery, onion, salt and garlic. Cook and stir until onion is tender, about 2 minutes.

Stir in pork and beans (with liquid), succotash (with liquid) and tomato paste. Heat to boiling; reduce heat. Simmer uncovered 10 minutes. Stir in olives; heat until hot. Sprinkle each serving with corn chips and cheese.   4 OR 5 SERVINGS.

Cheese and Franks

1 medium onion, sliced
1 small green pepper, chopped (about
  ½ cup)
2 tablespoons butter or margarine
1 can (16 ounces) whole tomatoes
1 teaspoon seasoned salt
1 teaspoon sugar
8 frankfurters, cut lengthwise in half
1 can (4 ounces) sliced mushrooms, drained
  Grilled Cheese Sandwiches (below)
¼ cup water
2 tablespoons cornstarch

Cook and stir onion and green pepper in butter in 3-quart saucepan over medium heat until onion is tender, about 3 minutes. Stir in tomatoes (with liquid), seasoned salt and sugar. Heat to boiling; reduce heat. Simmer uncovered 6 minutes. Stir in frankfurters and mushrooms. Simmer uncovered 12 minutes.

Prepare Grilled Cheese Sandwiches. Mix water and cornstarch; stir into frankfurter mixture. Cook, stirring constantly, until mixture thickens and boils. Boil and stir 1 minute. Top each sandwich with 2 frankfurter halves and about ¼ cup of the sauce.   8 SERVINGS.

GRILLED CHEESE SANDWICHES

Heat griddle or two 12-inch skillets over medium heat. Spread butter or margarine, softened, over 1 side of each of 8 slices bread. Place bread buttered sides down on hot griddle. Top with 8 slices cheese. Top cheese with 8 slices bread. Spread butter over bread. Grill sandwiches on both sides until cheese is melted and sandwiches are golden brown.

Slice frankfurters while the tomato mixture simmers.

Prepare Grilled Cheese Sandwiches while sauce simmers.

Grill the sandwiches until golden and cheese is melted.

Add water and cornstarch to franks; heat to boiling.

Frank Fiesta

Cut the frankfurters diagonally into ½-inch slices.

Cook and stir frankfurter slices and onion in skillet.

Stir in remaining ingredients except green pepper.

Cut green pepper into strips; add to mixture in skillet.

8 to 10 frankfurters, cut diagonally into
   ½-inch slices
1 medium onion, chopped (about ½ cup)
1 tablespoon vegetable oil
1 can (15 ounces) tomato sauce
1 can (8¾ ounces) whole kernel corn
1 can (8 ounces) kidney beans
5 ounces uncooked spiral macaroni or wide
   noodles
½ cup water
1½ to 2 teaspoons chili powder
1 teaspoon salt
½ medium green pepper, cut into strips

Cook and stir frankfurter slices and onion in oil in 12-inch skillet or Dutch oven until frankfurters are light brown and onion is tender. Stir in remaining ingredients except green pepper. Heat to boiling; reduce heat. Cover and simmer, stirring occasionally, until macaroni is tender, 20 to 25 minutes.

Add green pepper. Cover and simmer until green pepper is crisp-tender, about 5 minutes.　　4 TO 6 SERVINGS.

Easy Sausage Supper

2 cups water
2 teaspoons instant beef bouillon
2 large potatoes, cut lengthwise into fourths
4 medium carrots, cut into 3x½-inch strips
2 large onions, cut into fourths
½ medium head cabbage, cut into 4 wedges
1 teaspoon salt
1 medium apple, cut into wedges
4 to 6 knackwurst
Prepared mustard
Horseradish

Heat water and instant bouillon to boiling in Dutch oven. Layer potatoes, carrots, onions and cabbage in bouillon; sprinkle with salt. Layer apple and knackwurst on top. Heat to boiling; reduce heat. Cover and simmer until vegetables are tender, 25 to 30 minutes.

Remove knackwurst, apple and vegetables with slotted spoon and arrange on platter. Serve with mustard and horseradish.   4 SERVINGS.

CASSEROLE KNOW-HOW

For best results, always use the size and shape baking dish that is specified in your recipe. If your baking dish is too large, the liquid will evaporate and baking time will be affected. If it is too small, your casserole may bubble over in the oven. If your recipe calls for a cover and you do not have one, aluminum foil is a good substitute.

Pare the potatoes and cut lengthwise into fourths.

For variety, cut carrots into strips with lattice cutter.

Layer vegetables, apple and knackwurst in Dutch oven.

After simmering, remove with slotted spoon.

Glazed Ham with Spiced Grapes

Cut surface of ham ¼ inch deep in a diamond pattern.

Insert a whole clove in the center of each diamond.

Place 5- to 7-pound fully cooked ham fat side up on rack in shallow roasting pan. Insert meat thermometer so tip is in center of thickest part of meat and does not touch bone or rest in fat. Roast uncovered in 325° oven until meat thermometer registers 140°, 1½ to 2½ hours.

About 30 minutes before ham is done, remove from oven and cut surface ¼ inch deep in diamond pattern. If desired, insert whole clove in each diamond. Spoon one of the Ham Glazes (below) onto ham every 10 minutes. Serve with Spiced Grapes (below). 6 SERVINGS—with ham for leftovers.

HAM GLAZES

Mix ¼ cup honey, ½ teaspoon dry mustard and ¼ teaspoon ground cloves or ground ginger.

Heat ½ cup red cinnamon jelly, ¼ cup corn syrup and ⅛ teaspoon dry mustard over low heat, stirring constantly, until jelly is melted.

SPICED GRAPES

   1 pound Tokay grapes, cut in half and
      seeds removed (about 2⅓ cups)
1½ cups sugar
  ½ cup cider vinegar
  ¼ cup maraschino cherry juice
  3 sticks cinnamon

Place grapes in 1-quart jar or glass container. Heat remaining ingredients to boiling in small saucepan, stirring constantly until sugar is dissolved; reduce heat. Simmer uncovered 5 minutes. Pour hot syrup on grapes; cool. Cover and refrigerate at least 2 hours.

Broiled Ham Platter

1 can (24 ounces) fully cooked ham
  Whole cloves
1 can (11 ounces) mandarin orange
  segments, drained (reserve 2 tablespoons
  syrup)
½ teaspoon prepared horseradish
1 can (16 ounces) whole new potatoes,
  drained
1 can (16 ounces) whole green beans,
  drained
1 can (4 ounces) mushroom stems and
  pieces, drained
2 tablespoons butter or margarine, softened
⅛ teaspoon paprika
  Dried thyme leaves

Cut ham horizontally in half, then score and insert cloves.

Drizzle the mixture of syrup and horseradish over ham.

Heat oven to 350°. Cut ham horizontally in half. Cut top of each half ¼ inch deep in 1-inch diamond pattern; insert cloves in cuts. Place in broiler pan. Mix reserved orange syrup and horseradish; drizzle over ham. Bake 10 minutes.

Arrange potatoes, beans and mushrooms around ham; place orange segments between ham slices. Dot vegetables with butter. Sprinkle potatoes with paprika, and beans and mushrooms with thyme.

Set oven control to broil and/or 550°. Broil with tops 4 to 5 inches from heat about 5 minutes.   4 OR 5 SERVINGS.

Glazed Ham with Peaches

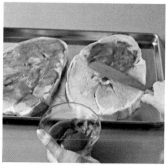

Spread ham slices with seasoned paste. Bake uncovered in 325° oven 30 minutes.

About ten minutes before serving, stir peaches in butter sauce until coated.

2 slices fully cooked center smoked ham,
   1 inch thick (about 3½ pounds)
½ cup packed brown sugar
¾ teaspoon dry mustard
¼ teaspoon ground allspice
1 can (16 ounces) peach halves, drained
   (reserve syrup)
3 tablespoons orange-flavored liqueur
2 tablespoons packed brown sugar
2 tablespoons butter or margarine
   Lemon leaves or parsley

Cut ham slices ¼ inch deep in diamond pattern as pictured. Place in ungreased jelly roll pan, 15½x10½x1 inch. Mix ½ cup brown sugar, the mustard and allspice. Add enough syrup (about 1 tablespoon) to make paste; spread over ham. Bake uncovered in 325° oven 30 minutes.

About 10 minutes before serving, cut each peach half in two. Heat peaches, liqueur, 2 tablespoons brown sugar and the butter over medium heat, stirring constantly, until sugar is dissolved and peaches are coated. Arrange the peaches around ham; garnish with lemon leaves. Serve peach sauce with ham.   10 SERVINGS.

Ham Loaf Swirl

1 pound ground fully cooked ham
1 pound ground lean pork
2 eggs, beaten
1 cup quick-cooking oats
¾ cup tomato juice
1 medium onion, chopped (about ½ cup)
½ teaspoon salt
¼ teaspoon pepper
1 package (10 ounces) frozen cut green
    beans
¼ teaspoon salt
3 slices mozzarella, American or Swiss
    cheese, cut diagonally into triangles

Heat oven to 350°. Mix ground ham, ground pork, eggs, oats, tomato juice, onion, ½ teaspoon salt and the pepper. Pat meat mixture into rectangle, 12x10 inches, on 18x15-inch piece of aluminum foil.

Rinse frozen beans under running cold water to separate; drain. Arrange beans evenly on meat mixture, leaving ½-inch margin on all sides. Sprinkle with ¼ teaspoon salt. Roll up meat, beginning at narrow end, using foil to lift meat as pictured. Press edges and ends of loaf to seal. Place on rack in ungreased baking pan, 13x9x2 inches. Bake uncovered until brown, 1¼ to 1½ hours.

Just before serving, overlap cheese triangles on loaf; bake until cheese begins to melt, about 2 minutes.   8 SERVINGS.

Pat the meat mixture into a rectangle on aluminum foil.

Arrange beans evenly on meat, leaving ½-inch margin.

Roll up meat, using the foil to lift meat as it is rolled.

Place the loaf on rack in baking pan and pat into shape.

Red-Eye Ham with Biscuit Squares

Brown ham slices 5 minutes on each side; remove from pan.

Cook and stir coffee with particles from ham until blended.

Brush dough with half of the melted butter or margarine.

Fold rectangle in half. Brush with remaining butter; cut.

Soak 2 packages (12 ounces each) thin boneless country-style ham slices in warm water 1 hour. Trim excess fat from ham. Heat fat pieces in 12-inch skillet until crisp; remove from skillet. Add ham. Brown over medium-high heat 5 minutes on each side. Remove to warm platter.

Drain fat from skillet. Stir in 1 cup hot coffee or boiling water. Heat to boiling; cook and stir until particles from ham are blended with coffee. Serve ham with gravy and Biscuit Squares (below).   6 SERVINGS.

BISCUIT SQUARES
- ½ cup shortening
- 2 cups all-purpose flour*
- 1½ teaspoons baking powder
- 1 teaspoon salt
- ½ teaspoon baking soda
- ⅔ cup buttermilk or sweet milk
- ¼ cup butter or margarine, melted

Heat oven to 450°. Cut shortening into flour, baking powder, salt and baking soda until particles are size of small peas. Stir in buttermilk.

Gather dough into a ball. Knead lightly 10 to 15 times. Roll dough into rectangle, 16x8 inches, on lightly floured cloth-covered board; brush with half of the butter. Fold rectangle crosswise in half; brush with remaining butter. Cut into 2-inch squares. Place on ungreased baking sheet. Bake until golden brown, 10 to 12 minutes.

*If using self-rising flour, omit baking powder, salt and baking soda.

Ham Rolls

1 package (10 ounces) frozen asparagus
   spears
8 thin slices fully cooked ham
1 can (10¾ ounces) condensed cream of
   shrimp soup
¼ cup dry white wine or water

Heat oven to 350°. Cook asparagus spears as directed on package; drain. Wrap each ham slice around 2 or 3 asparagus spears. Place in ungreased baking dish,10x6x1¾ inches. Mix soup and wine; pour on ham rolls. Bake uncovered until bubbly, 20 to 25 minutes.   4 SERVINGS.

Wrap each ham slice around 2 or 3 asparagus spears.

Pour the soup-wine mixture evenly on the Ham Rolls.

Ham Hawaiian

¾ pound fully cooked ham, cut into 2x½x¼-
   inch strips (about 2 cups)
2 medium stalks celery, thinly sliced (about
   1 cup)
1 medium red apple, cut up (about 1 cup)
1 can (15¼ ounces) pineapple chunks,
   drained
½ cup mayonnaise or salad dressing
1 teaspoon soy sauce
½ teaspoon ground ginger
4 ounces spinach or ½ small head lettuce,
   torn into bite-size pieces (about 2 cups)

Toss ham, celery, apple and pineapple. Mix mayonnaise, soy sauce and ginger; stir into ham mixture. Refrigerate at least 1 hour. Just before serving, toss ham mixture with spinach.   4 TO 6 SERVINGS.

Ham and Green Noodle Bake

Add the Swiss cheese to the onion sauce and ham.

Alternate noodles and sauce mixture in casserole.

1 medium onion, chopped (about ½ cup)
2 tablespoons butter or margarine
2 tablespoons flour
½ teaspoon salt
¼ teaspoon pepper
¼ teaspoon dry mustard
1¾ cups milk*
2 cups cut-up fully cooked ham
½ cup shredded Swiss cheese (about 2 ounces)
4 ounces uncooked spinach egg noodles
2 tablespoons grated Parmesan cheese
Twist of lemon
Celery leaves

Heat oven to 375°. Cook and stir onion in butter until tender. Blend in flour, salt, pepper and mustard. Heat over low heat, stirring constantly, until bubbly; remove from heat. Add milk; heat to boiling, stirring constantly. Boil and stir 1 minute. Stir in ham and Swiss cheese.

Cook noodles as directed on package; drain. Alternate layers of noodles and sauce mixture in ungreased 1½-quart casserole; sprinkle with Parmesan cheese. Bake uncovered until bubbly and light brown, about 20 minutes. Garnish with twist of lemon and celery leaves.
6 SERVINGS.

* ¼ cup dry sherry can be substituted for ¼ cup of the milk.

Ham and Spaghetti Casserole

7 ounces uncooked thin spaghetti, broken
   into 2-inch pieces
2 cups cubed fully cooked ham
1 cup dairy sour cream
1 can (10¾ ounces) condensed cream of
   chicken soup
1 jar (4½ ounces) sliced mushrooms, drained
   (reserve ¼ cup liquid)
½ cup sliced pimiento-stuffed olives
2 tablespoons instant minced onion
½ teaspoon seasoned salt
1 teaspoon dry mustard
1 teaspoon Worcestershire sauce
¾ cup bread crumbs
2 tablespoons butter or margarine, melted
1 cup shredded Cheddar cheese (about 4
   ounces)

Heat oven to 325°. Cook spaghetti as directed on package; drain. Mix spaghetti, ham, sour cream, soup, mushrooms, reserved mushroom liquid, olives, onion, seasoned salt, mustard and Worcestershire sauce. Pour into ungreased baking dish, 11¾ x 7½ x 1¾ inches.

Mix bread crumbs and butter. Mix ½ cup of the cheese and the buttered bread crumbs; sprinkle in diagonal rows over casserole. Sprinkle remaining cheese between rows. Bake until casserole begins to bubble, about 30 minutes.

8 SERVINGS.

Mix all ingredients except bread crumbs, butter and the shredded Cheddar cheese.

Mix ½ cup of the shredded Cheddar cheese and the buttered bread crumbs.

Sprinkle the cheese–bread crumb mixture in diagonal rows over the casserole.

Sprinkle the remaining Cheddar cheese between the rows. Bake about 30 minutes.

Lamb Cucumber and Pineapple Ice

Place 4- to 5-pound lamb rolled shoulder roast fat side up on rack in shallow roasting pan. Insert meat thermometer so tip is in thickest part of lamb and does not rest in fat. Roast uncovered in 325° oven until meat thermometer registers 175 to 180°, 2¾ to 3¾ hours.

About 40 minutes before lamb is done, prepare Cucumber Topping (below). Overlap cucumber slices on lamb. Spoon liquid onto slices; repeat every 10 minutes. Serve with Pineapple Ice (below). 6 SERVINGS—with lamb for leftovers.

CUCUMBER TOPPING
  2 small cucumbers, cut into ⅛-inch slices
  1 cup water
1½ teaspoons salt
  1 teaspoon instant chicken bouillon
½ teaspoon pepper
½ teaspoon rosemary

Place cucumber slices in small bowl. Mix remaining ingredients; pour on cucumbers.

PINEAPPLE ICE
  2 cans (6 ounces each) pineapple juice
½ cup light corn syrup
  2 tablespoons lemon juice
⅛ teaspoon mint extract

Mix all ingredients. Pour into ice cube tray. Freeze until edges are firm, about 2 hours.

Turn frozen mixture into chilled small mixer bowl; beat on low speed until smooth. Beat on high speed just until foamy, about 1 minute. Pour into ice cube tray. Freeze until firm, about 2 hours.

Mandarin Lamb

1½ pounds lean lamb boneless shoulder, cut
    into ½-inch strips
¼ teaspoon garlic powder
  2 tablespoons butter or margarine
  1 medium onion, chopped (about ½ cup)
  1 cup water
1½ cups water
½ teaspoon salt
  1 cup uncooked instant brown rice
¼ cup water
  3 tablespoons soy sauce
  2 tablespoons cornstarch
½ teaspoon salt
¼ teaspoon pepper
  1 medium green pepper, cut into rings
  1 can (11 ounces) mandarin orange
    segments, drained

Cook and stir lamb strips and garlic powder in butter in 10-inch skillet until lamb is brown, about 6 minutes. Stir in onion and 1 cup water. Heat to boiling; reduce heat. Cover and simmer 15 minutes.

Heat 1½ cups water and ½ teaspoon salt to boiling in 1½-quart saucepan. Stir in rice; reduce heat. Cover and steam 15 minutes.

Mix ¼ cup water, the soy sauce, cornstarch, ½ teaspoon salt and the pepper; stir into lamb mixture. Add green pepper rings, reserving 2 or 3 rings for garnish. Cook, stirring constantly, until mixture thickens and boils. Boil and stir 1 minute. Fold in orange segments. Serve over rice and garnish with reserved green pepper rings. 4 SERVINGS.

Lamb and Bean Stew

½ pound dry white beans (about 1¼ cups)
3 medium onions, thinly sliced
3 medium carrots, cut into 1-inch pieces
¼ cup butter or margarine
2 pounds lamb stew meat, cut into 1-inch
    pieces
1 clove garlic, finely chopped
¼ cup vegetable oil
¾ cup dry white wine
1 cup boiling water
1 teaspoon instant chicken bouillon
2 medium tomatoes, peeled and chopped
1 teaspoon dried thyme leaves
2½ teaspoons salt
⅛ teaspoon pepper
1 bouquet garni (see note)

Place browned lamb on onions and carrots in Dutch oven.

Pour on wine mixture; stir in beans. Cover and simmer.

Place beans in 3-quart saucepan. Add water to 1 inch above beans. Heat to boiling; boil 2 minutes. Remove from heat; cover and let stand 1 hour. Drain.

Cook and stir onions and carrots in butter in Dutch oven over low heat, stirring occasionally, about 10 minutes.

Cook and stir lamb and garlic in oil in 10-inch skillet over medium heat until lamb is light brown. Remove lamb, reserving pan juices. Place lamb on onions and carrots in Dutch oven. Stir wine into reserved pan juices. Heat to boiling; boil and stir 2 minutes. Stir in remaining ingredients. Heat to boiling; pour on lamb in Dutch oven. Stir in beans. Heat to boiling; reduce heat. Cover and simmer until beans are tender, about 1½ hours. Refrigerate several hours. Skim off fat; reheat to serve.   4 TO 6 SERVINGS.

Note: For a bouquet garni, tie 2 sprigs parsley, ⅓ bay leaf and ⅛ teaspoon dried rosemary leaves in cheesecloth.

Spanish Lamb

Heat tomato mixture to boiling, stirring occasionally.

Add the cut-up lamb and olives to the tomato mixture.

1 medium onion, chopped (about ½ cup)
2 tablespoons vegetable oil
1 can (15 ounces) tomato sauce
1 can (2 ounces) mushroom stems and
　　pieces
½ teaspoon garlic salt
½ teaspoon dried basil leaves
1 bay leaf
2 cups cut-up cooked lamb
¼ cup sliced pimiento-stuffed olives
　　Hot cooked spaghetti
¼ cup grated Parmesan cheese

Cook onion in oil in 2-quart saucepan until tender. Stir in tomato sauce, mushrooms (with liquid), garlic salt, basil and bay leaf. Heat to boiling; reduce heat. Cover and simmer 20 minutes.

Stir in lamb and olives; heat until lamb is hot. Serve over hot spaghetti. Sprinkle with cheese. Garnish with additional sliced pimiento-stuffed olives.　4 TO 6 SERVINGS.

Lamb Romanoff

1 package (5.5 ounces) noodles Romanoff mix
1½ cups cut-up cooked lamb
1 medium stalk celery, chopped
1 tablespoon snipped chives
½ teaspoon curry powder
　　Paprika

Heat oven to 350°. Prepare noodles Romanoff as directed on package except—increase milk to ⅔ cup. Stir in remaining ingredients except paprika. Pour into ungreased 1-quart casserole. Cover and bake until lamb is hot, about 15 minutes. Sprinkle with paprika.　4 SERVINGS.

Bacon-Lamb Burgers

8 slices bacon (about ½ pound)
1 pound ground lamb
2 slices bread, torn into small pieces
1 egg
1 small onion, finely chopped (about ¼ cup)
¼ cup grated Parmesan cheese or American cheese food
¼ cup milk
3 tablespoons snipped parsley
1¼ teaspoons salt
Dash of pepper

Arrange bacon slices on plastic wrap so they overlap slightly. Mix remaining ingredients and spread over bacon. Roll up like jelly roll as pictured; wrap in plastic wrap and secure with wooden picks if necessary. Refrigerate at least 2 hours but no longer than 8 hours.

Set oven control to broil and/or 550°. Unwrap lamb roll and cut into 8 slices; flatten slightly. Broil with tops 4 to 5 inches from heat 6 to 8 minutes on each side.   4 TO 6 SERVINGS.

Overlap bacon slices on piece of plastic wrap.

Spread lamb mixture evenly over the bacon slices.

Roll up, using plastic wrap to ease roll together.

Cut chilled roll into slices, using sharp knife.

Veal Strips Stroganoff

Start veal; slice mushrooms. Simmer veal; cook noodles.

Mix soup and milk; add to veal. Toss noodles, butter and seed.

1 pound veal round steak, ¼ inch thick, cut
   into ¼-inch strips
¼ cup butter or margarine
¼ teaspoon salt
⅛ teaspoon dried thyme leaves
⅛ teaspoon pepper
½ pound mushrooms, sliced
¼ cup frozen chopped onion (optional)
¼ cup water
5 ounces uncooked noodles (about 2⅔ cups)
1 can (10¾ ounces) condensed cream of
   mushroom soup
½ cup milk
1 tablespoon butter or margarine
1 teaspoon poppy seed

Cook veal strips in ¼ cup butter in 10-inch skillet over medium heat, stirring occasionally, until light brown, about 3 minutes. Sprinkle veal with salt, thyme and pepper. Stir in mushrooms, onion and water. Heat to boiling; reduce heat. Cover and simmer until veal is tender, about 20 minutes.

Cook noodles as directed on package. Mix soup and milk; stir into veal mixture. Heat until soup is hot. Drain noodles; toss with 1 tablespoon butter and the poppy seed. Serve stroganoff over noodles.   4 SERVINGS.

Veal Chop Suey

1 pound veal round steak, cut into ½-inch
    cubes
1 medium onion, thinly sliced
2 large stalks celery, cut diagonally into
    slices (about 1½ cups)
2 tablespoons vegetable oil
1 can (16 ounces) bean sprouts, drained
1¾ cups water
1 teaspoon salt
3 tablespoons cornstarch
3 tablespoons cold water
3 tablespoons soy sauce
1 teaspoon packed brown sugar
1 jar (2½ ounces) sliced mushrooms,
    drained
1 cup cherry tomatoes, cut in half
    Chow mein noodles

Slice onion while veal cooks.

Cut celery while onion cooks.

Cook and stir veal cubes, onion and celery in oil in 10-inch skillet over medium heat until veal is brown and onion is tender, about 5 minutes. Stir in bean sprouts, 1¾ cups water and the salt. Heat to boiling; reduce heat. Cover and simmer until veal is tender, about 15 minutes.

Mix cornstarch, 3 tablespoons cold water, the soy sauce and brown sugar; stir into veal mixture. Cook, stirring constantly, until mixture thickens and boils. Boil and stir 1 minute. Stir in mushrooms; fold in tomatoes. Serve over chow mein noodles.　4 SERVINGS.

Braised Veal Shanks

Use veal (left) or beef shanks (right) for this recipe.

Cook and turn coated veal in oil until brown on all sides.

Add broth, wine, garlic and bay leaf. Cover and simmer.

To skim fat from broth, wrap ice cubes in a paper towel.

4 pounds veal or beef shanks, cut into
   2½-inch pieces
1 teaspoon salt
¼ teaspoon pepper
¼ cup all-purpose flour
3 tablespoons olive or vegetable oil
1 can (10½ ounces) condensed beef broth
⅓ cup dry white wine
1 clove garlic, crushed
1 bay leaf
7 ounces uncooked spaghetti
2 tablespoons snipped parsley
1 teaspoon grated lemon peel
  Grated Romano cheese

Trim excess fat from veal shanks if necessary. Sprinkle veal with salt and pepper; coat with flour. Cook and turn veal in oil in 4-quart Dutch oven over medium heat until brown on all sides, about 20 minutes.

Stir in broth, wine, garlic and bay leaf. Heat to boiling; reduce heat. Cover and simmer until veal is tender, 1½ to 2 hours. Remove veal; skim fat from broth. Return veal to broth.

Cook spaghetti as directed on package; drain. Sprinkle veal mixture with parsley and lemon peel. Heat to boiling; reduce heat. Cover and simmer 5 minutes. Serve on spaghetti; sprinkle with cheese.   4 TO 6 SERVINGS.

Poultry and Seafood

Roast Orange-Stuffed Chicken

After stuffing wishbone area, fasten neck skin with skewer.

Fill each body cavity with about 2 cups of orange stuffing.

Tie drumsticks to tails; place the chickens in roasting pan.

Crisscross 2 slices of bacon on each chicken; roast uncovered.

Three 2½- to 3-pound broiler-fryer
 chickens
1 can (11 ounces) mandarin orange
 segments, drained
1 cup coarsely chopped walnuts
2 medium apples, chopped (about 2 cups)
2 cups herb-seasoned stuffing mix
⅓ cup orange marmalade
6 slices bacon
 Parsley sprigs
 Orange slices
 Cranberries

Stuff chickens just before roasting, not ahead of time. To prepare stuffing, toss orange segments, walnuts, apples and stuffing mix. Add orange marmalade and toss.

Fill each wishbone area with about ¼ cup stuffing. Fasten neck skins to backs with skewers. Fold wings across backs with tips touching. Fill each body cavity with about 2 cups stuffing. (Stuffing will expand while cooking.) Tie drumsticks to tails.

Heat oven to 375°. Place chickens breast sides up on rack in shallow roasting pan or jelly roll pan, 15½x10½x1 inch. Crisscross 2 bacon slices on top of each chicken. Do not add water. Roast uncovered until drumstick meat feels soft when pressed between fingers, 1¼ to 1¾ hours. Garnish with parsley sprigs, orange slices and cranberries.

12 TO 16 SERVINGS.

Country-Style Chicken

2½- to 3-pound broiler-fryer chicken
½ teaspoon salt
⅛ teaspoon pepper
2 tablespoons butter or margarine
4 thin strips salt pork
2 tablespoons butter or margarine
8 medium carrots, cut into fourths
8 medium turnips, cut into fourths
1 can (10¾ ounces) condensed chicken broth
½ teaspoon salt
⅛ teaspoon pepper
½ cup dry white wine
1 tablespoon plus 1½ teaspoons cornstarch
3 tablespoons water

Rub skin of chicken with ½ teaspoon salt and ⅛ teaspoon pepper. Fold wings across back with tips touching; tie drumsticks to tail.

Melt 2 tablespoons butter in Dutch oven. Brown chicken in butter over medium heat about 30 minutes. Place 2 strips salt pork over breast and 1 strip over each drumstick.

Heat oven to 325°. Melt 2 tablespoons butter in 10-inch skillet. Toss half of the carrots and turnips in butter; place in Dutch oven around chicken. Toss remaining vegetables in butter; place around chicken. Pour broth over chicken and vegetables; sprinkle with ½ teaspoon salt and ⅛ teaspoon pepper. Cover and bake until thickest pieces of chicken are done, about 1¾ hours.

Remove chicken and vegetables to warm platter; remove salt pork strips and string from chicken. Keep chicken warm while preparing sauce.

Stir wine into chicken broth. Heat to boiling, stirring constantly. Boil and stir 3 minutes. Mix cornstarch and water; stir into wine broth. Heat to boiling, stirring constantly. Boil and stir 3 minutes; skim off fat. Serve sauce with chicken.   6 OR 7 SERVINGS.

Do-Ahead Chicken in White Wine

2½- to 3-pound broiler-fryer chicken, cut up
2 tablespoons vegetable oil
½ pound fresh mushrooms
¼ pound tiny pearl onions or 8 small white onions
1 cup dry white wine
1 cup water
1 chicken bouillon cube
1 clove garlic, finely chopped
1 teaspoon salt
¼ teaspoon pepper
  Bouquet garni
½ pound fresh green beans, cut lengthwise into strips

Brown chicken pieces in oil in Dutch oven; remove chicken. Add mushrooms and onions. Cook and stir until tender, adding more oil if necessary. Return chicken to Dutch oven; stir in wine, water, bouillon cube, garlic, salt, pepper and bouquet garni. Heat to boiling; reduce heat. Cover and simmer 45 minutes.

Add beans. Heat to boiling; reduce heat. Cover and simmer until chicken is done, 15 to 20 minutes; remove bouquet garni. Cover and refrigerate up to 24 hours.

■20 minutes before serving, spoon off fat. Heat chicken mixture to boiling; reduce heat. Cover and simmer 10 minutes. Garnish with snipped parsley.   4 SERVINGS.

Note: For a bouquet garni, tie 2 sprigs parsley, ⅓ bay leaf and ⅛ teaspoon dried rosemary leaves in cheesecloth.

Chicken-Squash Skillet

Zucchini, yellow crookneck and scalloped squash.

Cut zucchini or crookneck lengthwise in half.

Cut fresh green beans lengthwise into strips.

Place squash, beans and onions on chicken.

2½- to 3-pound broiler-fryer chicken, cut up
2 tablespoons vegetable oil
1½ cups water
2 teaspoons instant chicken bouillon
½ teaspoon dried basil leaves
1 bay leaf
1 pound soft-shelled summer squash (crookneck, zucchini or scalloped)
½ pound fresh green beans, cut lengthwise into strips*
2 medium onions, cut into ½-inch slices
1 teaspoon salt
½ cup pitted ripe olives, drained
1 tablespoon cornstarch
2 tablespoons cold water

Brown chicken pieces in oil in 12-inch skillet or Dutch oven; drain. Add 1½ cups water, the instant bouillon, basil and bay leaf. Heat to boiling; reduce heat. Cover and simmer 30 minutes.

Remove stem and blossom ends from squash, but do not pare. Cut crookneck and zucchini lengthwise in half; cut scalloped crosswise in half. Place squash, beans and onions on chicken. Sprinkle with salt. Heat to boiling; reduce heat. Cover and simmer until chicken is done and vegetables are tender, 20 to 25 minutes.

Remove chicken and vegetables to serving platter; top with olives. Mix cornstarch and 2 tablespoons water; stir into liquid in skillet. Cook over medium heat, stirring constantly, until mixture thickens and boils. Boil and stir 1 minute. Serve over chicken and vegetables.   6 SERVINGS.

*1 package (9 ounces) frozen French-style green beans, thawed, can be substituted for the fresh beans.

Chicken Moroccan Style

3 medium onions, sliced
2 tablespoons vegetable oil
2½- to 3-pound broiler-fryer chicken, cut up
1 can (8 ounces) tomato sauce
1 cup water
2 medium carrots, cut into 2-inch slices
2 teaspoons salt
½ teaspoon chili powder
⅓ cup bulgur or instant barley
3 medium sweet potatoes, cut into ½-inch
   slices
1 can (15 ounces) garbanzo or kidney beans
½ pound pepperoni, cut into ½-inch slices,
   or ½ pound fully cooked ham, cut up

Stir barley into liquid, lifting chicken if necessary; add potatoes and beans.

Add pepperoni to cooked mixture in Dutch oven; heat until pepperoni is hot.

Cook and stir onions in oil in Dutch oven until tender; remove onions. Brown chicken pieces in Dutch oven, adding more oil if necessary; drain. Return onions to Dutch oven. Stir in tomato sauce, water, carrots, salt and chili powder. Heat to boiling; reduce heat. Cover and simmer 30 minutes.

Stir bulgur into liquid in Dutch oven, lifting chicken if necessary. Add sweet potatoes and beans (with liquid). Heat to boiling; reduce heat. Cover and simmer until sweet potatoes are tender, 25 to 30 minutes. Add pepperoni; heat until pepperoni is hot.　6 SERVINGS.

Simmer the chicken with the carrots, onion, salt, broth, wine and 1 bouquet garni.

Heat onions, remaining butter, wine and bouquet garni to boiling; cover and simmer.

Cook strained broth mixture, mushrooms and lemon juice until reduced to 2½ cups.

Beat 1 cup broth by table-spoonfuls into cream mixture; beat in remaining broth.

Chicken Fricassee

2 medium carrots, thinly sliced
1 medium onion, thinly sliced
6 tablespoons butter or margarine
3-pound broiler-fryer chicken, cut up
½ teaspoon salt
2 cans (10¾ ounces each) condensed
    chicken broth
1 cup dry white wine or dry vermouth
2 bouquets garnis (see note)
16 small white onions
½ pound mushrooms, sliced
1 tablespoon lemon juice
2 egg yolks
½ cup whipping cream

Cook and stir carrots and onion slices in 4 tablespoons of the butter in Dutch oven; push aside. Add chicken; cook until golden, about 5 minutes. Add salt, broth, ½ cup wine and 1 bouquet garni. Heat to boiling; reduce heat. Cover; simmer until done, about 40 minutes.

Heat 16 onions and the remaining butter, wine and bouquet garni to boiling; reduce heat. Cover; simmer until onions are tender, 20 to 25 minutes. Remove onions and chicken pieces to warm platter with slotted spoon. Strain chicken broth and onion liquid together, discarding carrots and onion slices. Skim fat from broth. Heat broth, mushrooms and lemon juice to boiling; reduce to 2½ cups.

Mix egg yolks and cream. Beat 1 cup hot broth by table-spoonfuls into cream mixture. Beat in remaining broth. Heat to boiling, stirring constantly. Boil and stir 1 minute; pour on chicken and onions.   6 SERVINGS.

Note: For each bouquet garni, tie 2 sprigs parsley, ⅓ bay leaf and ⅛ teaspoon dried rosemary leaves in cheesecloth.

Chicken and Vegetable Dinner

⅓ cup all-purpose flour
1 teaspoon salt
1 teaspoon paprika
⅛ teaspoon pepper
2½- to 3-pound broiler-fryer chicken, cut up
3 tablespoons vegetable oil
1½ cups water
½ teaspoon dried savory leaves
¼ teaspoon dried thyme leaves
3 medium carrots, cut into 3x¼-inch strips
½ package (16-ounce size) frozen crinkle-cut
    potato slices (about 2 cups)
1 package (10 ounces) frozen asparagus
    spears or cuts, broken apart
1½ teaspoons salt

Mix flour, 1 teaspoon salt, the paprika and pepper; coat chicken pieces. Brown chicken in oil in 12-inch skillet or Dutch oven; drain. Add water, savory and thyme. Heat to boiling; reduce heat. Cover and simmer 30 minutes.

Add carrots; cover and simmer 10 minutes. Add frozen potatoes and asparagus; sprinkle with 1½ teaspoons salt. Heat to boiling; reduce heat. Cover and simmer until chicken is done and vegetables are tender, 10 to 15 minutes.
6 SERVINGS.

Brown chicken pieces on all sides, turning with tongs.

Add the frozen potato slices and asparagus spears.

Chicken Gumbo

Remove the cooked and cooled chicken meat from the bones, then cut into bite-size pieces.

Add vegetables, rice and red pepper sauce to Dutch oven; break up tomatoes with fork.

3½-pound broiler-fryer chicken, cut up
2 cups water
2 teaspoons salt
1 clove garlic, finely chopped
1 large bay leaf, crumbled
2 large stalks celery (with leaves), cut diagonally into slices (about 1½ cups)
1 medium onion, chopped (about ½ cup)
1 can (28 ounces) whole tomatoes
1 package (10 ounces) frozen okra
1 can (7 ounces) whole kernel corn
⅓ cup uncooked regular rice
½ teaspoon red pepper sauce

Heat chicken pieces, water, salt, garlic and bay leaf to boiling in Dutch oven; reduce heat. Cover and simmer until chicken is done, about 45 minutes.

Remove chicken from broth; strain broth. Refrigerate chicken and broth. When cool, remove chicken from bones (skin can be removed if desired). Cut chicken into bite-size pieces. Skim excess fat from broth and place broth and chicken in Dutch oven. Stir in celery, onion, tomatoes (with liquid), frozen okra, corn (with liquid), rice and pepper sauce; break up tomatoes with fork. Heat to boiling; reduce heat. Cover and simmer until okra and rice are tender, 20 to 30 minutes. Garnish with snipped parsley.   8 SERVINGS.

Chicken and Rice

4- pound stewing chicken, cut up
2 large onions, sliced
2 teaspoons salt
1 cup finely chopped bacon or salt pork
  (about 6 ounces)
1 medium onion, chopped (about ½ cup)
1 medium green pepper, chopped (about
  1 cup)
1 can (28 ounces) whole tomatoes
1½ teaspoons salt
1 teaspoon ground cumin
½ cup water
1½ cups uncooked regular rice
½ cup seedless raisins

To cut breast of stewing hen into thirds, cut crosswise behind wishbone; follow bone.

Cut through cartilage at "V" of neck, then pull away the remaining breast in 2 parts.

Heat chicken, onion slices, 2 teaspoons salt and just enough water to cover to boiling in Dutch oven; reduce heat. Cover and simmer until thickest pieces of chicken are done, 2½ to 3 hours. Refrigerate chicken and broth. When cool, remove skin and bones from chicken. Cut chicken into 1-inch pieces. (Broth can be strained and refrigerated up to 2 days or frozen up to 6 months.)

Cook and stir bacon in Dutch oven until crisp. Drain on paper towels; reserve. Cook and stir chopped onion and green pepper in bacon fat until onion is tender. Stir in tomatoes (with liquid), 1½ teaspoons salt, the cumin and ½ cup water. Stir in rice. Heat to boiling; reduce heat. Simmer uncovered 10 minutes.

Place chicken pieces on rice. Cover and cook 15 minutes. Stir chicken into rice; stir in raisins. Cover and let stand 5 minutes before serving. Sprinkle with reserved bacon.
8 SERVINGS.

Family-Style Broiled Chicken

Brush butter mixture over chicken pieces before and at intervals during broiling.

Turn the chicken as it browns until the thickest pieces are done, 40 to 50 minutes.

2½-pound broiler-fryer chicken, cut up
½ cup butter or margarine
¼ cup vegetable oil
1 small onion, finely chopped (about ¼ cup)
2 tablespoons lemon juice
1 medium clove garlic, crushed
2 teaspoons salt
2 teaspoons sugar
½ teaspoon paprika
½ teaspoon ground ginger

Place chicken pieces skin sides down on rack in broiler pan. Heat remaining ingredients, stirring occasionally, until butter is melted; brush over chicken.

Set oven control to broil and/or 550°. Broil with tops 5 to 7 inches from heat, brushing with butter mixture every 10 to 15 minutes and turning chicken as it browns, until thickest pieces are done, 40 to 50 minutes.   6 SERVINGS.

Chicken and Peppers Sicilian

½ pound Italian link sausages or pork link
    sausages, cut into ½-inch slices
1 tablespoon vegetable oil
3½ to 4 pounds chicken parts
½ cup hot water
2 cloves garlic, finely chopped
1 teaspoon instant chicken bouillon
½ teaspoon salt
¼ teaspoon dried basil leaves
¼ teaspoon pepper
2 medium onions, sliced and separated into
    rings
2 medium green peppers, cut into rings
2 medium tomatoes, peeled and chopped

Heat oven to 350°. Cook and stir sausage slices in oil in Dutch oven or 12-inch skillet until light brown; remove sausage. Brown chicken in Dutch oven; drain. Add sausage, water, garlic, instant bouillon, salt, basil and pepper. Cover and bake 45 minutes.

Add onions, green peppers and tomatoes. Cover and bake until green peppers are crisp-tender, 10 to 15 minutes.
8 SERVINGS.

Especially For The Kids: Reserve the drumsticks from the chicken parts; dip in ¼ cup melted butter or margarine, then roll in ¼ cup crushed corn flake cereal. Place in ungreased baking pan, 8x8x2 inches; drizzle with any remaining butter. Sprinkle with ¼ teaspoon salt. Bake uncovered until done, 50 minutes to 1 hour. (Drumsticks can be baked at the same time as Chicken and Peppers Sicilian.)

For children, dip reserved drumsticks in melted butter.

Then carefully roll in the crushed corn flake cereal.

Add browned sausage to the remaining chicken pieces.

Add onions, green peppers and tomatoes to baked chicken.

Ginger-Curry Chicken

Prepare Condiments ahead of time. (Choose 3 to 6 that contrast in color and flavor.)

Just before serving, remove chicken and apple rings from Dutch oven; prepare sauce.

4 pounds broiler-fryer chicken parts
  Juice of 1 lemon
2 teaspoons salt
¼ cup water
¼ cup raisins
2 teaspoons ground ginger
2 teaspoons curry powder
1 teaspoon sugar
½ teaspoon ground nutmeg
2 medium red apples, cored and cut into
  rings
1 carton (8 ounces) dairy sour cream
6 cups hot cooked rice
  Condiments (below)

Heat oven to 375°. Place chicken in Dutch oven. Sprinkle with lemon juice and salt. Cover and bake 1 hour.

Add water, raisins, ginger, curry powder, sugar, nutmeg and apple rings. Cover and bake 15 minutes. Remove chicken and apple rings; keep warm. Stir sour cream into mixture in Dutch oven. Heat 3 to 5 minutes (do not boil). Serve chicken with sauce, rice and Condiments.
8 SERVINGS.

CONDIMENTS

Choose from the following: chopped green pepper, chopped tomatoes, sliced sweet gherkin pickles, chutney, grated lemon peel, toasted shredded coconut, chopped peanuts and preserved kumquats.

Honey-Ginger Chicken

3 tablespoons shortening
3 tablespoons butter or margarine
⅓ cup all-purpose flour
¾ teaspoon salt
½ teaspoon ground ginger
¼ teaspoon pepper
3 pounds chicken drumsticks and thighs
⅓ cup honey
⅓ cup chili sauce
⅓ cup soy sauce
½ teaspoon ground ginger

Heat oven to 425°. Heat shortening and butter in baking pan, 13x9x2 inches, in oven until melted. Mix flour, salt, ½ teaspoon ginger and the pepper. Coat chicken pieces thoroughly with flour mixture. Place chicken skin sides down in pan. Bake uncovered 30 minutes. Turn chicken; bake 15 minutes. Remove chicken. Drain fat; line pan with aluminum foil. Return chicken to pan.

Mix honey, chili sauce, soy sauce and ½ teaspoon ginger; pour on chicken. Bake 15 minutes, spooning honey mixture onto chicken every 5 minutes. Serve immediately or refrigerate and serve chilled.   6 SERVINGS.

Place the chicken pieces skin sides down in baking pan.

Pour honey mixture on the partially baked chicken.

Pound chicken to ¼-inch thickness. Fold chicken over frozen butter, making sure the butter is enclosed. Fasten with picks.

Roll the chicken in flour, dip in eggs and coat with bread crumbs. Then repeat the process. Wrap carefully in the aluminum foil.

Freezer Chicken Kiev

1 cup butter or margarine, softened
2 tablespoons snipped parsley
1½ teaspoons dried tarragon leaves
1 teaspoon snipped chives
½ to 1 clove garlic, crushed
1 teaspoon salt
⅛ teaspoon pepper
6 whole chicken breasts, boned, split and skin removed
½ cup all-purpose flour
5 eggs, well beaten
2 cups dry bread crumbs

Blend butter, parsley, tarragon, chives, garlic, salt and pepper. Shape into 4-inch square on aluminum foil. Wrap and freeze until firm, 30 to 40 minutes.

Place chicken breasts between two pieces waxed paper; pound to ¼-inch thickness. Cut frozen butter square into 12 pieces. Place 1 piece butter in the center of each chicken breast. Fold chicken over butter, making sure butter is sealed completely inside chicken as pictured. Fasten with wooden picks.

Roll chicken in flour, dip in eggs and coat with bread crumbs; repeat. Shape into triangular pieces. Wrap in heavy-duty aluminum foil and label; freeze up to 1 month.

■20 to 24 hours before serving, thaw in refrigerator. Heat vegetable oil or fat (3 to 4 inches deep) in deep fat fryer to 340°. Fry chicken, 3 pieces at a time, until deep golden brown, about 8 minutes, turning if necessary; drain. (See note.)   12 SERVINGS.

Note: Chicken can be refrigerated covered after frying for up to 6 hours. Forty-five minutes before serving, heat oven to 350°. Cover and bake chicken 30 minutes. Uncover and bake 5 minutes.

Chicken Scallopini

2 cooked chicken breasts, cut in half
¼ cup all-purpose flour
1½ teaspoons garlic salt
¼ teaspoon paprika
¼ cup butter or margarine
3 tablespoons water
1 tablespoon lemon juice
¼ teaspoon instant chicken bouillon
4 thin lemon slices

Remove skin and bones from chicken breasts. Mix flour, garlic salt and paprika. Coat chicken with flour mixture. Brown chicken in butter in 10-inch skillet. Remove chicken from skillet to serving platter and keep warm. Stir water, lemon juice and instant bouillon into skillet, loosening brown particles on bottom. Add lemon slices and heat over low heat 1 minute. Pour broth on chicken; garnish with the lemon slices and snipped parsley.   4 SERVINGS.

Brown chicken breasts evenly on both sides in butter, turning carefully with tongs.

Stir water, lemon juice and bouillon into skillet, loosening brown particles on bottom.

FREEZING POULTRY

Freeze cooked poultry in recipe-size quantities. Cut up and pack tightly in freezer containers with or without the broth. Cooked poultry without broth can be frozen up to 1 month; with broth up to 6 months. Thaw in refrigerator up to 24 hours before using.

A handy way to freeze chicken or meat stock is to pour it into ice cube trays, then remove frozen cubes and pack in plastic bags. Store in freezer up to 6 months at 0°.

Ahead of time, prepare chicken filling and brown ½ cup potato puffs. Cook remaining potato puffs; divide into 8 equal parts.

Spoon potatoes into 8 mounds; hollow centers, fill and sprinkle with potato puffs. Heat soup and sour cream for the sauce.

Chicken in Potato Boats

2 cups cut-up cooked chicken
1 medium stalk celery, sliced (about ½ cup)
¼ cup pitted ripe olives
1 tablespoon chopped pimiento
½ teaspoon chili powder
¼ cup dairy sour cream
1 can (10¾ ounces) condensed cream of chicken soup
½ cup mashed potato mix
3 tablespoons butter or margarine
  Potato Boats (below)
¾ cup dairy sour cream
¼ teaspoon salt

Heat oven to 350°. Mix chicken, celery, olives, pimiento, chili powder, ¼ cup sour cream and ½ cup of the soup; reserve. Cook and stir potato mix in butter until golden; reserve for topping.

Prepare Potato Boats. Spoon chicken mixture into Potato Boats. Sprinkle with browned potato mix. Bake 30 minutes.

Mix remaining soup, ¾ cup sour cream and the salt. Heat just to boiling. Serve over chicken.   8 SERVINGS.

POTATO BOATS

Prepare mashed potato mix for 8 servings as directed on package except—reduce water to 2 cups. Stir in 1 egg, slightly beaten, and ¼ cup grated American cheese food. Spoon into 8 mounds on greased baking sheet. Hollow centers with the back of a spoon.

Cheesy Chicken over Rice

Rice Pilaf (below)
1 small onion, chopped (about ¼ cup)
¼ small green pepper, cut into 1x¼-inch
  pieces
2 tablespoons finely chopped celery
¼ cup butter or margarine
2 cups cut-up cooked chicken
¼ cup diced cooked ham
1 can (11 ounces) condensed Cheddar
  cheese soup
¼ cup milk

Prepare Rice Pilaf; keep warm.   Cut meat while onion cooks.

Prepare Rice Pilaf. Cook and stir onion, green pepper and celery in butter in 10-inch skillet until celery is crisp-tender, about 4 minutes. Stir in chicken, ham, soup and milk. Heat until chicken is hot. Serve over Rice Pilaf.
6 SERVINGS.

RICE PILAF

1 small onion, chopped (about ¼ cup)
2 tablespoons butter or margarine
2⅔ cups boiling water
1⅓ cups uncooked regular rice
1 tablespoon instant chicken bouillon
½ teaspoon salt
1 bay leaf
½ cup raisins

Cook and stir onion in butter in 2-quart saucepan until tender, about 3 minutes. Stir water, rice, instant bouillon, salt, bay leaf and raisins into onion. Heat to boiling; reduce heat. Cover and simmer 18 minutes.

Chicken-Avocado Salad

Dip slices for garnish into a mixture of water and lemon juice to prevent darkening.

Add remaining avocado slices and lettuce to salad; toss with the Chili Mayonnaise.

2 cups cut-up cooked chicken
4 ounces hot pepper cheese, cut into strips
1 can (15 ounces) kidney beans, drained
2 medium stalks celery, thinly sliced (about 1 cup)
10 cherry tomatoes, cut in half
1 small onion, thinly sliced
Chili Mayonnaise (below)
1 medium avocado
1 small head iceberg lettuce, torn into bite-size pieces (about 4 cups)
1 package (6¼ ounces) tortilla chips

Place chicken, cheese, beans, celery, tomatoes and onion in large bowl. Cover and refrigerate 4 to 6 hours. Prepare Chili Mayonnaise.

Just before serving, peel avocado and cut into thin slices. Reserve a few avocado slices for garnish. Add remaining avocado slices and the lettuce to salad; toss with Chili Mayonnaise. Top with 1 cup of the tortilla chips. Garnish with reserved avocado slices. Serve with remaining tortilla chips.   6 SERVINGS.

CHILI MAYONNAISE
½ cup mayonnaise or salad dressing
¼ cup chili sauce
½ teaspoon salt
2 drops red pepper sauce

Mix all ingredients. Cover and refrigerate 1 hour.

Lemon Barbecue Chicken Salad

2 cups cut-up cooked chicken or turkey,
  chilled
1 tablespoon lemon juice
½ teaspoon salt
2 cups cooked rice, chilled
2 large stalks celery, sliced (about 1½ cups)
½ cup sliced pimiento-stuffed olives
  Barbecue Dressing (below)
3 tablespoons imitation bacon

Sprinkle chicken with lemon juice and salt. Add rice, celery, olives and Barbecue Dressing; toss. Sprinkle with imitation bacon and garnish with parsley sprigs.   5 SERVINGS.

BARBECUE DRESSING

Mix ¾ cup mayonnaise or salad dressing, 1 tablespoon barbecue sauce and ¼ teaspoon liquid smoke.

Ahead of time, cook and cut up chicken and cook the rice.

Mix mayonnaise and barbecue sauce for salad dressing.

RICE KNOW-HOW

Rely on rice to stretch a small amount of meat into a nourishing treat. It can be mounded and fluffy, each grain whole, separate and tender—if you prepare it properly. Do not overstir or overcook. When you do stir or fluff, use a fork to avoid crushing the grains. Don't use just one kind of rice—enjoy them all! For 2 cups cooked rice, start with:

    ⅔ cup regular white rice

    ½ cup processed rice

    1 cup precooked (instant) rice

    ½ cup brown rice

Almond-Chicken Oriental

1 package (6 ounces) frozen pea pods
1 package (10 ounces) frozen green peas
2 cups cut-up cooked chicken
½ cup sliced water chestnuts
1 can (2 ounces) mushroom stems and
   pieces
⅓ cup water
1 teaspoon instant chicken bouillon
¼ cup water
2 teaspoons cornstarch
2 teaspoons soy sauce
   Orange Rice (below)
¼ cup sliced almonds

Heat frozen pea pods, frozen peas, chicken, water chestnuts, mushrooms (with liquid), ⅓ cup water and the instant bouillon to boiling in covered 3-quart saucepan; reduce heat. Simmer until chicken is hot and pea pods are crisp-tender, about 5 minutes.

Mix ¼ cup water, the cornstarch and soy sauce; stir gradually into chicken mixture. Heat to boiling, stirring constantly. Boil and stir 1 minute. Serve over Orange Rice; sprinkle with almonds.   6 SERVINGS.

ORANGE RICE
Prepare instant rice for 6 servings as directed on package. Stir in ½ teaspoon grated orange peel.

Chicken India

2 cans (5 ounces each) boned chicken,
   broken into chunks
1 can (8¼ ounces) pineapple chunks, drained
1 cup chilled cooked rice
1 large stalk celery, sliced (about ¾ cup)
¼ to ⅓ cup mayonnaise or salad dressing
3 tablespoons chutney or chopped sweet
   pickle
½ teaspoon curry powder
   Dried parsley flakes
   Whole cranberry sauce

Mix chicken, pineapple, rice and celery. Mix mayonnaise, chutney and curry powder; toss with chicken mixture. Refrigerate 1 hour. Garnish with parsley flakes; serve with cranberry sauce.   4 SERVINGS.

Chicken Canton

1 large stalk celery, chopped (about ¾ cup)
2 tablespoons vegetable oil
1 can (11 ounces) condensed Cheddar cheese
   soup
2 cans (5 ounces each) boned chicken, broken
   into chunks
1 can (5 ounces) Vienna sausages, drained
   and sliced
1 jar (2 ounces) sliced pimiento, drained
1 tablespoon instant minced onion
1 can (5 ounces) chow mein noodles

Cook and stir celery in oil until celery is crisp-tender. Stir in soup, chicken, sausages, pimiento and onion. Heat to boiling; reduce heat. Simmer uncovered, stirring occasionally, 5 minutes. Serve over noodles.   4 TO 6 SERVINGS.

Chicken over Corn Bread

Corn Bread (below)
1 package (10 ounces) frozen chopped
   broccoli
1 tablespoon finely chopped onion
1 clove garlic, finely chopped
¼ cup butter or margarine
2 tablespoons flour
1½ teaspoons salt
¾ cup milk
2 egg yolks, slightly beaten
1 carton (8 ounces) unflavored yogurt
1 can (5 ounces) boned chicken, broken
   into chunks
¼ cup shredded Cheddar cheese

Bake Corn Bread. Rinse frozen broccoli under running cold water to separate. Cook and stir broccoli, onion and garlic in butter in 10-inch skillet over low heat 5 minutes; remove from heat. Blend in flour and salt. Cook, stirring constantly, until bubbly; remove from heat. Stir in milk. Heat to boiling, stirring constantly. Boil and stir 1 minute.

Mix egg yolks and yogurt. Stir yogurt mixture and chicken chunks into broccoli mixture. Heat over low heat, stirring frequently, until chicken is hot; serve over Corn Bread. Sprinkle with cheese.　6 SERVINGS.

CORN BREAD
2 eggs
1 cup biscuit baking mix
1 cup cornmeal
1½ cups buttermilk
2 tablespoons vegetable oil
½ teaspoon poultry seasoning

Heat oven to 450°. Grease baking pan, 9x9x2 inches. Beat eggs until fluffy; beat in remaining ingredients just until smooth. Bake until golden brown, 25 minutes.

Blend flour and salt into broccoli mixture in skillet.

After cooking mixture, remove from heat; stir in milk.

To make corn bread, grease pan generously.

Beat eggs; beat in remaining ingredients until smooth.

Herbed Game Hens

Dry cavities of hens. Mix the croutons and olives. Stuff each hen.

Fasten with skewers; lace. Bake breast sides up; baste frequently.

6 Rock Cornish hens (1 to 1¼ pounds each), thawed
2 cups herb-seasoned croutons
½ cup sliced ripe olives
¼ cup lemon juice
¼ cup vinegar
¼ cup vegetable oil
1 clove garlic, crushed
½ teaspoon dried thyme leaves
¼ to ½ teaspoon salt
Grape clusters

Heat oven to 350°. Dry cavities of hens (do not rub cavities with salt). Mix croutons and olives. Stuff each hen loosely with ⅓ cup stuffing; fasten openings with skewers and lace shut with string. Place hens breast sides up in ungreased shallow baking pan.

Mix lemon juice, vinegar, oil, garlic, thyme and salt; pour on hens. Bake uncovered 2 hours, spooning lemon mixture onto hens every 20 minutes.

Place hens on warm platter. Garnish with grape clusters and parsley sprigs.   6 SERVINGS.

Note: If desired, hens can be cut into halves before serving. Cut along backbone from tail to neck with kitchen scissors.

Duckling with Apricot Sauce

4- to 5-pound ready-to-cook duckling
½ small onion, chopped (about 2 tablespoons)
¼ teaspoon dried tarragon leaves
2 tablespoons butter or margarine
1 can (8¼ ounces) crushed pineapple, drained (reserve syrup)
½ cup finely chopped dried apricots
2 tablespoons soy sauce
2 tablespoons brandy
¼ teaspoon ground ginger
⅛ teaspoon salt
2 tablespoons brandy

Fasten neck skin to back of duckling with skewers; lift wing tips up and over back to make a natural brace. Place duckling breast side up on rack in shallow roasting pan.

Heat oven to 325°. Cook and stir onion and tarragon in butter until onion is tender. Add enough water to reserved pineapple syrup to measure ½ cup. Stir pineapple, pineapple syrup mixture, apricots, soy sauce, 2 tablespoons brandy, the ginger and salt into the onion. Heat until mixture is hot.

Spread half of the apricot mixture on duckling. Roast uncovered 2½ to 3 hours, pricking skin with fork occasionally. (If duckling becomes too brown, place piece of aluminum foil lightly over breast.) Duckling is done when drumstick meat feels very soft.

Stir 2 tablespoons brandy into remaining apricot mixture; heat about 5 minutes. Serve with duckling.   4 SERVINGS.

After presenting duckling at the table, cut it lengthwise in half with poultry shears.

Then cut each half into 2 pieces. Serve duckling with the brandied apricot sauce.

Holiday Turkey

Stuff wishbone area first. Fasten neck skin to back.

Carefully fold wings across back with the tips facing.

Fill body cavity lightly—the stuffing will expand.

Tie legs together with tail or tuck under band of skin.

3 medium onions, finely chopped (about 1½ cups)
¾ cup butter or margarine
3 cups toasted croutons
2 cups chopped walnuts
2 large stalks celery, chopped (about 1½ cups)
2 cups dry white wine
¾ cup raisins
¼ to ½ cup water (optional)
2¼ teaspoons salt
1½ teaspoons ground sage
10- to 12-pound turkey
2 tablespoons butter or margarine, melted
1 teaspoon instant chicken bouillon
1 cup boiling water

Cook and stir onions in ¾ cup butter in Dutch oven until tender; remove from heat. Stir in croutons, walnuts, celery, 1 cup of the wine, the raisins, ¼ to ½ cup water (depending on desired moistness of stuffing), the salt and sage. Stuff turkey as pictured just before roasting.

Heat oven to 325°. Place turkey breast side up on rack in shallow roasting pan. Brush with 2 tablespoons melted butter. Pour remaining wine on turkey. Dissolve instant bouillon in 1 cup boiling water; pour on turkey. Insert meat thermometer so tip is in thickest part of inside thigh muscle or breast meat and does not touch bone. Roast uncovered until thermometer registers 185° or until drumstick can be moved easily, 3½ to 4½ hours. Place aluminum foil loosely over turkey when it begins to turn golden. When turkey is done, remove from oven and let stand 20 minutes for easier carving.   ABOUT 10 SERVINGS.

Turkey Dressing Bake

2 cups cut-up cooked turkey
2 eggs
1 cup warm water
1 package (about 1 ounce) turkey or
  chicken gravy mix
1⅓ cups herb-seasoned stuffing mix
¼ cup slivered almonds
  Mushroom-Corn Sauce (below)

Heat oven to 350°. Place turkey in greased baking pan, 8x8x2 inches. Beat eggs, water and gravy mix; pour on turkey. Sprinkle turkey with stuffing mix, then with almonds. Bake uncovered 40 minutes. Top each serving with Mushroom-Corn Sauce.   6 SERVINGS.

MUSHROOM-CORN SAUCE

1 can (12 ounces) whole kernel corn with
  sweet peppers, drained
1 can (10¾ ounces) condensed cream of
  mushroom soup
1 can (4 ounces) mushroom stems and pieces
  (with liquid)

Heat all ingredients to boiling, stirring frequently.

Note: To double this recipe, double all ingredients and bake in greased baking pan, 13x9x2 inches, in 350° oven 55 minutes.

Pour egg-gravy mixture on cut-up turkey pieces.

Sprinkle with seasoned stuffing mix, then with almonds.

Deep Dish Turkey Pie

Cut shortening into the flour mixture with pastry blender.

Add enough milk to the mixture to make a soft dough.

Drop half of dough by spoonfuls onto hot turkey pie.

Drop the remaining dough onto a greased baking sheet.

1 can (18 ounces) vacuum-pack sweet
  potatoes
2 cups cut-up cooked turkey
1 medium onion, chopped (about ½ cup)
1 package (10 ounces) frozen green peas,
  broken apart
1 package (1 ounce) chicken gravy mix
1 teaspoon salt
½ teaspoon grated lemon peel
  Sweet Potato Biscuits (below)

Heat oven to 400°. Mash enough of the sweet potatoes to measure ¼ cup; reserve for Sweet Potato Biscuits. Cut remaining sweet potatoes into ½-inch slices.

Alternate layers of turkey, onion, frozen peas and sweet potato slices in ungreased 2-quart casserole. Prepare gravy mix as directed on package except—stir in salt and lemon peel; pour into casserole. Bake uncovered 15 minutes.

Prepare Sweet Potato Biscuits dough. Drop half of the dough (5 to 7 spoonfuls) onto hot turkey pie. Bake until biscuit topping is light brown, about 20 minutes.
6 SERVINGS.

SWEET POTATO BISCUITS
3 tablespoons shortening
1 cup all-purpose flour
¼ cup mashed sweet potato
2 teaspoons sugar
2 teaspoons baking powder
½ teaspoon salt
¼ to ⅓ cup milk

Cut shortening into flour, sweet potato, sugar, baking powder and salt. Stir in milk. Divide dough in half. Use one half for pie. Drop remaining dough by spoonfuls onto greased baking sheet. Bake until light brown, 12 to 15 minutes.

Tamale Turkey

4 cups cut-up cooked turkey or chicken
1 can (28 ounces) whole tomatoes, drained
  (reserve liquid)
1 can (16 ounces) whole kernel corn,
  drained (reserve liquid)
1 cup sliced ripe olives
1 medium onion, chopped (about ½ cup)
½ medium green pepper, chopped (about
  ¼ cup)
2 to 3 tablespoons chili powder
2 tablespoons butter or margarine, softened
1 clove garlic, finely chopped
1 tablespoon salt
1¼ cups yellow cornmeal
4 eggs, beaten
1½ teaspoons instant chicken bouillon
  Crushed tortilla chips
  Sliced ripe olives

Heat oven to 375°. Mix turkey, tomatoes, corn, olives, onion, green pepper, chili powder, butter, garlic and salt. Add enough water to reserved tomato and corn liquids to measure 1½ cups. Mix liquid, cornmeal, eggs and instant bouillon; stir into turkey mixture. Divide among 10 ungreased individual casseroles.

Bake uncovered until knife inserted in centers comes out clean, about 30 minutes. Garnish with crushed tortilla chips and sliced ripe olives.   10 SERVINGS.

Ahead of time, cook turkey and cool. Cut up enough of the turkey to fill 4 cups.

Mix turkey, tomatoes, corn, olives, onion, green pepper, butter and seasonings.

Add mixture of liquid, cornmeal, eggs and instant bouillon; pour into casseroles.

Bake in 375° oven until knife inserted in centers comes out clean, about 30 minutes.

Fill each trout with about ½ cup of the stuffing; arrange trout in greased baking dish.

Lightly butter 4 strips (6x3 inches each) of foil, then wrap tails of trout and bake.

Stuffed Baked Trout

2 medium green peppers, chopped (about 2 cups)
1 jar (4½ ounces) sliced mushrooms, drained
½ cup butter or margarine
20 cherry tomatoes, cut in half
2 cups herb-seasoned croutons
¼ cup lemon juice
2 teaspoons salt
¼ teaspoon pepper
¼ teaspoon dried marjoram leaves
  Salt
4 trout (10 to 12 ounces each)
  Lemon slices
  Cucumber slices
  Cherry tomatoes

Heat oven to 350°. Cook and stir green pepper and mushrooms in butter until green pepper is tender, about 5 minutes. Remove from heat. Stir in cherry tomato halves, croutons, lemon juice, 2 teaspoons salt, the pepper and marjoram.

Lightly salt the cavity of each trout; fill with ½ cup of the stuffing. Place remaining stuffing in greased 1-quart casserole. Arrange trout in greased baking dish, 13½x8¾x1¾ inches. Wrap tails in buttered aluminum foil. Bake stuffing and trout until trout flakes easily with fork, 30 to 35 minutes.

Remove foil from tails. Garnish with lemon slices, cucumber slices and cherry tomatoes.   4 SERVINGS.

Halibut with Shrimp Sauce

2 pounds halibut steaks
Salt
Pepper
Paprika
⅓ cup mashed potato mix
3 tablespoons butter or margarine
⅛ teaspoon garlic powder
3 large tomatoes, cut in half
Shrimp Sauce (below)

Set oven control to broil and/or 550°. Cut halibut steaks into 6 serving pieces; sprinkle with salt, pepper and paprika. Broil with tops 3 inches from heat until light brown, 5 to 8 minutes.

Cook and stir potato mix in butter and garlic powder until golden; sprinkle over tomato halves. Place tomatoes on broiler pan with halibut. Turn halibut; sprinkle with salt, pepper and paprika. Broil until halibut flakes easily with fork, 5 to 8 minutes. (Broiling time varies according to thickness of halibut.) Serve with Shrimp Sauce.
6 SERVINGS.

SHRIMP SAUCE

Heat 1 can (10¾ ounces) condensed cream of shrimp soup, 1 can (4¼ ounces) broken shrimp, drained, and ¼ teaspoon dried dill weed over medium heat, stirring constantly, until hot and bubbly.

Season cut halibut; broil 1 side.

Cook potato mix in butter.

Add tomatoes; turn the fish.

Heat Shrimp Sauce until hot.

Add croutons, corn, tomato, cheese, onion to egg mixture.

Arrange halibut on croutons; top with remaining croutons.

Crouton-Halibut Bake

2 pounds frozen skinless halibut fillets, thawed*
1 teaspoon salt
½ cup mayonnaise or salad dressing
2 tablespoons lemon juice
1 egg, beaten
2 cups seasoned croutons
1 cup drained whole kernel corn with sweet peppers
1 medium tomato, chopped (about ¾ cup)
¼ cup grated American cheese food
2 tablespoons instant minced onion
Lemon slices

Heat oven to 350°. Sprinkle halibut with salt. Mix mayonnaise, lemon juice and egg in medium bowl. Stir in croutons, corn, tomato, cheese and onion. Spread 2 cups of the crouton mixture in greased baking dish, 11¾x7½x1¾ inches. Arrange halibut on top; spread with remaining crouton mixture.

Bake uncovered until halibut flakes easily with fork, 45 to 50 minutes. Garnish with lemon slices.   8 TO 10 SERVINGS.

*Cod, pollack, flounder or sole can be substituted for the halibut.

Baked Codfish

2 medium onions, thinly sliced
2 tablespoons butter or margarine
2 tablespoons olive or vegetable oil
2 pounds codfish, cut into 1-inch pieces
  Broth Béchamel (below)
2 pounds small new potatoes, cooked,
  peeled and cut into ¼-inch slices
6 hard-cooked eggs, sliced
¼ cup snipped parsley
½ teaspoon salt
½ teaspoon lemon pepper

Cook and stir onion slices in butter and oil in 12-inch skillet until tender. Stir in codfish. Cook uncovered over low heat 30 minutes. Prepare Broth Béchamel.

Heat oven to 350°. Layer half each of the codfish and onions, potatoes, eggs and Broth Béchamel in ungreased baking dish, 11¾x7½x1¾ inches. Sprinkle with half each of the parsley, salt and lemon pepper. Repeat. Bake uncovered until light brown and bubbly, about 45 minutes.
10 TO 12 SERVINGS.

BROTH BECHAMEL

¼ cup butter or margarine
¼ cup all-purpose flour
½ teaspoon salt
⅛ teaspoon pepper
1 cup chicken broth
1 cup milk
2 tablespoons catsup

Cook and stir butter, flour, salt and pepper over low heat until mixture is smooth and bubbly, about 2 minutes. Remove from heat. Stir in broth, milk and catsup. Heat to boiling, stirring constantly. Boil and stir 1 minute.

Stir the codfish into sautéed onions; cook 30 minutes.

Layer ingredients; add parsley, salt, lemon pepper. Repeat.

To make fancy garnishes for fish, use carrots, carrot tops, eggs, dill pickles topped with onions and mild sweet peppers.

Or try whole or grated radishes, lemon slices or peel, cherry tomatoes on lettuce or cucumber slices with parsley sprigs.

Dilled Torsk

2 pounds frozen skinless torsk or cod fillets, thawed
3 tablespoons butter or margarine, softened
2 tablespoons lemon juice
1 teaspoon dried dill weed
½ teaspoon salt
¼ teaspoon paprika
  Tomato wedges

Heat oven to 375°. Place torsk fillets in ungreased baking dish, 11¾x7½x1¾ inches. Brush both sides of torsk with butter. Sprinkle both sides with lemon juice, dill and salt. Sprinkle tops with paprika. Bake uncovered until torsk flakes easily with fork, 30 to 35 minutes. Garnish with tomato wedges and parsley.   8 TO 10 SERVINGS.

Barbecued Fish

1 pound frozen skinless fish fillets, thawed
¼ cup catsup
3 tablespoons lemon juice
1 tablespoon Worcestershire sauce
2 teaspoons sugar
2 teaspoons instant minced onion
¼ teaspoon salt
  Dash of red pepper sauce
  Lemon wedges

Place fish fillets in ungreased baking pan, 13x9x2 inches. Mix catsup, lemon juice, Worcestershire sauce, sugar, onion, salt and pepper sauce. Pour on fish; turn until both sides are coated. Cover and refrigerate 30 minutes.

Heat oven to 400°. Bake uncovered until fish flakes easily with fork, 15 to 20 minutes. Garnish with lemon wedges. Serve with pan juices.   5 OR 6 SERVINGS.

Sole with Green Grapes

    2 tablespoons finely chopped shallots
    2 pounds sole fillets
    1 teaspoon salt
    ¼ teaspoon pepper
    1 cup dry white wine
    1 tablespoon lemon juice
    1 can (16 ounces) seedless green grapes,
         drained (reserve liquid)
    2 tablespoons butter or margarine
    2 tablespoons flour
    ½ cup whipping cream
    2 tablespoons butter or margarine

Sprinkle shallots in 10-inch skillet. Sprinkle fillets with salt and pepper. Fold in half; arrange in skillet. Add wine, lemon juice and reserved grape liquid. Heat to boiling; reduce heat. Cover and simmer until fillets flake easily, 4 to 5 minutes. Remove fillets with slotted spatula to oven-proof platter; keep warm.

Add grapes to liquid in skillet. Heat to boiling; reduce heat. Simmer uncovered 3 minutes. Remove grapes with slotted spoon.

Heat liquid in skillet to boiling; boil until reduced to 1 cup. Melt 2 tablespoons butter. Stir in flour. Stir flour mixture, a small amount at a time, into reduced liquid. Cook over low heat, stirring constantly, until thickened. Remove from heat. Stir in cream. Heat to boiling. Add 2 tablespoons butter; stir until melted. Drain excess liquid from platter if necessary. Spoon sauce over fillets.

Set oven control to broil and/or 550°. Broil fillets just until sauce is glazed, about 3 minutes. Garnish with grapes. 8 TO 10 SERVINGS.

Greek-Style Baked Fish

    ¼ cup olive oil
    ½ cup dry bread crumbs
    2 pounds red snapper fillets*
    1 teaspoon salt
    ¼ cup lemon juice
    ½ cup olive oil
    ¼ cup tomato sauce
    1 cup snipped parsley
    ½ cup dry white wine
    2 cloves garlic, finely chopped
    1 teaspoon salt
    ¼ teaspoon pepper
    ½ cup dry bread crumbs

Heat oven to 350°. Pour ¼ cup oil into baking dish, 13x9x2 inches. Sprinkle ½ cup bread crumbs over oil. Place fillets in single layer in baking dish; sprinkle with 1 teaspoon salt. Pour lemon juice on top.

Mix ½ cup oil, the tomato sauce, parsley, wine, garlic, 1 teaspoon salt and the pepper; spoon over fillets. Sprinkle with ½ cup bread crumbs. Bake uncovered until golden brown, about 40 minutes.   8 TO 10 SERVINGS.

*2 pounds fresh or frozen (thawed) cod, haddock, halibut or yellow pike fillets can be substituted for the red snapper fillets.

Seafood Slaw

Simmer flounder until it flakes easily with a fork. Drain and flake the flounder.

Place flounder, shredded cabbage, celery and shrimp in a large bowl.

Mix the mayonnaise, 3 tablespoons lemon juice, the salt and the dried basil leaves.

Pour the dressing on the flounder mixture and toss. Cover and refrigerate 2 hours.

1 pound skinless flounder, torsk or cod fillets
2 tablespoons lemon juice
½ small head cabbage, shredded (about 3 cups)
1 large stalk celery, cut into thin diagonal slices (about 1 cup)
1 can (4¼ ounces) tiny shrimp, rinsed and drained
¾ cup mayonnaise or salad dressing
3 tablespoons lemon juice
¾ to 1 teaspoon salt
½ teaspoon dried basil leaves
   Salad greens
   Cherry tomatoes
   Parsley sprigs

Heat water (1½ inches) to boiling in 10-inch skillet or Dutch oven. Add flounder fillets and 2 tablespoons lemon juice; reduce heat. Simmer uncovered until flounder flakes easily with fork, 8 to 10 minutes. (Cooking time varies according to thickness of flounder.) Remove flounder from skillet; drain and flake.

Place flounder, cabbage, celery and shrimp in large bowl. Mix mayonnaise, 3 tablespoons lemon juice, the salt and basil; pour on flounder mixture and toss. Cover and refrigerate about 2 hours.

Spoon slaw onto salad greens. Core tomatoes; insert a parsley sprig in each tomato. Garnish salad with tomatoes. 6 TO 8 SERVINGS.

Seafood Choice Salad

1 package (10 ounces) frozen cooked shrimp,
   thawed (2 cups)
½ pound scallops, cooked and drained
1 medium green pepper, cut into ¼-inch
   strips
½ pound mushrooms, sliced
1 medium lemon, cut into wedges
1 medium onion, sliced and separated into
   rings
⅔ cup tarragon vinegar
½ cup vegetable oil
1 teaspoon sugar
1 teaspoon salt
⅛ teaspoon dried tarragon leaves
1 bay leaf, crumbled
1 teaspoon snipped parsley
1 small head lettuce, torn into bite-size
   pieces
   Salt
   Coarsely ground pepper

Mix shrimp, scallops, green pepper, mushrooms, lemon and onion in baking dish, 13½x8¾x1¾ inches. Mix vinegar, oil, sugar, 1 teaspoon salt, tarragon and bay leaf; pour on shrimp mixture. Cover and refrigerate 8 hours, spooning marinade onto shrimp mixture occasionally.

Drain shrimp mixture, reserving marinade. Stir parsley into marinade. Serve shrimp mixture, lettuce and reserved marinade in separate bowls. Toss salads and season with salt and pepper.   6 TO 8 SERVINGS.

Mix shrimp, scallops, pepper, mushrooms, lemon and onion.

Mix marinade; pour it on the shrimp mixture. Refrigerate.

Stir parsley into marinade reserved from drained shrimp.

Serve shrimp mixture, lettuce and the marinade separately.

ARTICHOKE HEARTS are actually tiny whole artichokes which are canned and bottled before the thistle-like cores have toughened. On a fresh, mature artichoke the thistles are to be avoided; only the tender base of the artichoke leaves and the bottom layer beneath the core are edible — and delicious too!

Seafood Kabobs

Anchovy Sauce (below)
½ pound mushrooms
1 package (8 ounces) frozen cooked large shrimp, thawed
1 package (7 ounces) frozen breaded scallops, thawed
1 can (8½ ounces) artichoke hearts, drained and cut into fourths
1 medium green pepper, cut into 1-inch pieces (about 1 cup)
2 medium lemons, cut into eighths
½ teaspoon dried dill weed
3 to 4 cups hot cooked rice
Paprika

Prepare Anchovy Sauce. Cut caps from mushrooms; reserve stems. Alternate shrimp, scallops, mushroom caps, artichoke hearts, green pepper pieces and lemon wedges on six 10- to 12-inch skewers as pictured.

Set oven control to broil and/or 550°. Brush Anchovy Sauce over kabobs. Broil with tops 3 to 4 inches from heat, brushing occasionally with sauce, until tender, 8 to 10 minutes.

Chop reserved mushroom stems. Heat stems, dill and rice in 2-quart saucepan over low heat, stirring occasionally, 5 minutes. Serve kabobs over rice; sprinkle with paprika.
6 SERVINGS.

ANCHOVY SAUCE
Heat ⅓ cup butter or margarine, 1½ teaspoons anchovy paste, 1 teaspoon lemon juice and ¼ teaspoon onion juice, stirring constantly, until mixture is smooth.

Shrimp and Artichokes au Vin

1 package (6 ounces) long-grain and wild
   rice
5 ounces mushrooms, sliced
¼ cup butter or margarine
3 tablespoons flour
½ teaspoon salt
¾ cup half-and-half
2 packages (6 ounces each) frozen cooked
   shrimp, thawed
2 jars (7 ounces each) marinated artichoke
   hearts, drained
¼ cup dry white wine
¼ cup grated Parmesan cheese

Ahead of time, cook the rice and the mushrooms and prepare the shrimp mixture.

Transfer shrimp mixture to a chafing dish. Stir in mushrooms and wine; heat.

Prepare rice as directed on package. While rice is cooking, cook and stir mushrooms in butter until tender, 3 to 4 minutes. Remove mushrooms with slotted spoon; reserve. Stir flour and salt into butter. Cook, stirring constantly, until smooth and bubbly; remove from heat. Stir in half-and-half. Heat to boiling, stirring constantly. Boil and stir 1 minute. Stir in shrimp and artichoke hearts; heat about 5 minutes.

Transfer shrimp mixture to chafing dish or skillet. Stir in mushrooms and wine; heat until hot. Sprinkle with cheese. Serve shrimp over rice.   5 SERVINGS.

Shrimp Curry

Cook and stir soup mixture until it is hot and bubbly.

Stir jam mixture, shrimp and cucumber into soup mixture.

1 small onion, chopped (about ¼ cup)
1 small apple, chopped (about ½ cup)
¼ cup butter or margarine
1 can (10¾ ounces) condensed cream of chicken soup
½ cup milk
2 to 3 teaspoons curry powder
1 teaspoon ground ginger
1 teaspoon salt
2 tablespoons plum jam
1 tablespoon lemon juice
2 cups fresh or frozen shrimp, cleaned and cooked
1 small cucumber, pared and cut into cubes (about ¾ cup)
3 cups hot cooked rice
  Condiments (below)

Cook and stir onion and apple in butter in 10-inch skillet over medium heat until onion is tender. Mix soup, milk, curry powder, ginger and salt; stir into onion and apple. Cook and stir over low heat until hot and bubbly, about 4 minutes.

Mix jam and lemon juice until smooth; stir into soup mixture. Stir in shrimp and cucumber. Heat 3 minutes. Serve with rice and Condiments.   4 TO 6 SERVINGS.

CONDIMENTS
Serve the following in ramekins or custard cups: chopped peanuts, chutney, coconut, raisins, chopped green pepper, India relish and chopped hard-cooked eggs.

Crabmeat Curry: Substitute crabmeat (cartilage removed), cut into 1-inch pieces, for the shrimp.

Shrimp Cantonese

1 cup uncooked regular rice
¼ cup sugar
2 tablespoons cornstarch
1 can (15½ ounces) pineapple chunks, drained (reserve syrup)
¼ cup vinegar
2 teaspoons soy sauce
2 medium stalks celery, chopped (about 1 cup)
4 green onions (with tops), sliced (about ½ cup)
½ medium green pepper, cut into ¼-inch strips
1 large tomato, cut into eighths
2 cans (4¼ ounces each) jumbo shrimp, drained
1½ cups shredded Swiss cheese (about 6 ounces)
⅓ cup toasted sliced almonds

Cook rice as directed on package. Mix sugar and cornstarch in 3-quart saucepan. Add enough water to reserved pineapple syrup to measure 1 cup. Stir pineapple liquid, vinegar and soy sauce into sugar mixture gradually. Cook over medium heat, stirring constantly, until mixture thickens and boils. Boil and stir 1 minute.

Stir pineapple, celery, onions and green pepper into sauce mixture. Fold in tomato and shrimp. Heat until shrimp is hot. Toss cheese and rice; pack into buttered 4-cup mold. Immediately invert on large serving plate. Top with shrimp mixture; sprinkle with almonds. 6 TO 8 SERVINGS.

Prepare the vegetables while the rice is cooking.

Add fruit, vegetables and shrimp to the sauce.

Toss the cheese and rice; pack into 4-cup mold.

Invert mold on serving plate; top with shrimp mixture.

To make rice ring, pack rice mixture lightly in greased mold; let stand 2 minutes.

Cover mold with serving platter. Invert, then lift off mold. Serve with hot seafood.

Seafood with Rice Ring

Crunchy Rice Ring (below)
2 cans (10¾ ounces each) condensed cream
   of shrimp soup
3 cans (4½ ounces each) deveined small
   shrimp, rinsed and drained*
1 can (6½ ounces) tuna, drained and broken
   into chunks
1 jar (2 ounces) sliced pimiento, drained
¼ cup apple cider

Prepare Crunchy Rice Ring. Heat soup, shrimp, tuna, pimiento and cider just to boiling in 2-quart saucepan over medium heat, stirring occasionally. Serve with Crunchy Rice Ring.   8 TO 10 SERVINGS.

*1 can (7 ounces) fish flakes can be substituted for 1 can of the shrimp.

CRUNCHY RICE RING
4½ cups water
  2 cups uncooked regular rice
  2 tablespoons butter or margarine
  2 teaspoons salt
  1 can (8 ounces) water chestnuts, drained
    and sliced

Heat water to boiling in 2-quart saucepan. Stir in rice, butter and salt; reduce heat. Cover and simmer until water is absorbed, about 25 minutes.

Stir in water chestnuts. Grease 6-cup ring mold or coat with vegetable spray-on for cookware. Pack rice mixture lightly in mold. Let stand 2 minutes. Unmold on serving platter.

Crabby Joes

2 medium stalks celery, chopped (about 1 cup)
1 tablespoon butter or margarine
1 can (10¾ ounces) condensed cream of shrimp soup
2 cans (7½ ounces each) crabmeat, drained and flaked*
½ cup dairy sour cream
1 tablespoon grated lemon peel
    Dash of aromatic bitters
4 English muffins, split and toasted
    Paprika

Cook and stir celery in butter until the celery is tender.

Stir in soup, crabmeat, sour cream, lemon peel and bitters.

Cook and stir celery in butter in 10-inch skillet until celery is tender, about 5 minutes. Stir in soup, crabmeat, sour cream, lemon peel and bitters. Heat just to boiling. Serve over hot muffins; sprinkle with paprika.   4 SERVINGS.

*1 can (7 ounces) fish flakes, drained, can be substituted for 1 can of the crabmeat.

ABOUT CRABMEAT

Crabmeat lends a touch of elegance to any fish dish, as well as a good supply of protein, calcium and minerals. You can combine it with less expensive fish to stretch it in sauces, salads, chowders and dips. Crabs are available live (close to the place of capture), frozen (cooked in the shell) and canned. Some processors have floating canneries to facilitate immediate packing of the fresh crabs.

Salmon-Corn Cakes

Drop the salmon mixture onto a hot griddle; flatten slightly.

Cook until cakes are golden brown, about 3 minutes; turn.

3 eggs
2 tablespoons flour
2 teaspoons lemon juice
1 teaspoon salt
2 drops red pepper sauce
  Dash of pepper
1 can (12 ounces) whole kernel corn, drained
1 can (7¾ ounces) salmon, drained and
  flaked
  Pimiento Sauce (below)

Grease heated griddle if necessary. Mix eggs, flour, lemon juice, salt, pepper sauce and pepper with hand beater until foamy. Stir in corn and salmon.

Drop mixture by generous ¼ cupfuls onto hot griddle; flatten slightly. Cook until golden brown, about 3 minutes on each side. Grease griddle as necessary. Serve corn cakes with Pimiento Sauce.   4 SERVINGS.

PIMIENTO SAUCE

½ cup dairy sour cream
¼ cup grated American cheese food
2 tablespoons chopped pimiento

Heat all ingredients just to boiling over low heat, stirring constantly.

Salmon Strata

12 slices sandwich bread
¼ cup soft butter or margarine
2 teaspoons prepared mustard
2 cans (7¾ ounces each) red salmon,
　　drained
1 cup shredded Cheddar cheese (about
　　4 ounces)
¼ cup sliced pimiento-stuffed olives
1 small onion, chopped (about ¼ cup)
1 package (10 ounces) frozen green peas
1 can (10¾ ounces) condensed cream of
　　shrimp soup
¼ cup milk
　　Dill pickles

Toast bread; trim crusts. Mix butter and mustard; spread over 1 side of each bread slice. Arrange 6 slices bread buttered sides up in ungreased baking dish, 11¾x7½x1¾ inches.

Heat oven to 350°. Flake salmon, removing skin and bones. Mix salmon, cheese, olives and onion. Spread salmon mixture evenly over bread in baking dish. Cut remaining 6 slices bread diagonally in half; place buttered sides up on salmon mixture. Rinse frozen peas under running cold water to separate; layer on bread. Mix soup and milk; pour evenly on and around sandwiches. Bake uncovered until hot and bubbly, 25 to 30 minutes. Serve with dill pickles.
6 TO 9 SERVINGS.

Spread butter mixture over bread. Arrange 6 slices bread in baking dish. Spread salmon mixture evenly over bread in dish.

Cut remaining bread diagonally in half; place on salmon mixture. Layer peas on bread. Pour soup mixture evenly on top.

Salmon Platter

½ pound uncooked asparagus
¼ cup Italian salad dressing
Leaf lettuce
1 can (16 ounces) red salmon, drained
6 medium tomatoes
1 large cucumber, thinly sliced
Carrot sticks
1 carton (8 ounces) unflavored yogurt
½ cup mayonnaise or salad dressing
1 tablespoon snipped chives
½ teaspoon garlic salt

Break off tough ends of asparagus at point where stalks snap easily. Cut diagonally into very thin slices; toss with salad dressing. Cover and refrigerate 1 hour.

Arrange lettuce on large platter. Break salmon into chunks, removing skin and bones; mound salmon on lettuce in center of platter. Cut each tomato into a flower as pictured. Drain asparagus; spoon into tomato flowers. Arrange tomatoes, cucumber and carrot sticks around salmon.

Mix yogurt, mayonnaise, chives and garlic salt; spoon 2 tablespoons onto salmon. Serve remaining dressing with salad.   6 SERVINGS.

Salmon Quiches

1 package (11 ounces) pie crust mix or
   sticks
1 can (about 16 ounces) salmon, drained
   and flaked
4 green onions, chopped (about 6
   tablespoons)
8 eggs
4 cups whipping cream or half-and-half
1½ teaspoons salt
½ teaspoon sugar
¼ teaspoon cayenne red pepper

Prepare pastry for two One-Crust Pies as directed on package. Divide salmon and onions between pastry-lined pie plates.

Beat eggs slightly; beat in whipping cream, salt, sugar and red pepper.

Heat oven to 425°. Pour half of the egg mixture on salmon and onions in each pie plate. Bake 15 minutes. Reduce oven temperature to 300° and bake until knife inserted 1 inch from edge comes out clean, about 45 minutes. Let stand 10 minutes before cutting.   10 TO 12 SERVINGS.

Tuna Salad with Biscuits

7 ounces uncooked elbow macaroni (about
    2 cups)
1 jar (8 ounces) pasteurized process
    pimiento cheese spread
1 jar (2 ounces) broken pimiento-stuffed
    olives, drained
2 cans (6½ ounces each) tuna, drained and
    broken into chunks
2 medium stalks celery, sliced (about 1 cup)
⅓ cup mayonnaise or salad dressing
2 teaspoons lemon juice
½ teaspoon seasoned salt
    Dried parsley flakes
    Corn Flake Biscuits (below)

Cook macaroni as directed on package; drain. Stir in
cheese until melted. Reserve 2 tablespoons olives. Stir remaining olives, the tuna, celery, mayonnaise, lemon juice
and seasoned salt into macaroni. Cover and refrigerate 2
hours. Garnish with reserved olives and parsley flakes.
Serve with Corn Flake Biscuits. 6 TO 8 SERVINGS.

CORN FLAKE BISCUITS

¼ cup butter or margarine, melted
1 cup crushed corn flake cereal (about 1¾
    cups uncrushed)
2 cups biscuit baking mix
½ cup cold water

Heat oven to 425°. Spread half of the butter in baking pan,
9x9x2 inches; sprinkle with half of the cereal. Stir baking
mix and water until a soft dough forms; beat vigorously 20
strokes. Drop dough by tablespoonfuls onto cereal; drizzle
with remaining butter. Press remaining cereal into dough.
Bake until light brown, 12 to 15 minutes.

Stir pimiento cheese spread into hot drained macaroni until the cheese is melted.

Add part of the olives, the tuna, celery, mayonnaise, lemon juice and seasoned salt.

To make biscuits, sprinkle half of the crushed cereal over half the butter in pan.

Drop dough onto cereal in pan; drizzle with remaining butter. Add remaining cereal.

Press yolks through a sieve. Reserve for topping.

Chop egg whites to heat with the rice-tuna mixture.

Tuna with Rice

2 cups water
1 cup uncooked regular rice
1 teaspoon salt
1 clove garlic
3 hard-cooked eggs
¼ cup butter or margarine
2 green onions (with tops), sliced (about ¼ cup)
1 to 2 teaspoons curry powder
1 can (12½ ounces) tuna, drained and flaked
½ teaspoon salt
¼ teaspoon ground ginger
⅛ teaspoon cayenne red pepper
2 tablespoons snipped parsley
1 jar (9 ounces) mango chutney

Heat water, rice, 1 teaspoon salt and the garlic to boiling in 3-quart saucepan, stirring once or twice; reduce heat. Cover and simmer 15 minutes. (Do not lift cover or stir.) Remove from heat; discard garlic. Fluff rice lightly with fork. Cover and let steam about 10 minutes.

Separate egg yolks from whites. Press yolks through sieve and chop whites; reserve. Heat butter in 12-inch skillet until melted. Cook and stir onions and curry powder in butter over low heat 1 minute. Stir in rice, tuna, ½ teaspoon salt, the ginger, red pepper and egg whites. Cook and stir until tuna is hot, about 3 minutes; transfer to warm serving plate. Sprinkle tuna mixture with egg yolks and parsley. Serve with chutney.   6 SERVINGS.

Tuna-Tomato Polenta

¾ cup cornmeal
¾ cup cold water
½ teaspoon salt
¼ teaspoon garlic salt
1½ cups boiling water
1 can (15 ounces) tomato sauce
2 cans (6½ ounces each) tuna, drained and
    flaked
1 medium stalk celery, chopped (about ½
    cup)
¼ teaspoon dried basil leaves
¾ cup grated Parmesan cheese
    Sliced ripe olives

Mix cornmeal, cold water, salt and garlic salt thoroughly in 1-quart saucepan. Stir in boiling water. Cook over medium heat, stirring constantly, until mixture thickens and boils, about 2 minutes. Reduce heat; cover and simmer 10 minutes. Spread cornmeal in ungreased baking dish, 11¾x7½x1¾ inches. Refrigerate until firm, about 8 hours.

Heat oven to 350°. Mix tomato sauce, tuna, celery and basil. Spread ⅔ of the tuna mixture in ungreased baking dish, 12x8x1¾ or 13½x8¾x1¾ inches. Cut cornmeal into 10 parts; place on tuna mixture in dish. Top cornmeal with remaining tuna mixture; sprinkle with cheese. Bake uncovered 25 minutes. Garnish with olives.   8 SERVINGS.

Cook the cornmeal in 1-quart pan. Spread in dish; refrigerate 8 hours. Mix tomato sauce, tuna, celery, basil.

Spread ⅔ of the tuna mixture in dish. Place pieces of cornmeal on sauce. Top with remaining sauce and cheese.

Tuna Short Pie

Layer tuna, broccoli and celery in baking dish.

Overlap Biscuit Rounds on soup mixture.

2 cans (6½ ounces each) tuna, drained and flaked
1 package (10 ounces) frozen chopped broccoli, thawed and drained
2 medium stalks celery, sliced (about 1 cup)
1 can (11 ounces) condensed Cheddar cheese soup
2 tablespoons milk
½ teaspoon onion salt
½ teaspoon dried marjoram leaves
Biscuit Rounds (below)

Heat oven to 400°. Layer tuna, broccoli and celery in ungreased baking dish, 8x8x2 inches. Mix soup, milk, onion salt and marjoram; pour on tuna and vegetables. Heat in oven 15 minutes. While tuna mixture is heating, prepare Biscuits Rounds.

Overlap the Biscuit Rounds on tuna mixture. Bake uncovered until Biscuit Rounds are golden, 15 to 20 minutes. 6 SERVINGS.

BISCUIT ROUNDS
1 cup biscuit baking mix
¼ cup butter or margarine, softened
3 tablespoons boiling water

Combine baking mix and butter. Stir in water with fork until dough forms a ball and cleans side of bowl. (Dough will be puffy and soft.) Divide into 6 parts; flatten each into 3- to 4-inch round.

Salmon Short Pie: Substitute 1 can (16 ounces) salmon for the tuna. Flake salmon, removing skin and bones.

Tuna-Lemon Puff

2 slices white bread, torn into ¼-inch pieces (about 2 cups)
1 cup shredded Cheddar cheese (about 4 ounces)
1 can (6½ ounces) tuna, drained and flaked
¾ cup milk
3 eggs, separated
    Grated peel of 1 medium lemon (optional)
1 tablespoon lemon juice
1 teaspoon instant minced onion
½ teaspoon salt
¼ teaspoon dry mustard
3 tablespoons butter or margarine, melted
½ teaspoon poppy seed

Heat oven to 350°. Mix 1½ cups of the bread, the cheese, tuna, milk, egg yolks, lemon peel, lemon juice, onion, salt and mustard. Beat egg whites until stiff but not dry; fold into tuna mixture. Pour into greased 1-quart casserole. Toss remaining bread, the butter and poppy seed; sprinkle over casserole. Bake uncovered until golden and set in center, about 40 minutes. Garnish with parsley.
6 SERVINGS.

Fold egg whites into tuna mixture; pour into casserole.

Toss remaining bread, butter and poppy seed for topping.

Mix ingredients in the casserole in which they will bake.

Sprinkle with cheese; add reserved tomato and chips.

Tuna-Corn Bake

1 can (10¾ ounces) condensed cream of
   chicken soup
1 can (9¼ ounces) tuna, drained and flaked
1 can (8 ounces) stewed tomatoes (reserve
   3 tomato pieces)
1 cup coarsely crumbled corn chips
½ small green pepper, chopped (about ¼
   cup)
2 teaspoons instant minced onion
½ teaspoon chili powder
   Dash of garlic salt
1 cup shredded Cheddar cheese (about 4
   ounces)
1 cup coarsely crumbled corn chips
   Chili sauce (optional)

Heat oven to 350°. Mix soup, tuna, tomatoes, 1 cup corn chips, the green pepper, onion, chili powder and garlic salt in greased 1½-quart casserole. Sprinkle with cheese and arrange reserved tomato pieces in center. Sprinkle 1 cup corn chips around tomatoes. Bake uncovered until bubbly, about 30 minutes. Serve with chili sauce.   6 SERVINGS.

Eggs, Cheese and Dried Beans

Mushroom Omelet

Pour beaten eggs over mushrooms while sauce simmers.

Sprinkle omelet with cheese and bake 5 minutes.

    Asparagus-Cheese Sauce (below)
1   cup sliced mushrooms
2   tablespoons butter or margarine
8   eggs, beaten
1   teaspoon salt
¼   teaspoon pepper
⅓   cup grated Parmesan cheese

Prepare Asparagus-Cheese Sauce. Heat oven to 450°. Cook and stir mushrooms in butter in 10-inch ovenproof omelet pan or skillet over medium heat until tender. Mix eggs, salt and pepper; pour on mushrooms.

As mixture begins to set at bottom and side, gently lift cooked portion with spatula so thin uncooked portion can flow to bottom. Cook until eggs are set, about 5 minutes. Sprinkle omelet with cheese. Bake 5 minutes. Let stand 1 minute before cutting into wedges. Top each serving with about ½ cup of the sauce.   4 SERVINGS.

ASPARAGUS-CHEESE SAUCE

Mix 1 can (11 ounces) condensed Cheddar cheese soup and ½ cup water in 2-quart saucepan. Stir in 1 package (10 ounces) frozen cut asparagus, partially thawed. Heat to boiling; reduce heat. Simmer uncovered, stirring occasionally, until asparagus is tender.

Mozzarella Eggs

1 tablespoon butter or margarine
4 eggs
½ teaspoon salt
Dash of pepper
1½ teaspoons water
4 slices mozzarella cheese
½ teaspoon dried oregano leaves
Paprika

Heat butter in 10-inch skillet until just hot enough to sizzle a drop of water. Break each egg into measuring cup or saucer; carefully slip eggs one at a time into skillet. Cook eggs over low heat until whites are set; sprinkle with salt and pepper.

Pour water into skillet. Place a cheese slice on each egg; sprinkle with oregano and paprika. Remove from heat. Cover and let stand 5 minutes before serving. 4 SERVINGS.

Break each egg into measuring cup or saucer; slip into skillet. Cook until whites are set.

Add salt and pepper, water, cheese, oregano and paprika. Cover; let stand 5 minutes.

EGG KNOW-HOW

Store eggs in the refrigerator up to 1 week. Keep them insulated in their original carton (saves flavor) with the large ends up to hold the yolks in the centers.

Leftover egg whites can be refrigerated covered up to 10 days. Leftover yolks should be covered with water in a closed container and refrigerated up to 3 days.

Eggs separate best when they are cold, but beat faster and lighter when they are at room temperature; so separate them first and then let them stand 1 hour before beating.

Eggs in a Ring

Mix the batter just to moisten flour. Batter will be lumpy.

Spoon batter into greased ring mold; bake until golden brown.

To prepare Creamed Eggs, heat frozen peas and chicken soup.

Fold in the remaining ingredients. Simmer 3 to 5 minutes.

1 egg
1 cup milk
¼ cup vegetable oil
1 cup all-purpose flour
1 cup whole wheat flour
1 cup shredded Cheddar cheese (about 4 ounces)
2 tablespoons sugar
1 tablespoon baking powder
½ teaspoon salt
Creamed Eggs (below)

Heat oven to 400°. Grease 6-cup ring mold. Beat egg; stir in milk and oil. Stir in flours, cheese, sugar, baking powder and salt just until flour is moistened. (Batter will be lumpy.) Spoon into mold. Bake until golden brown, 20 to 25 minutes; unmold. Prepare Creamed Eggs; serve in center of hot muffin ring.   4 TO 6 SERVINGS.

CREAMED EGGS

1 package (10 ounces) frozen green peas
1 can (10¾ ounces) condensed cream of chicken soup
3 hard-cooked eggs, sliced
6 to 8 pimiento-stuffed olives, sliced
2 tablespoons chopped onion
⅛ teaspoon poultry seasoning

Heat frozen peas and soup in 2-quart saucepan over medium heat, stirring occasionally. Fold in eggs, olives, onion and poultry seasoning; reduce heat. Simmer uncovered 3 to 5 minutes.

Eggs with Cheese Potatoes

2 cups water
1 teaspoon salt
6 small new potatoes
6 hard-cooked eggs, sliced
2 green onions (with tops), chopped (about
  ¼ cup)
1 jar (2 ounces) sliced pimiento, drained
  (about 2 tablespoons)
1 can (10¾ ounces) condensed cream of
  chicken soup
½ cup milk
1 clove garlic, crushed
½ teaspoon onion salt
⅛ teaspoon pepper
1 cup shredded Cheddar cheese (about 4
  ounces)
4 slices bacon, crisply fried and crumbled

Heat water and salt to boiling. Add potatoes; heat to boiling. Cover and cook until tender, 20 to 25 minutes. Drain; cool slightly. Remove skins; cut potatoes into fourths.

Heat oven to 375°. Layer potatoes, eggs, onions and pimiento in ungreased 1½-quart casserole. Mix soup, milk, garlic, onion salt and pepper; pour on top. Sprinkle with cheese and bacon. Bake uncovered until potatoes are hot and cheese is melted, about 25 minutes.   4 TO 6 SERVINGS.

Layer potatoes, eggs, onions and pimiento in casserole.

Pour on soup mixture; sprinkle with cheese and bacon.

Baked Eggs

1 can (11 ounces) condensed Cheddar
   cheese soup
2 tablespoons milk
⅛ teaspoon chili powder
   Dash of garlic powder
6 eggs
½ cup shredded Cheddar cheese
3 English muffins, split and toasted
   Chopped green onion

Heat oven to 350°. Mix soup, milk, chili powder and garlic powder in saucepan. Heat to boiling; reduce heat. Simmer uncovered, stirring occasionally, 5 minutes. Pour into ungreased baking dish, 11¾x7½x1¾ inches.

Break 1 egg at a time into measuring cup. Slip into soup mixture, spacing evenly; sprinkle with cheese. Cover and bake until eggs are set, 20 to 25 minutes. Serve on muffin halves; garnish with onion.   3 SERVINGS.

Eggs-in-Cups

Heat oven to 350°. For each serving, spoon 1 tablespoon chopped canned mushrooms or 1 tablespoon finely snipped sliced smoked ham into buttered 4- to 6-ounce baking dish or custard cup. Break egg into dish; sprinkle with salt and pepper. Top with 1 tablespoon milk; sprinkle with paprika and snipped parsley. Bake uncovered until egg is desired doneness, about 25 minutes.

Impossible Quiche

12 slices bacon (about ½ pound), crisply fried
   and crumbled
1 cup shredded natural Swiss cheese (about 4
   ounces)
⅓ cup finely chopped onion
2 cups milk
½ cup biscuit baking mix
4 eggs
¼ teaspoon salt
⅛ teaspoon pepper
   Fruit Wedges (below)

Heat oven to 350°. Lightly grease 9- or 10-inch pie plate. Sprinkle bacon, cheese and onion evenly over bottom of pie plate.

Place remaining ingredients in blender container. Cover and blend on high speed 1 minute. Pour into pie plate. Bake until golden brown and knife inserted in center comes out clean, 50 to 55 minutes. Let stand 5 minutes before cutting. Serve with Fruit Wedges. Refrigerate any leftover pie. 6 TO 8 SERVINGS.

FRUIT WEDGES

Mound 1 to 2 tablespoons packed brown sugar in center of each of 6 small plates. Cut top from 1 small pineapple. Cut pineapple into 6 slices; remove core. Cut each slice into wedges and arrange around brown sugar on plates.

Cut 2 oranges into 4 slices each. Cut slices into wedges and arrange on pineapple. Top each serving with a strawberry. Fruit can be dipped in the brown sugar.

Ham Oven Omelet

    4 eggs
    ½ cup biscuit baking mix
    ½ cup milk
    1 teaspoon salt
    1 teaspoon Worcestershire sauce
    ½ teaspoon garlic salt
    ½ teaspoon cayenne red pepper
    2 medium zucchini, chopped (about 2 cups)
    2 medium tomatoes, chopped (about 1½
       cups)
    1 small onion, chopped (about ¼ cup)
    1 cup cut-up cooked ham
    1 cup shredded Cheddar cheese (about 4
       ounces)

Heat oven to 325°. Beat eggs slightly; beat in baking mix, milk, salt, Worcestershire sauce, garlic salt and red pepper. Layer zucchini, tomatoes, onion and ham in ungreased baking dish, 8x8x2 inches; pour egg mixture on top. Sprinkle with cheese.

Bake uncovered until knife inserted 1 inch from edge comes out clean, 40 to 50 minutes. Let stand 10 minutes before serving.   4 TO 6 SERVINGS.

Cut the zucchini into lengthwise strips, then cut crosswise.

Layer the zucchini, tomatoes, onion and ham in baking dish.

Pour the egg mixture on top.

Sprinkle evenly with cheese.

Cheese and Egg Puffs

Cook the vegetables while the eggs are beating.

Cook the egg puffs while the sauce simmers.

6 eggs
1 medium green pepper, chopped (about 1 cup)
1 medium onion, chopped (about ½ cup)
2 tablespoons butter or margarine
2 teaspoons cornstarch
1 can (15 ounces) tomato sauce
1 can (4 ounces) sliced mushrooms, drained
¾ cup all-purpose flour
1½ teaspoons baking powder
½ teaspoon salt
1½ cups shredded Cheddar cheese (about 6 ounces)

Beat eggs in large mixer bowl until very thick and lemon colored, about 10 minutes. Cook and stir green pepper and onion in butter in 2-quart saucepan over medium heat until tender, about 2 minutes. Stir in cornstarch; add tomato sauce and mushrooms. Cook, stirring constantly, until mixture thickens; reduce heat. Cover and simmer 15 minutes.

Heat lightly greased griddle over medium heat. Mix flour, baking powder and salt; beat into eggs gradually. Fold in cheese. Drop batter by ¼ cupfuls onto hot griddle. Cook until light brown, about 2 minutes on each side. For each serving, top 2 egg puffs with ½ cup of the sauce.
4 OR 5 SERVINGS.

Fruit-Topped Oven Pancakes

Fruit Topping (below)
3 eggs
½ teaspoon salt
½ cup all-purpose flour*
½ cup milk
2 tablespoons butter or margarine
1½ cups shredded Cheddar or Swiss cheese
(about 6 ounces)
Powdered sugar

Heat oven to 450°. Prepare Fruit Topping. Place 2 round layer pans, 8x1½ inches, in oven. Beat eggs and salt in small mixer bowl on high speed 1 minute. Beat on low speed, adding flour and milk alternately in 3 additions; continue beating 1 minute.

Remove pans from oven. Place 1 tablespoon butter in each pan; brush pans with butter. Divide batter equally between pans. Bake uncovered 15 minutes. Reduce oven temperature to 350°. Bake 5 minutes.

Place pancakes on 2 warm serving plates; sprinkle with cheese. Spoon topping onto each pancake; sprinkle with sugar. Cut into wedges.   4 SERVINGS.

*Do not use self-rising flour in this recipe.

FRUIT TOPPING

Squeeze juice of ½ medium lemon over 2 cups sweetened sliced fresh fruit or berries.

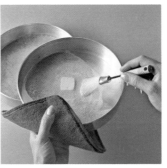

Heat 2 round layer pans in the oven. Brush each pan with 1 tablespoon butter.

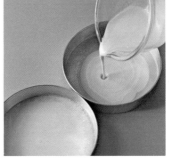

Divide batter between pans; bake 15 minutes at 450°, 5 minutes at 350°.

Sprinkle toast with 1 cup of the cheese; add asparagus.

Pour on seasoned custard; top with paprika. Refrigerate.

Swiss Cheese Bake

6 slices white bread, toasted
2 tablespoons butter or margarine, softened
2 cups shredded Swiss cheese (about 8 ounces)
1 package (10 ounces) frozen asparagus cuts, cooked and drained
2 cups milk
4 eggs, slightly beaten
2 tablespoons snipped parsley
1 teaspoon salt
1 teaspoon Worcestershire sauce
½ teaspoon dry mustard
¼ to ½ teaspoon red pepper sauce
¼ teaspoon paprika

Spread 1 side of each toast slice with butter; cut crosswise into thirds. Arrange 9 toast pieces, buttered sides up, in ungreased baking dish, 10x6x1¾ inches. Sprinkle with 1 cup of the cheese; top with asparagus. Sprinkle remaining cheese over asparagus. Top with remaining toast pieces, buttered sides down.

Mix milk, eggs, parsley, salt, Worcestershire sauce, mustard and pepper sauce until smooth; pour on toast. Sprinkle with paprika. Cover and refrigerate 4 to 6 hours.

Heat oven to 325°. Bake uncovered until knife inserted halfway between center and edge comes out clean, about 1 hour 15 minutes. Garnish with parsley.   6 SERVINGS.

Broccoli-Cheese Pie

6 cups water
1 teaspoon salt
3 ounces uncooked macaroni rings (about
　¾ cup)
1 egg yolk
1 tablespoon snipped chives
1 cup shredded Cheddar cheese (about
　4 ounces)
1 package (10 ounces) frozen chopped
　broccoli
½ teaspoon salt
4 eggs
1 egg white
1 cup creamed cottage cheese
1 tablespoon snipped chives
1 teaspoon salt
　Paprika

Heat oven to 375°. Heat water and 1 teaspoon salt to boiling; stir in macaroni. Boil until tender, 5 to 8 minutes. Drain; rinse in cold water.

Beat egg yolk; stir in macaroni and 1 tablespoon chives. Press mixture against bottom and side of greased 9-inch pie plate with back of spoon. Bake 10 minutes; remove from oven. Cool 10 minutes.

Increase oven temperature to 425°. Sprinkle Cheddar cheese over crust. Prepare broccoli as directed on package, using ½ teaspoon salt; drain. Arrange broccoli on cheese. Beat eggs, egg white, cottage cheese, 1 tablespoon chives and 1 teaspoon salt; pour on broccoli. Sprinkle with paprika.

Bake uncovered 15 minutes. Reduce oven temperature to 300°. Bake until knife inserted 1 inch from edge comes out clean, about 30 minutes. Cool 10 minutes before serving.
5 SERVINGS.

Stir the cooked macaroni and chives into the egg yolk.

Press the macaroni mixture in greased 9-inch pie plate.

Sprinkle cheese over crust; top with hot cooked broccoli.

Pour egg mixture on broccoli; sprinkle with paprika.

Cheese-Clam Casserole

Mix uncooked macaroni with other ingredients except the potato chips and tomatoes.

Refrigerate 3 to 4 hours; stir. Bake uncovered 45 minutes; add chips. Bake 15 minutes.

3½ ounces uncooked macaroni (about 1 cup)
1 can (10¾ ounces) condensed New England clam chowder
1 cup shredded Cheddar cheese (about 4 ounces)
1 cup milk
⅓ large onion, chopped (about ⅓ cup)
½ small green pepper, chopped (about ¼ cup)
1 jar (2 ounces) sliced pimiento, drained
1 teaspoon salt
¼ teaspoon dry mustard
¼ cup crushed potato chips
   Cherry tomatoes, cut in half

Mix uncooked macaroni, chowder, cheese, milk, onion, green pepper, pimiento, salt and mustard in greased 1½-quart casserole. Cover and refrigerate 3 to 4 hours; stir.

Heat oven to 350°. Bake uncovered 45 minutes; sprinkle with potato chips. Bake 15 minutes. Garnish with tomatoes.   4 TO 6 SERVINGS.

KNOW THE DIFFERENCE

Grated cheese is dry, almost powdery cheese that has been put through the small holes of a grater. Cheese that has become dry and hard can be grated and stored in a covered container, or you can purchase grated cheese in shaker-top cans.

Shredded cheese is moist, fresh cheese put through the small holes of a shredder. You can shred it yourself or buy it in packages at most stores.

Tomato-Cheese Macaroni

7 ounces uncooked macaroni (about 2 cups)
1 medium green pepper, chopped
4 green onions (with tops), sliced (about ½ cup)
2 tablespoons vegetable oil
1 can (16 ounces) whole tomatoes
1 can (8 ounces) tomato sauce
¼ teaspoon pepper
3 cups shredded process American cheese (about 12 ounces)

Heat oven to 350°. Cook macaroni as directed on package; drain. Pour hot macaroni into ungreased 2-quart casserole. Reserve 3 tablespoons chopped green pepper. Cook and stir remaining green pepper and the onions in oil in 2-quart saucepan until onions are tender, about 5 minutes. Stir in tomatoes (with liquid), tomato sauce and pepper; break up tomatoes with fork. Heat until tomatoes are hot; pour on hot macaroni.

Stir 2½ cups of the cheese into macaroni mixture. Bake uncovered 25 minutes. Sprinkle with remaining cheese; bake uncovered until cheese is melted, about 5 minutes. Garnish with reserved green pepper.   6 TO 8 SERVINGS.

You can stir the macaroni into 6 cups boiling salted water and cook and stir 3 minutes.

Remove from heat; cover tightly. Let stand 10 minutes. (It cooks as it stands.)

Do-Ahead Macaroni and Cheese

Add cheese to the uncooked macaroni in the casserole.

To crush potato chips easily, place in plastic bag and roll.

7 ounces uncooked elbow macaroni
2 cups shredded Cheddar cheese (about 8 ounces)
1 can (11 ounces) condensed Cheddar cheese soup
1¾ cups milk
1 jar (2 ounces) sliced pimiento, drained
¾ teaspoon salt
1 cup crushed potato chips
Chicken-Pepper Sauce (below)

Mix all ingredients except potato chips and Chicken-Pepper Sauce in greased 2-quart casserole or baking dish, 8x8x2 inches. Cover and refrigerate up to 24 hours.

∎1 hour 30 minutes before serving, heat oven to 350°. Stir macaroni mixture; sprinkle with crushed potato chips. Cover and bake 1 hour. Uncover and bake 20 minutes. Serve with Chicken-Pepper Sauce.   4 TO 6 SERVINGS.

CHICKEN-PEPPER SAUCE
1 package (about 1 ounce) chicken gravy mix
½ cup water
½ cup dairy sour cream
2 tablespoons chopped green pepper
Paprika

Heat gravy mix, water, sour cream and green pepper to boiling, stirring constantly. Sprinkle with paprika.

Meatless Lasagne

Lasagne Sauce (below)
2 cartons (12 ounces each) creamed
    cottage cheese (small curd)
1 cup grated Parmesan cheese
1 tablespoon dried parsley flakes
2 teaspoons salt
1½ teaspoons dried oregano leaves
8 ounces uncooked lasagne noodles
3 cups shredded mozzarella cheese

Prepare Lasagne Sauce. Mix cottage cheese, ½ cup of the Parmesan cheese, the parsley, salt and oregano; reserve. Cook noodles as directed on package; drain.

Heat oven to 350°. Reserve ½ cup sauce. Layer ⅓ each of the noodles, remaining sauce, mozzarella cheese and cottage cheese mixture in ungreased lasagne pan, 14x8x2 inches, or baking pan, 13x9x2 inches. Repeat 2 times. Top with reserved sauce; sprinkle with remaining Parmesan cheese. Bake uncovered 45 minutes. Let stand 15 minutes. 12 SERVINGS.

LASAGNE SAUCE

2 cans (15 ounces each) tomato sauce
1 can (16 ounces) whole tomatoes (with
    liquid)
3 cans (4 ounces each) mushroom stems and
    pieces (with liquid)
1 medium onion, chopped (about ½ cup)
2 tablespoons sugar
2 tablespoons dried parsley flakes
1 teaspoon salt
1 teaspoon dried basil leaves
1 clove garlic, finely chopped

Heat all ingredients to boiling, stirring occasionally; reduce heat. Simmer uncovered 45 minutes.

Layer ⅓ of the hot noodles in ungreased lasagne pan.

Reserve ½ cup sauce. Pour on ⅓ of the remaining sauce.

Add ⅓ each of the mozzarella cheese and cheese mixture.

Repeat layers 2 times. Add reserved sauce and cheese.

Fettuccine Alfredo

While noodles are cooking, heat butter in chafing dish at the table until melted.

Stir in cream, grated cheese and salt; heat, stirring occasionally, until smooth.

8 ounces medium egg noodles (about 6 cups)
¼ cup butter or margarine
1 cup whipping cream
¾ cup grated Parmesan cheese
½ teaspoon salt
Grated Parmesan cheese
Freshly ground pepper

Cook noodles as directed on package. While noodles are cooking, heat butter over water bath in chafing dish until melted. Stir in cream, ¾ cup Parmesan cheese and the salt. Heat, stirring occasionally, until smooth. Drain noodles; toss with cream mixture until evenly coated. Serve with Parmesan cheese and pepper.   4 SERVINGS.

AT THE TABLE

The chafing dish is really a star performer when you want to prepare a show-stopping main dish or dessert at the table. It consists of a burner, stand, water pan, blazer pan and lid. When the blazer pan is placed over the source of heat and used as a skillet, you can cook at high temperatures at the table. The water pan below the blazer pan is used to keep food warm or for slow cooking at low temperatures. There are a wide variety of chafing dishes available which use alcohol, canned heat or butane; electric chafing dishes are also available.

Cheese-Fruit Mold

2 cups boiling water
1 package (6 ounces) orange-flavored
  gelatin*
½ cup sugar
1 package (8 ounces) cream cheese,
  softened
2 cans (15¼ ounces each) crushed
  pineapple in juice
2 cups shredded Cheddar cheese (about
  8 ounces)
2 cups creamed cottage cheese
2 teaspoons lemon juice
  Salad greens
  Honey Dressing (below)
  Crackers

Beat the cream cheese into the gelatin mixture until smooth.

Stir in the pineapple, remaining cheeses and lemon juice.

Pour boiling water on gelatin and sugar in large bowl; stir until gelatin and sugar are dissolved. Beat in cream cheese until smooth. Stir in pineapple (with juice), Cheddar cheese, cottage cheese and lemon juice. Pour into 12-cup mold. Refrigerate until firm, about 8 hours. Unmold on salad greens and serve with Honey Dressing and crackers. 8 TO 10 SERVINGS.

*Lime-flavored gelatin can be substituted for the orange-flavored gelatin.

HONEY DRESSING
Mix 2 cups unflavored yogurt and ½ cup honey. Sprinkle with ground nutmeg.

Soak beans first, then while they are cooking, cut pork into pieces and slice onion.

Layer beans, pork pieces and onion slices. Add bean liquid and seasonings; bake.

Baked Beans with Pork

1 pound navy or pea beans (about 2½ cups)
1 tablespoon vegetable oil
5 cups water
½ pound pork boneless Boston shoulder, cut into ½-inch pieces
1 medium onion, sliced
2 cups water
⅓ cup dark molasses
1 small carrot, grated (about ⅓ cup)
2 tablespoons brown sugar
2½ teaspoons salt
1 teaspoon dry mustard
¼ teaspoon ground sage
⅛ teaspoon pepper
⅛ teaspoon liquid smoke

Heat beans, oil and 5 cups water to boiling in Dutch oven. Boil 2 minutes; remove from heat. Cover and let stand 1 hour.

Heat beans to boiling; reduce heat. Cover and simmer until beans are tender, about 50 minutes. Drain, reserving 1 cup liquid (if necessary, add enough water to measure 1 cup).

Heat oven to 300°. Layer beans, pork pieces and onion slices in ungreased 3-quart casserole. Mix reserved liquid and remaining ingredients; pour over beans. Cover and bake 2 hours. Uncover and bake, stirring occasionally, 1½ hours.   8 SERVINGS.

Pinto Beans with Chilies

1 pound dried pinto beans (about 2½ cups)
5 cups water
1 tablespoon vegetable oil
½ pound salt pork (without rind), cut into
   1-inch pieces
1 can (8 ounces) tomato sauce
1 medium onion, chopped (about ½ cup)
2 to 3 tablespoons chopped canned chilies
1½ teaspoons garlic salt
2 slices Cheddar cheese

Heat beans, water and oil to boiling in Dutch oven. Boil 2 minutes; remove from heat. Cover and let stand 1 hour.

Heat beans to boiling; reduce heat. Cover and simmer until beans are tender, about 50 minutes. (Do not boil or beans will burst.)

Heat oven to 300°. Place beans (with liquid) in ungreased 2-quart casserole. Stir in salt pork, tomato sauce, onion, chilies and garlic salt. Bake uncovered, stirring occasionally, 1½ hours.

Ten minutes before serving, top with cheese slices. Bake until cheese is melted.　8 SERVINGS.

Cut salt pork into 1-inch pieces; add to casserole.

Stir the beans occasionally while they are baking.

Burgundy Bean Stew

1 pound bacon
3 cans (15 ounces each) kidney beans, drained (reserve 1 cup liquid)
1 Bermuda onion, chopped (about 1 cup)
1 medium green pepper, chopped (about 1 cup)
1 can (8 ounces) tomato sauce
1 cup red Burgundy or dry red wine
1 tablespoon brown sugar
1 teaspoon horseradish
  Bermuda onion rings

Fry bacon over medium heat until crisp; drain. Heat oven to 350°. Layer beans, onion and green pepper in ungreased 3-quart casserole. Crumble bacon and mix with reserved bean liquid and remaining ingredients except onion rings; pour over bean mixture. Top with onion rings. Cover and bake 1 hour.   8 SERVINGS.

Beany Rarebit

1 small green pepper, chopped (about ½ cup)
2 tablespoons butter or margarine
1 can (15 ounces) kidney beans
2 cups shredded American cheese
½ teaspoon chili powder
6 hard rolls

Reserve 2 tablespoons green pepper. Cook and stir remaining green pepper in butter in 2-quart saucepan until tender, about 5 minutes. Stir in beans (with liquid), cheese and chili powder. Cook over low heat, stirring occasionally, until cheese is melted, about 5 minutes. Split rolls; serve rarebit over rolls. Garnish with reserved green pepper.
4 TO 6 SERVINGS.

Party Baked Beans

½ pound fully cooked ham, cut into ½-inch pieces
1 can (27½ ounces) baked beans in molasses sauce, drained
1 can (17 ounces) lima beans, drained
1 can (15½ ounces) butter beans, drained
1 can (15½ ounces) kidney beans, drained
  Barbecue Sauce (below)
1 can (20 ounces) sliced pineapple, drained
  Paprika

Heat oven to 350°. Mix ham and beans in ungreased 3-quart casserole. Pour Barbecue Sauce on ham and beans. Bake uncovered 1¼ hours. Stir before serving. If beans are too liquid, let stand 10 minutes. Garnish with pineapple slices; sprinkle slices with paprika.   6 SERVINGS.

BARBECUE SAUCE

⅔ cup light corn syrup
⅓ cup catsup
¼ cup vinegar
1 medium onion, chopped (about ½ cup)
1 tablespoon prepared mustard
½ teaspoon garlic powder

Mix all ingredients.

Crunchy Baked Soybeans

12 ounces dried soybeans (about 2 cups)
 6 cups water
 1 teaspoon salt
½ cup imitation bacon
⅓ cup packed brown sugar
¼ cup molasses
 1 medium onion, chopped (about ½ cup)
 1 teaspoon salt
 1 teaspoon dry mustard
 1 can (15 ounces) tomato sauce

Heat soybeans, water and 1 teaspoon salt to boiling; boil
2 minutes. Remove from heat. Cover and let stand 1 hour.
Drain soybeans, reserving ¾ cup liquid.

Heat oven to 325°. Mix soybeans, reserved bean liquid,
imitation bacon, brown sugar, molasses, onion, 1 teaspoon
salt and the mustard. Pour into ungreased 1½-quart casserole. Cover and bake 3 hours. Stir in tomato sauce; bake
1 hour.   6 SERVINGS.

SOYBEANS contain 1½
times as much protein as
other dried beans, and that
protein is high quality. Use
as meat substitutes and ex-
tenders. Store and soak as
you would other dried
beans, but expect them to
be firmer after cooking. Add
acid foods after beans are
tender. One cup dried yields
2½ cups cooked.

Simmer soaked beans until tender; drain. Layer the beans and corn. Mix flour, sugar, seasonings, tomato liquid; shake.

Stir the mixture into tomatoes; add green pepper. Pour on soybeans and corn; top with bread crumbs and cheese, then bake.

Soybean Vegetable Casserole

6 ounces dried soybeans (about 1 cup)
4 cups water
1 teaspoon salt
1 can (17 ounces) whole kernel corn, drained
2 tablespoons flour
1 teaspoon sugar
¼ teaspoon Italian seasoning
⅛ teaspoon pepper
1 can (16 ounces) whole tomatoes, drained
  (reserve ½ cup liquid)
½ small green pepper, chopped (about
  ¼ cup)
1 cup soft bread crumbs
1 cup shredded Cheddar cheese (about
  4 ounces)

Heat soybeans and water to boiling in Dutch oven; boil 2 minutes. Remove from heat. Cover and let stand 1 hour.

Add salt to soybeans. Heat to boiling; reduce heat. Simmer uncovered until soybeans are tender, 2 to 3 hours; drain.

Heat oven to 375°. Layer soybeans and corn in ungreased 1½-quart casserole. Add flour, sugar, Italian seasoning and pepper to reserved tomato liquid. Shake in covered container; stir into tomatoes. Add green pepper. Pour on soybeans and corn. Top with bread crumbs and cheese. Bake uncovered 40 minutes.   6 SERVINGS.

Sandwiches and Soups

Fiesta Beef Roll Sandwiches

After patting beef mixture to edges of foil, sprinkle with cheese, chips and olives.

Roll up beef carefully, beginning at long side and using foil to lift mixture.

1½ pounds ground beef
⅓ cup dry bread crumbs
⅓ cup catsup
2 tablespoons finely chopped onion
2 tablespoons finely chopped green pepper
1 teaspoon salt
1 teaspoon chili powder
1 egg
1 cup shredded Cheddar cheese (about 4 ounces)
1 cup crushed corn chips
½ cup chopped pitted ripe olives
½ loaf (1-pound size) French bread
   Hot taco sauce or prepared mustard

Mix ground beef, bread crumbs, catsup, onion, green pepper, salt, chili powder and egg. Pat ground beef mixture evenly to edges of piece of aluminum foil, 12x11 inches. Sprinkle with cheese, corn chips and olives.

Heat oven to 350°. Roll up beef carefully, beginning at long side and using foil to lift beef mixture. Press edge and ends of roll to seal. Place roll on rack in jelly roll pan, 15½x10½x1 inch. (At this point, roll can be refrigerated covered up to 24 hours.) Bake uncovered until done, about 1 hour.

Cut French bread diagonally into 12 slices. Toast slices. Serve sliced beef roll on toast with taco sauce.
12 OPEN-FACE SANDWICHES.

Taco Submarines

6 brown and serve French-style rolls (each
    about 6 inches long)
1 pound ground beef
½ cup dairy sour cream
¼ cup water
1 package (1¼ ounces) taco seasoning mix
    Mayonnaise or salad dressing
    Shredded lettuce
6 slices Swiss cheese, cut diagonally in half
3 medium tomatoes, each cut into 4 slices

Bake rolls as directed on package. Cook and stir ground beef in 10-inch skillet over medium heat until light brown; drain. Stir in sour cream, water and seasoning mix; reduce heat. Simmer uncovered 5 minutes.

Cut rolls in half; spread with mayonnaise. Place lettuce on bottoms. Layer about ⅓ cup beef mixture, 2 cheese slices and 2 tomato slices on each sandwich. Cover with top of roll; secure with wooden pick.   6 SUBMARINES.

Stir sour cream, water and taco seasoning mix into beef.

Layer beef mixture, 2 cheese and 2 tomato slices on rolls.

Arrange the toppers on lettuce-lined tray and uncooked hamburgers on bed of parsley.

Grill the hamburgers to desired doneness, and serve with a choice of toppers.

Grilled Hamburgers Royale

Toppers (below)
3 pounds ground beef
¾ cup finely chopped onion
¾ cup dry bread crumbs
⅔ cup Burgundy or dry red wine
3 teaspoons salt
¼ teaspoon pepper
Parsley
12 buttered hamburger buns

Prepare toppers. Mix remaining ingredients except parsley and buns. Shape into 12 patties, about ½ inch thick; place on bed of parsley. Adjust charcoal grill so it is about 4 inches from hot coals. Grill hamburger patties, place in buns and add toppers.   8 TO 12 SERVINGS.

CHEESE-BACON TOPPERS

Place 4 slices mozzarella cheese on lettuce-lined tray. Top each with 2 slices cooked bacon and 1 mushroom cap; sprinkle with chopped green onion.

DILL-TOMATO TOPPERS

Mix ¼ cup dairy sour cream, ¼ to ½ teaspoon dried dill weed and ⅛ teaspoon salt. Place 4 slices tomato on lettuce-lined tray. Top each with 1 spoonful sour cream mixture and thin slice cucumber.

PINEAPPLE TOPPERS

Mix ¼ cup mayonnaise or salad dressing and 1 tablespoon sweet-and-sour salad dressing. Place 4 pineapple rings on lettuce-lined tray. Top each with green pepper ring, 1 spoonful mayonnaise mixture and 1 to 3 mandarin orange segments; sprinkle with chopped salted peanuts.

Grilled Pineapple Burgers

2 pounds lean ground beef
3 tablespoons Italian salad dressing
1 teaspoon salt
⅛ teaspoon pepper
1 can (about 15¼ ounces) sliced pineapple,
   drained
8 slices bacon
¾ cup barbecue sauce
¼ cup packed brown sugar
¼ cup honey
1 tablespoon lemon juice

Mix ground beef, salad dressing, salt and pepper. Shape into 8 patties, 3 inches in diameter. Press pineapple slice into each patty. Wrap each patty with bacon slice; secure with wooden pick. Mix barbecue sauce, brown sugar, honey and lemon juice. Place patties in glass or plastic dish, 13x9x2 inches. Pour barbecue mixture on patties. Cover and refrigerate at least 2 hours.

Grill patties pineapple sides down 4 inches from hot coals 12 to 15 minutes. Turn; brush with barbecue mixture. Grill 10 to 15 minutes. Heat remaining barbecue mixture; serve with patties.   8 SERVINGS.

Press a pineapple slice into each ground beef patty.

Wrap each patty with a bacon slice; secure with pick.

Pour barbecue sauce mixture onto patties; refrigerate.

Cover and marinate at least 2 hours; keep chilled.

Beer Brisket Buns

3- pound corned beef brisket
1 large Bermuda onion, sliced
1 can (12 ounces) beer
¾ cup catsup
¼ cup barbecue sauce
8 Kaiser rolls

Heat oven to 325°. Place corned beef brisket on rack in baking pan, 9x9x2 inches. Roast uncovered 1 hour.

Remove rack from pan; drain. Place beef in pan and top with onion slices. Mix beer, catsup and barbecue sauce; pour on beef and onion. Bake uncovered until beef is tender, about 2 hours, spooning sauce onto beef and onion several times.

Cool beef in sauce. Cut thin diagonal slices across grain; heat beef and onion slices in sauce. Set oven control to broil and/or 550°. Split rolls and broil cut sides up 3 to 4 inches from heat until golden brown, about 1 minute. Serve hot beef and onion slices on rolls.   8 SERVINGS.

Pour the catsup mixture on the beef and onion, then bake.

Cut thin diagonal slices across faces of cooled beef.

Open-Face Reubens

7 slices dark rye bread, toasted
  Prepared mustard
1 can (8 ounces) sauerkraut, drained
1 package (3 ounces) sliced corned
  beef, finely snipped
2 cups shredded pizza or Swiss cheese
  (about 4 ounces)
¼ cup mayonnaise or salad dressing

Heat oven to 375°. Spread toast lightly with mustard; place on ungreased baking sheet. Cut through sauerkraut with scissors. Stir in corned beef, cheese and mayonnaise.

Spread about ⅓ cup sauerkraut mixture onto each slice of toast. Bake until sauerkraut mixture is hot and cheese is melted, about 10 minutes. Cut sandwiches in half if desired.　7 SANDWICHES.

Cut through sauerkraut with kitchen scissors; add corned beef, cheese and mayonnaise.

Spread about ⅓ cup of the sauerkraut mixture onto each slice of toast; bake 10 minutes.

SANDWICH KNOW-HOW

1. Choose interesting breads and colorful fillings. For color as well as taste, combine two kinds of bread in one sandwich.

2. Bland fillings can be pepped up with lemon juice, mustard or sauces. Crunchiness can be added with bacon bits, nuts, cucumber or celery; color with chopped pickles, pimiento, green pepper or parsley garnishes.

3. One way to keep sandwiches fresh is to place a damp towel in the bottom of a large shallow pan with edges of towel hanging over the sides. Cover with waxed paper. Stack sandwiches with waxed paper between layers and on top. Fold the edges of the towel snugly over the sandwiches.

Make diagonal cuts almost through to bottom of loaf.

Alternate 2 ham slices and 2 cheese slices in each cut.

Hot Ham Sandwich Loaf

1 loaf (1 pound) unsliced whole wheat bread
¼ cup butter or margarine, softened
2 tablespoons snipped chives
1 tablespoon prepared mustard
16 slices chopped ham luncheon meat
16 slices Swiss cheese
2 tablespoons butter or margarine, melted
1 tablespoon poppy seed

Heat oven to 400°. Make 8 diagonal cuts from top almost through to bottom of loaf.

Mix ¼ cup butter, the chives and mustard. Spread 1 side of each slice with butter mixture. Place loaf on piece of aluminum foil, 20x18 inches. Alternate 2 ham slices and 2 cheese slices in each cut. Brush loaf with 2 tablespoons butter; sprinkle with poppy seed. Wrap securely in foil. (At this point, loaf can be refrigerated up to 24 hours.) Bake on ungreased baking sheet 30 minutes.   8 SERVINGS.

Little Supper Pizzas

Sausage Topping (below)
2 cups all-purpose flour*
2 teaspoons baking powder
1 teaspoon salt
⅔ cup shortening
½ cup hot water
1 tablespoon lemon juice
1 egg yolk, beaten
1 can (15 ounces) tomato sauce
1 or 2 large mild onions, sliced
1 green pepper, cut into rings
1 tablespoon dried oregano leaves
Pickles, olives and cheese cubes

Prepare Sausage Topping. Heat oven to 450°. Mix flour, baking powder and salt. Stir in shortening, water, lemon juice and egg yolk. Mix until dough cleans side of bowl; divide into 24 parts. Pat into 3½-inch circles on ungreased baking sheets; prick with fork. Bake until light golden, 6 to 8 minutes. Remove from oven; leave crusts on baking sheets. (Crusts can be baked several hours ahead of time.) Reduce oven temperature to 400°.

Spread each pizza crust with 1 tablespoon tomato sauce; add 1 tablespoon Sausage Topping. Top with an onion or green pepper ring. Sprinkle with oregano; top with pickle, olive or cheese cube. Bake until bubbly, 5 to 10 minutes. 2 DOZEN PIZZAS.

*If using self-rising flour, omit baking powder and salt.

SAUSAGE TOPPING

Cook and stir ¾ pound pork bulk sausage over medium heat until light brown; drain. Stir in 3 green onions, sliced (about ¼ cup), 1 cup shredded mozzarella cheese (about 4 ounces) and ¼ teaspoon onion salt.

After you bake crusts, add sauce and topping.

Then onion or green pepper rings and oregano are added.

A marker (pickle, olive or cheese) identifies each pizza.

Then pizzas are baked until bubbly, 5 to 10 minutes.

Turkey-Ham Sandwiches

Pat the dough into a rectangle.

Cut the dough into 5 strips.

Bake the strips, then separate.

Layer turkey, cheese and ham.

1 cup biscuit baking mix
¼ cup cold water
5 slices cooked turkey (about 6x2 inches)
5 thin slices Swiss cheese (about 6x2 inches)
5 slices cooked ham (about 6x2 inches)
1 package (about 1 ounce) chicken gravy
   mix
¼ cup dry white wine
1 can (4 ounces) mushroom stems and
   pieces, drained

Heat oven to 450°. Mix baking mix and water; beat vigorously 20 strokes. Pat into rectangle, 10x5 inches, on ungreased baking sheet. Cut rectangle crosswise into five 2-inch strips, but do not separate. Bake until strips are golden brown, about 10 minutes.

Set oven control to broil and/or 550°. Separate biscuit strips; place slice of turkey, cheese and ham on each strip. Broil with tops 5 inches from heat until cheese is melted, about 4 minutes.

Prepare gravy mix as directed on package except—substitute the wine for ¼ cup of the water; stir in mushrooms. Serve gravy over sandwiches.   5 SANDWICHES.

Turkey Bake

6 slices bread, cut in half
2 cups cut-up cooked turkey
1 medium onion, chopped (about ½ cup)
1 small green pepper, chopped
2 tablespoons chopped pimiento
½ teaspoon salt
½ teaspoon dried sage leaves, crushed
2 eggs
½ cup mayonnaise or salad dressing
1 cup milk
1 can (10¾ ounces) condensed cream of
    chicken soup

Heat oven to 325°. Layer half of the bread in ungreased baking dish, 8x8x2 inches. Mix turkey, onion, green pepper, pimiento, salt and sage; spread over bread. Top with remaining bread. Beat eggs and mayonnaise; stir in milk and soup. Pour on bread. Sprinkle with paprika. Bake uncovered until casserole is set and top is golden, 1 to 1¼ hours. Serve immediately.   6 SERVINGS.

Spread turkey mixture over bread slices in baking dish.

Pour soup-mayonnaise mixture over top bread layer.

Turkey Rachels

¼ cup Thousand Island salad dressing
8 slices pumpernickel or rye bread
4 slices Swiss cheese
4 slices cooked turkey
1 cup coleslaw
    Soft butter or margarine

Spread salad dressing over 1 side of each bread slice. Arrange cheese, turkey and coleslaw on half of the slices; top with remaining slices. Spread butter over outsides of sandwiches. Brown sandwiches on both sides in skillet over low heat until cheese is melted.   4 SANDWICHES.

Place ham, pear slices and cheese on toasted rye bread.

Broil sandwiches until cheese is melted, 1½ to 2 minutes.

Hot Broiled Cheesewiches

CLUBHOUSE SANDWICH BROIL

1 slice whole wheat bread
   Blue cheese salad dressing
1 slice smoked chicken or turkey
3 or 4 slices tomato
2 slices bacon, crisply fried
1 slice American cheese

Set oven control to broil and/or 550°. Toast bread 5 inches from heat until brown on both sides. Spread with salad dressing and top with chicken, tomato, bacon and cheese. Broil until cheese is melted, 1½ to 2 minutes.   1 SANDWICH.

TOMATO-CHEESE BROIL

Set oven control to broil and/or 550°. Toast 1 slice bread 5 inches from heat until brown on both sides. Spread with butter or margarine and top with 3 or 4 slices tomato. Sprinkle with salt. Top with 1 slice American cheese; sprinkle with cinnamon. Broil until cheese is melted, 1½ to 2 minutes. Top with dill pickle slice.   1 SANDWICH.

PEAR-HAM BROIL

1 slice rye bread
   Prepared mustard
2 slices smoked ham
4 thin slices pear
1 slice Swiss cheese

Set oven control to broil and/or 550°. Toast bread 5 inches from heat until brown on both sides. Spread with mustard. Top with ham, pear and cheese. Broil until cheese is melted, 1½ to 2 minutes.   1 SANDWICH.

Tuna-Cheese Toasties

3 hamburger buns, split and buttered
1 can (9¼ ounces) tuna, drained and flaked
1 package (3 ounces) cream cheese, softened
2 tablespoons mayonnaise or salad dressing
2 teaspoons lemon juice
1 teaspoon instant minced onion
1 teaspoon prepared horseradish
1 can (16 ounces) cut green beans, drained
1 cup shredded process American cheese
   (about 4 ounces)

Set oven control to broil and/or 550°. Broil bun halves with tops 4 to 5 inches from heat until light brown, about 2½ minutes. Remove from oven. Reduce oven temperature to 350°. Mix tuna, cream cheese, mayonnaise, lemon juice, onion and horseradish; stir in beans. Spoon scant ½ cup tuna mixture onto each bun half; sprinkle with American cheese. Bake about 10 minutes.   6 SERVINGS.

Broil bun halves until light brown, about 2½ minutes.

Mix remaining ingredients except cheese; spread on buns.

TUNA KNOW-HOW

Tuna is a versatile cupboard-shelf standby and a protein bargain as well. For economy, stock grated or flaked tuna for sandwiches, medium-priced chunk-style for salads and casseroles; buy the costlier solid pack when appearance counts as much as flavor.

Tuna Hero

Cut loaf lengthwise into 3 layers; spread with butter.

Spread cream cheese mixture over bottom layer of bread.

Mix the remaining ingredients; spread over middle layer.

Assemble sandwich; wrap and refrigerate. Slice to serve.

 1 loaf (1 pound) French bread
   Soft butter or margarine
 2 packages (3 ounces each) cream cheese, softened
½ cup chopped pimiento-stuffed olives
½ to 1 teaspoon anchovy paste
 2 cans (6½ ounces each) tuna, drained and flaked
 1 medium cucumber, chopped (about ⅔ cup)
⅓ cup mayonnaise or salad dressing
1½ teaspoons lemon juice
¼ teaspoon onion salt

Cut loaf lengthwise into 3 layers; spread each layer with butter. Mix cheese, olives and anchovy paste; spread over bottom layer of bread. Mix remaining ingredients; spread over middle layer. Assemble sandwich; wrap and refrigerate. Just before serving, cut into 1-inch slices.

8 SERVINGS.

Shrimp Mini Pizzas

2 packages active dry yeast
2 cups warm water (105 to 115°)
¼ cup vegetable oil
2 teaspoons sugar
2 teaspoons salt
4½ to 5¼ cups all-purpose flour*
1 can (15 ounces) tomato sauce
1½ teaspoons Italian seasoning
3 cans (4¼ ounces each) small shrimp, drained
1 medium onion, chopped (about ½ cup)
¾ cup sliced ripe olives
½ large green pepper, chopped
1½ cups shredded mozzarella cheese (about 6 ounces)
⅔ cup grated Parmesan cheese

An empty 15-ounce can is about the right size for cutting the dough into 4-inch circles.

After placing circles on ungreased baking sheet, pinch edge of each to form a ridge.

Dissolve yeast in warm water in large bowl. Stir in oil, sugar, salt and 4 cups of the flour; beat until smooth. Turn dough onto floured surface. Knead in enough remaining flour to make dough easy to handle; knead until smooth, 3 to 5 minutes. Place in greased bowl; turn greased side up. Cover; let rise in warm place until double, about 45 minutes.

Heat oven to 400°. Mix tomato sauce and Italian seasoning. Punch down dough; divide in half. Roll each half into rectangle, 16x12 inches, on lightly floured surface. Cut each rectangle into twelve 4-inch circles; place circles on ungreased baking sheet. Pinch edge of each circle to form a ridge. Spoon 1 tablespoon of the tomato sauce mixture onto each pizza. Layer each pizza with remaining ingredients. (Pizzas can be prepared and refrigerated up to 3 hours before baking.) Bake until cheese is brown and bubbly, about 15 minutes.   2 DOZEN PIZZAS.

*If using self-rising flour, omit salt.

Spread French bread halves with the chicken mixture.

Add Muenster cheese, lettuce, mayonnaise and vegetables.

Cut each half into thirds; mix shrimp and mayonnaise.

Spoon on shrimp mixture, then top with Parmesan cheese.

Shrimpwiches

½ loaf (1-pound size) French bread
2 cans (4¾ ounces each) chicken spread
2 tablespoons mayonnaise or salad dressing
½ teaspoon poultry seasoning
1 cup shredded Muenster cheese (4 ounces)
   Leaf lettuce
   Mayonnaise or salad dressing
1 medium cucumber, thinly sliced
1 medium tomato, sliced
1 can (4¼ ounces) tiny shrimp, rinsed and
     drained
3 tablespoons mayonnaise or salad dressing
   Grated Parmesan cheese

Cut loaf lengthwise in half; place halves cut sides up. Mix chicken spread, 2 tablespoons mayonnaise and the poultry seasoning; spread over bread halves. Top with Muenster cheese, lettuce, mayonnaise, cucumber and tomato slices. Cut each half into thirds. Mix shrimp and 3 tablespoons mayonnaise; spoon onto each sandwich. Sprinkle with Parmesan cheese.   6 OPEN-FACE SANDWICHES.

Danish Smorgasbord

SHRIMP SANDWICH

For each sandwich, cover 1 buttered bread slice (see note) with a lettuce leaf. Arrange 1 to 2 tablespoons tiny shrimp, drained, on center of lettuce. Arrange hard-cooked egg slices and cherry tomato slices on either side of shrimp. Sprinkle with dried dill weed.

HAM AND EGG SANDWICH

For each sandwich, place 1 thin slice fully cooked ham on half of 1 buttered bread slice. Arrange hard-cooked egg slices on other half. Sprinkle with sliced green onion.

BEEF AND GHERKIN SANDWICH

For each sandwich, place 1 thin slice roast beef on 1 buttered bread slice. Top with sliced dill gherkin pickles, onion slices and sieved egg yolk.

BEEF AND HERRING SANDWICH

For each sandwich, place 2 thin slices roast beef on half of 1 buttered bread slice. Place 3 to 5 pieces pickled herring, well drained, on remaining half. Top with cherry tomato slices, cucumber slices and snipped parsley.

SARDINE SANDWICH

For each sandwich, place 3 to 5 sardines, well drained, on half of 1 buttered bread slice. Place 1 to 2 tablespoons scrambled egg on remaining half. Top with shredded Cheddar cheese and sliced green onion.

Note: Spread soft butter or margarine to edges of thinly sliced rye or whole wheat bread to prevent sandwiches from becoming dry or soaked by sandwich ingredients.

Spread soft butter or margarine to the edges of bread.

Arrange ingredients in rows, overlapping when necessary.

Trim excess fat from beef cross rib pot roast.

Separate cauliflower into bite-size cauliflowerets.

Cut potatoes lengthwise into ¼-inch strips.

Cut up spinach easily with kitchen shears.

Garden Vegetable Soup

2- to 2½-pound beef cross rib pot roast
2½ cups water
 2 teaspoons salt
 1 teaspoon lemon juice
 ½ teaspoon dried basil leaves
 ¼ teaspoon pepper
 2 beef bouillon cubes
 1 bay leaf, crumbled
 1 medium onion, chopped (about ½ cup)
 1 can (16 ounces) stewed tomatoes
 2 medium stalks celery (with leaves), cut
   into ½-inch slices (about 2 cups)
 3 medium carrots, cut into ¼-inch slices
   (about 1½ cups)
 1 cup cauliflowerets
 ½ cup sliced fresh mushrooms*
 4 medium potatoes, cut lengthwise into
   ¼-inch strips
 2 ounces fresh spinach or kale, cut up
   (about 1 cup)

Trim excess fat from beef pot roast. Cut beef into 1½-inch pieces; reserve bone. Brown beef pieces and bone in Dutch oven; drain. Stir in water, salt, lemon juice, basil, pepper, bouillon cubes, bay leaf and onion. Heat to boiling; reduce heat. Cover and simmer 1½ hours.

Stir in tomatoes, celery, carrots, cauliflowerets and mushrooms. Heat to boiling; reduce heat. Cover and simmer until beef is tender, about 40 minutes. Stir in potatoes. Cover and simmer until potatoes are tender, about 15 minutes. Sprinkle soup with spinach. Cover and simmer 5 minutes.   6 TO 8 SERVINGS.

*1 can (2 ounces) mushroom stems and pieces (with liquid) can be substituted for the fresh mushrooms.

Beef and Barley Soup

5 slices bacon
1-pound beef chuck roast or steak, cut into
   1-inch pieces
2 large onions, chopped (about 2 cups)
2 cloves garlic, finely chopped
2 cans (10½ ounces each) condensed beef
   broth
2 cups water
¼ cup regular barley
1½ teaspoons paprika
1 teaspoon salt
¼ teaspoon caraway seed
⅛ teaspoon dried marjoram leaves
3 medium potatoes, cut into ½-inch pieces
2 medium carrots, sliced (about 1 cup)
2 medium stalks celery, sliced
1 can (16 ounces) stewed tomatoes
1 package (10 ounces) frozen green peas,
   broken apart
1 can (4 ounces) mushroom stems and
   pieces

Fry bacon in Dutch oven over medium heat until crisp; remove bacon and drain on paper towel. Cook and stir beef pieces, onions and garlic in bacon fat in Dutch oven until beef is brown. Stir in broth, water, barley, paprika, salt, caraway seed and marjoram. Heat to boiling; reduce heat. Cover and simmer 1½ hours.

Stir in potatoes, carrots, celery, tomatoes, frozen peas and mushrooms (with liquid). Heat to boiling; reduce heat. Cover and simmer until vegetables are tender, 30 to 40 minutes. Crumble bacon; sprinkle over soup.   8 SERVINGS.

BARLEY, one of the first known cereal grains to be cultivated, is nutritious and nutlike in flavor. It is used in soups, stews and casseroles or served as a side dish in place of rice or potatoes. It is available in both regular and quick-cooking forms, both of which can be stored in a cool, dry place on the cupboard shelf.

Beef-Cheddar Chowder

Start ground beef, then slice celery, onion and pepper.

Shred the cabbage while the vegetables and beef cook.

1 pound ground beef
2 medium stalks celery, sliced (about 1 cup)
1 small onion, chopped (about ¼ cup)
½ small green pepper, chopped (about ¼ cup)
½ medium head cabbage, coarsely shredded
½ cup water
3 cups milk
2 cups shredded Cheddar or process American cheese (about 8 ounces)
3 tablespoons flour
1½ teaspoons salt
⅛ teaspoon ground nutmeg
⅛ teaspoon pepper
2 tablespoons sliced pimiento

Cook and stir ground beef, celery, onion and green pepper in Dutch oven until vegetables are tender; drain. Stir in cabbage and water. Cover and cook over low heat, stirring occasionally, until cabbage is desired doneness, about 10 minutes.

Stir in milk, cheese, flour, salt, nutmeg and pepper. Heat to boiling, stirring constantly. Boil and stir 1 minute. Garnish each serving with pimiento.   8 SERVINGS.

Savory Meatball Soup

1½ pounds ground beef
1 egg, slightly beaten
½ cup dry bread crumbs
1 medium potato, finely chopped (about ½ cup)
1 small onion, chopped (about ¼ cup)
¼ cup milk
1 tablespoon snipped parsley
1 teaspoon salt
1 tablespoon vegetable oil
1 can (28 ounces) whole tomatoes
1 can (10½ ounces) condensed beef broth
2 cups water
2 medium carrots, sliced (about 1 cup)
2 medium potatoes, cut into ½-inch pieces (about 1 cup)
1 small stalk celery, chopped (about ¼ cup)
¼ cup snipped parsley
1 envelope (about 1½ ounces) onion soup mix
½ teaspoon dried basil leaves
¼ teaspoon pepper
1 bay leaf

Cut the potato into lengthwise strips, then chop strips finely.

Add chopped potato to ground beef, egg and bread crumbs.

Mix ground beef, egg, bread crumbs, chopped potato, onion, milk, 1 tablespoon parsley and the salt. Shape into 1½-inch balls. Cook meatballs in oil in Dutch oven until light brown. Remove meatballs; drain fat from Dutch oven.

Mix tomatoes (with liquid) and remaining ingredients in Dutch oven; break up tomatoes with fork. Heat to boiling; reduce heat. Cover and simmer 30 minutes, stirring occasionally. Add meatballs; cover and simmer 20 minutes.
8 SERVINGS.

Sausage-Vegetable Soup

Add water, carrots, celery and seasonings; simmer until the vegetables are tender.

Cut the polish sausage into slices; add to Dutch oven with the remaining vegetables.

1 medium onion, chopped (about ½ cup)
2 tablespoons vegetable oil
4 cups water
3 medium carrots, thinly sliced (about 1½ cups)
2 medium stalks celery (with leaves), thinly sliced (about 1 cup)
2 teaspoons salt
½ teaspoon dried chervil leaves
½ teaspoon dried thyme leaves
2 medium zucchini, cut lengthwise in half, then into ¼-inch slices
1 pint cherry tomatoes, cut in half
1 pound Polish sausage, cut into ¼-inch slices
1 can (15 ounces) great northern beans

Cook and stir onion in oil in Dutch oven until tender. Stir in water, carrots, celery, salt, chervil and thyme. Heat to boiling; reduce heat. Cover and simmer until vegetables are tender, about 30 minutes.

Stir zucchini, tomatoes, sausage and beans (with liquid) into vegetables in Dutch oven. Heat to boiling; reduce heat. Cover and simmer 30 minutes. Skim fat if necessary.
6 TO 8 SERVINGS.

Frank and Bean Soup

4 slices bacon, cut up
2 green onions (with tops), sliced (about
    ¼ cup)
1 can (16 ounces) stewed tomatoes
4 frankfurters, cut diagonally into slices
3 cups water
3 teaspoons instant chicken bouillon
⅛ teaspoon salt
⅛ teaspoon pepper
1 can (15 ounces) kidney beans
4 ounces uncooked shell macaroni (about
    1⅓ cups)
    Garlic Toast (below)

Cook and stir bacon and onions in 3-quart saucepan over medium heat until onions are tender; drain. Stir in tomatoes, frankfurters, water, instant bouillon, salt and pepper. Heat to boiling; reduce heat. Cover and simmer until bouillon is dissolved, about 5 minutes.

Stir beans (with liquid) and macaroni into tomato mixture. Heat to boiling; reduce heat. Cover and simmer until macaroni is tender, about 10 minutes. Serve with Garlic Toast. 4 SERVINGS.

GARLIC TOAST

Heat oven to 400°. Spread butter or margarine, softened, over 1 side of each of 8 slices French bread. Sprinkle garlic powder and grated Parmesan cheese over butter. Bake on ungreased baking sheet until tops are golden brown, about 7 minutes. Turn slices; spread with butter and sprinkle with garlic powder and cheese. Bake 7 minutes longer.

Cut frankfurters while the bacon and onions cook.

Prepare the bread while the bouillon dissolves.

Add beans and macaroni to soup while bread toasts.

Toast second side while the macaroni simmers.

Gingerroot, the source of spicy ground ginger, is now widely available in many stores.

Place slice of gingerroot between sheets of waxed paper. Crush with mallet.

To store, cover gingerroot with sherry; refrigerate it up to 6 months. Or wrap and freeze.

Suggested equivalent: 1 teaspoon crushed gingerroot for ½ teaspoon ground ginger.

Chinese Chicken Noodle Soup

2½- to 3-pound broiler-fryer chicken, cut up
1 teaspoon salt
   About 5 cups water
2 cans (4 ounces each) mushroom stems and pieces (with liquid)
6 green onions (with tops), finely chopped (about ¾ cup)
2 large carrots, cut diagonally (about 1½ cups)
¼ cup soy sauce
1 tablespoon sugar
1 tablespoon dry sherry
1 teaspoon crushed gingerroot*
3½ ounces uncooked vermicelli

Heat chicken, salt and enough water to cover chicken to boiling in Dutch oven; reduce heat. Cover and simmer about 40 minutes.

Cool chicken and broth quickly. Remove chicken from broth; refrigerate broth. Remove skin and bones from chicken; cut chicken into bite-size pieces. Skim fat from broth.

Place chicken pieces, broth and remaining ingredients except vermicelli in Dutch oven. Heat to boiling; reduce heat. Simmer uncovered until carrots are crisp-tender, about 20 minutes; remove gingerroot. Stir in vermicelli. Simmer uncovered until vermicelli is tender, about 5 minutes.
10 SERVINGS.

* ½ teaspoon ground ginger can be substituted for the gingerroot.

Turkey and Wheat-Noodle Soup

1 turkey carcass
1 tablespoon salt
2 teaspoons Worcestershire sauce
1 teaspoon dried sage leaves
2 bay leaves
3 quarts water
   Whole Wheat Noodles (below)
1 medium stalk celery, cut diagonally into
   1-inch slices (about ½ cup)
1 medium turnip, cut into ½-inch pieces
2 medium carrots, cut into ½-inch slices
   (about 1 cup)
1 medium onion, chopped (about ½ cup)
1 package (10 ounces) frozen lima beans

Break up turkey carcass to fit 6-quart kettle or Dutch oven. Add salt, Worcestershire sauce, sage, bay leaves and water. Heat to boiling; reduce heat. Cover and simmer 1 hour. While broth is simmering, prepare Whole Wheat Noodles.

Remove bones from broth; remove turkey from bones and cut turkey into small pieces. Skim fat from broth; strain and measure 10 cups broth into Dutch oven. Add turkey and remaining ingredients except noodles. Heat to boiling; reduce heat. Cover and simmer 15 minutes. Stir in noodles gradually. Heat to boiling; reduce heat. Cover and simmer 15 minutes.   8 SERVINGS.

WHOLE WHEAT NOODLES

Mix ½ cup whole wheat flour, ½ cup all-purpose flour,* 3 tablespoons milk, 1 egg, 1 teaspoon salt and ½ teaspoon paprika. Roll half of the dough into paper-thin rectangle, 18x8 inches, on floured cloth-covered board. Cut into 8x¼-inch strips. Repeat with remaining dough. Let noodles stand uncovered 1 hour.

*If using self-rising flour, reduce salt to ½ teaspoon.

Roll half of the dough into an 18x8-inch rectangle on a floured cloth-covered board.

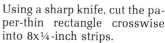

Using a sharp knife, cut the paper-thin rectangle crosswise into 8x¼-inch strips.

Hearty Fish Chowder

Heat halibut and water to boiling. Reduce heat; cover and simmer 10 to 15 minutes.

Remove halibut from Dutch oven; reserve broth. Flake or cut fish into bite-size pieces.

Simmer potatoes, onion and green pepper in 1 cup broth until potatoes are tender.

Stir in remaining broth, the halibut, tomato, half-and-half, salt and pepper.

2 pounds frozen halibut or haddock fillets, thawed
3 cups water
4 medium potatoes, cut into ½-inch pieces (about 4 cups)
1 large onion, chopped (about 1 cup)
1 medium green pepper, chopped (about 1 cup)
1 medium tomato, peeled and chopped (about ¾ cup)
1 cup half-and-half
1¾ teaspoons salt
¼ teaspoon pepper
⅓ cup shredded Cheddar cheese

Heat halibut fillets and water to boiling in Dutch oven; reduce heat. Cover and simmer just until halibut flakes easily with fork, 10 to 15 minutes. (Cooking time varies according to thickness of halibut.) Remove halibut and broth from Dutch oven. Flake or cut halibut into bite-size pieces; reserve broth.

Simmer potatoes, onion and green pepper in 1 cup of the reserved broth just until potatoes are tender, about 15 minutes. Stir in remaining broth, the halibut, tomato, half-and-half, salt and pepper. Heat until chowder is hot. Sprinkle with cheese.   8 SERVINGS.

Creole Shrimp Soup

1 pound frozen jumbo shrimp in the shell,
   cleaned and deveined
1 can (10¾ ounces) condensed chicken
   gumbo soup
1 can (28 ounces) whole tomatoes
1 jar (2 ounces) sliced pimiento, drained
3 small onions, cut into fourths
2 cloves garlic, finely chopped
1 cup water
¼ cup uncooked regular rice
1 teaspoon salt
½ teaspoon dried basil leaves
1 bay leaf
   Dash of red pepper sauce

Heat all ingredients to boiling; reduce heat. Cover and simmer until shrimp is tender and rice is done, 20 to 25 minutes. Garnish with parsley.　8 SERVINGS.

To devein peeled shrimp, cut about ⅛ inch deep along outside curve of each shrimp.

Lift out the black sand vein with the point of the knife. Rinse under cold water.

SHRIMP KNOW-HOW

Delicious and protein laden, shrimp are low in calories—only 100 calories per 3-ounce serving. Raw shrimp (heads removed) are greenish or pink and are sold by the pound, frozen or refrigerated. 1½ pounds raw shrimp will yield ¾ pound cooked (about 2 cups). Cooked shrimp (shells removed) are pink and are sold by the pound. Canned shrimp can be used interchangeably with cooked shrimp.

Cauliflower-Cheese Soup

Cook and stir cauliflower in butter over low heat until crisp-tender, about 6 minutes.

Stir in the water, cheese, half-and-half, instant bouillon and spices; heat to boiling.

½ small head cauliflower, separated into flowerets and cut into ½-inch pieces
2 tablespoons butter or margarine
1¼ cups water
⅔ cup pasteurized process cheese spread
½ cup half-and-half
1 teaspoon instant chicken bouillon
Dash of ground nutmeg
Dash of ground allspice
⅓ cup dry white wine
½ small green pepper, finely chopped (about ¼ cup)
Paprika

Cook and stir cauliflower in butter in 3-quart saucepan over low heat until crisp-tender, about 6 minutes.

Stir in water, cheese, half-and-half, instant bouillon, nutmeg and allspice. Heat to boiling over medium heat, stirring constantly. Stir in wine; heat about 2 minutes. Sprinkle green pepper and paprika over soup.   6 SERVINGS.

Peanut Butter Soup

  6 cups water
  2 pounds beef bones
  1 medium onion, chopped (about ½ cup)
  4 peppercorns
  2 cardamom seeds
  ½ cup creamy peanut butter
1½ teaspoons salt
1½ teaspoons lemon juice
  ¼ teaspoon red pepper sauce
  2 tablespoons snipped chives
  ¼ cup chopped salted peanuts

Heat water, beef bones, onion, peppercorns and cardamom seeds to boiling in 3-quart saucepan; reduce heat. Cover and simmer 1½ hours. Refrigerate several hours; skim off fat.

Strain stock, discarding bones, onion and seasonings. Gradually beat 1 cup stock into peanut butter; stir into remaining stock. Stir in salt, lemon juice and pepper sauce. Cook over low heat, stirring occasionally, 15 minutes. Sprinkle each serving with chives and peanuts.
6 SERVINGS.

Short-Cut Peanut Butter Soup: Substitute 2 cans (14½ ounces each) condensed beef broth and 1 teaspoon onion salt for the stock and salt; omit refrigeration step.
4 SERVINGS.

Strain stock; discard bones, onion, peppercorns and seeds.

Beat 1 cup stock into peanut butter; add to stock in pan.

Matzo Ball Soup

Stir the matzo meal mixture to make a soft dough.

Drop matzo balls into the simmering chicken broth.

2 eggs, slightly beaten
2 tablespoons melted chicken fat, butter
   or margarine
½ cup matzo meal
1 teaspoon snipped parsley
½ teaspoon salt
   Dash of white pepper
1 to 2 tablespoons chicken broth or water
6 cups chicken broth
1 medium carrot, cut into 2x¼-inch strips

Mix eggs and chicken fat. Stir in matzo meal, parsley, salt, pepper and 1 to 2 tablespoons broth to make a soft dough. Cover and refrigerate at least 30 minutes.

Heat 6 cups broth and the carrot to boiling in 3-quart saucepan or Dutch oven; reduce heat. Shape matzo dough into 12 balls. (For easy shaping, dip hands in cold water from time to time.) Drop matzo balls into simmering broth. Cover and cook 30 to 40 minutes.   6 SERVINGS.

HOMEMADE CHICKEN BROTH

To make broth from a stewing chicken, place 4- to 5-pound chicken, cut up, with giblets and 7 cups water in kettle. Add 1 medium stalk celery (with leaves), cut up, 1 small onion, sliced, 2 teaspoons salt and ½ teaspoon pepper. Heat to boiling; reduce heat. Cover and simmer until chicken is done, about 2½ hours.

Refrigerate chicken and broth. When cool, remove chicken from bones. Cut up chicken and strain broth. Use immediately or freeze chicken up to 1 month, broth up to 6 months.   ABOUT 5 CUPS CUT-UP COOKED CHICKEN AND 6 CUPS BROTH.

Vegetables and Salads

Lime Asparagus

1 to 1¼ pounds fresh asparagus
¼ cup butter or margarine
2 teaspoons lime juice
½ teaspoon garlic salt
Dash of pepper

Heat oven to 400°. Break off tough ends of asparagus at point where stalks snap easily. Arrange asparagus in ungreased baking dish, 11¾x7½x1¾ inches. Cover and bake until tender, 15 to 20 minutes.

Heat butter, lime juice, garlic salt and pepper over low heat until butter is melted; drizzle over asparagus.
4 SERVINGS.

Beans Deluxe

1 pound fresh green beans
1 cup water
½ teaspoon salt
1 medium stalk celery, sliced
¼ cup butter or margarine
1 tablespoon lemon juice
½ teaspoon seasoned salt
¼ cup sliced ripe olives
1 to 2 tablespoons chopped pimiento

Cut beans crosswise into 1-inch pieces. Heat beans, water and salt to boiling in 2-quart saucepan; reduce heat. Simmer uncovered 5 minutes. Add celery. Cover and cook until beans are tender, about 10 minutes; drain.

Heat butter, lemon juice, seasoned salt, olives and pimiento over low heat until butter is melted. Toss with beans.   4 TO 6 SERVINGS.

To store fresh asparagus, wrap the stem ends in damp paper towels and refrigerate.

Arrange the asparagus in an ungreased baking dish; cover and bake until tender.

Do-Ahead Beans au Gratin

1 package (10 ounces) frozen lima beans
1 package (9 ounces) frozen cut green
  beans
1 package (9 ounces) frozen cut wax beans
2 tablespoons butter or margarine
2 tablespoons flour
¾ teaspoon salt
¼ teaspoon dried basil leaves
⅛ teaspoon pepper
1¼ cups milk
2 tablespoons chopped pimiento (optional)
⅓ cup grated Parmesan cheese

Cook lima, cut green and cut wax beans as directed on packages, omitting salt; drain. Place beans in ungreased baking dish, 8x8x2 inches.

Heat butter in 2-quart saucepan over low heat until melted. Blend in flour, salt, basil and pepper. Cook over low heat, stirring constantly, until mixture is smooth and bubbly; remove from heat. Stir in milk. Heat to boiling, stirring constantly. Boil and stir 1 minute; remove from heat. Stir in pimiento. Pour sauce on beans; sprinkle with cheese. Cover and refrigerate up to 24 hours.

■**30 minutes before serving,** heat oven to 375°. Bake beans uncovered until bubbly and sauce is light brown, about 20 minutes.   6 TO 8 SERVINGS.

Cook the flour mixture until it is smooth and bubbly.

Remove the saucepan from the heat and stir in milk.

Heat the white sauce to boiling, stirring constantly.

Pour sauce on the beans in an ungreased baking dish.

Layer half each of the beans, mushrooms, bean sprouts and the soup mixture; repeat.

Sprinkle with thinly sliced almonds and bake uncovered until bubbly, 30 minutes.

Almond Beans

1 can (10¾ ounces) condensed cream of
   celery soup
1 teaspoon soy sauce
1 can (16 ounces) cut green beans, drained
1 can (4 ounces) mushroom stems and
   pieces, drained
1 can (16 ounces) bean sprouts, drained
½ cup thinly sliced almonds

Heat oven to 350°. Mix soup and soy sauce. Layer half each of the beans, mushrooms, bean sprouts and soup mixture in ungreased 1½-quart casserole; repeat. Sprinkle with almonds. Bake uncovered until hot and bubbly, about 30 minutes.　4 TO 6 SERVINGS.

Bean-Corn Relish

1 can (16 ounces) succotash
1 can (8 ounces) stewed tomatoes, drained
2 large stalks celery, coarsely chopped
   (about 1½ cups)
¼ cup Italian salad dressing
1 tablespoon instant minced onion
¼ teaspoon dried basil leaves
¼ teaspoon seasoned salt
   Celery leaves

Toss succotash, tomatoes, celery, salad dressing, onion, basil and seasoned salt. Cover and refrigerate until chilled, about 1 hour. Garnish with celery leaves.　6 SERVINGS.

Broccoli and Chinese Cabbage

3 tablespoons vegetable oil
1½ pounds broccoli, separated into flowerets
   and cut in half (about 3 cups)
2 small onions, sliced
1 small head Chinese or celery cabbage,
   sliced (about 2 cups)
1 can (8 ounces) water chestnuts, drained
   and sliced
¼ cup water
½ teaspoon salt
1 tablespoon soy sauce

Heat all ingredients except soy sauce to boiling in 10-inch skillet; reduce heat. Cover and simmer until vegetables are crisp-tender, 8 to 10 minutes. Toss with soy sauce. Serve with additional soy sauce.   6 SERVINGS.

Broccoli and Bean Sprouts: Substitute 1 can (16 ounces) bean sprouts, drained, for the Chinese cabbage.

SAVE THE NUTRIENTS

To save the nutrients in your fresh vegetables:

1. Pare vegetables as thinly as possible.

2. Cook vegetables without paring when possible. Use a vegetable brush to scrub potatoes, carrots and beets clean.

3. Do not discard thick stems of broccoli or beet tops; use as a separate vegetable.

4. Slice, shred, cube or cut vegetables into strips to reduce cooking time. Save the cooking liquid to serve with the vegetables or to use in soups and gravies.

Broccoli Puff

1 package (10 ounces) frozen chopped
   broccoli
¼ cup butter or margarine
¼ cup all-purpose flour
¼ teaspoon salt
⅛ teaspoon pepper
¾ cup milk
¼ cup dry white wine
1 teaspoon instant minced onion
1 teaspoon salt
3 eggs, separated
¼ teaspoon cream of tartar

Cook broccoli as directed on package; drain. Heat oven to 350°. Butter 1-quart soufflé dish. Melt butter over low heat. Stir in flour, ¼ teaspoon salt and the pepper. Cook over low heat, stirring constantly, until smooth and bubbly. Remove from heat.

Stir in milk and wine. Heat to boiling, stirring constantly. Boil and stir 1 minute. Remove from heat. Stir in onion and 1 teaspoon salt.

Beat egg whites and cream of tartar in large mixer bowl until stiff, about 5 minutes. Beat yolks in small mixer bowl until thick and lemon colored, about 4 minutes. Stir egg yolks into sauce mixture. Stir in broccoli.

Stir about ¼ of the egg whites into the sauce mixture; gently fold into remaining egg whites. Carefully pour into soufflé dish. Set dish in pan of water (1 inch deep).

Bake until puffed and golden and knife inserted halfway between edge and center comes out clean, about 60 minutes. Serve immediately.   4 TO 6 SERVINGS.

Cabbage with Pepper Sauce

Cut 1 large head of green cabbage into 12 wedges.

Heat cabbage wedges and water to boiling in skillet.

Cook and stir green pepper in butter until crisp-tender.

Remove the flour mixture from heat and stir in the milk.

1 large head green cabbage (about 2 pounds)
1 cup water
½ teaspoon salt
1 small green pepper, chopped (about ½ cup)
3 tablespoons butter or margarine
2 tablespoons flour
½ teaspoon onion salt
⅛ teaspoon pepper
1 cup milk
¼ cup grated Parmesan cheese

Cut cabbage into 12 wedges. Heat water and salt to boiling in 10-inch skillet; add cabbage wedges. Heat to boiling; reduce heat. Cover and simmer until cabbage is crisp-tender, 10 to 15 minutes; drain.

Cook and stir green pepper in butter over medium heat until pepper is crisp-tender, about 1 minute. Blend in flour, onion salt and pepper. Cook and stir over low heat until mixture is smooth and bubbly. Remove from heat; stir in milk. Heat to boiling, stirring constantly. Boil and stir 1 minute.

Place hot cabbage wedges in serving dish. Pour sauce on cabbage; sprinkle with cheese.   6 SERVINGS.

Carrot Bake

6 medium fresh carrots (about 1 pound), cut
    into 2x¼-inch strips
1 medium head cauliflower (about 2
    pounds), separated into flowerets
¼ cup butter or margarine
1 teaspoon salt
¼ teaspoon ground nutmeg
    Grated Parmesan cheese (optional)

Heat oven to 375°. Arrange carrots in ungreased baking dish, 11¾x7½x1¾ inches. Layer cauliflowerets over carrots. Dot with butter and sprinkle with salt and nutmeg. Cover and bake until vegetables are tender, 50 to 55 minutes. Sprinkle with cheese and garnish with parsley. 6 SERVINGS.

Arrange carrots and cauliflowerets in baking dish.

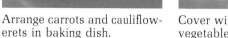

Cover with foil and bake until vegetables are tender.

Ginger Carrots

6 medium fresh carrots (about 1 pound),
    cut lengthwise into 3x⅜-inch strips
½ cup water
¼ cup butter or margarine
3 tablespoons honey
1 tablespoon lemon juice
½ to ¾ teaspoon ground ginger
¼ teaspoon salt

Heat carrots and water to boiling in 10-inch skillet; reduce heat. Cover and simmer until tender, 15 to 20 minutes.

Drain; remove carrots from skillet. Cook and stir butter, honey, lemon juice, ginger and salt in skillet until bubbly; add carrots. Cook uncovered, stirring occasionally, until carrots are glazed, about 5 minutes. Garnish with parsley. 4 SERVINGS.

Cauliflower Stir-Fry

Cover and cook vegetables 4 to 5 minutes; break them apart with fork if necessary.

Stir-fry the vegetables for 4 minutes. Add the pea pods; stir-fry until crisp-tender.

¼ cup butter or margarine
1 teaspoon instant chicken bouillon
1 package (10 ounces) frozen cauliflower
1 package (10 ounces) frozen baby Brussels sprouts
1½ cups frozen sliced carrots
1 package (6 ounces) frozen pea pods
2 tablespoons sliced almonds
½ teaspoon salt
¼ teaspoon lemon pepper

Heat butter in electric skillet until melted; stir in instant bouillon. Add cauliflower, Brussels sprouts and carrots. Cover and cook over medium heat 4 to 5 minutes; break vegetables apart with fork if necessary. Stir-fry vegetables 4 minutes. Add pea pods; stir-fry until pea pods are crisp-tender, about 5 minutes. Stir in almonds, salt and lemon pepper. 8 SERVINGS.

AT THE TABLE

Stir-frying, the ancient Oriental method of rapid cooking, is the newest thing in tabletop cooking. It's simple and elegant: Food is prepared (washed, dried and cut) beforehand, then stirred and tossed rapidly for a few minutes in a small amount of very hot oil in an electric skillet or wok. To ensure maximum cooking in the shortest time, ingredients are cut to uniform size. Most vegetables are sliced thinly, stalk or root vegetables are sliced diagonally to create a greater surface for heat absorption and pulpy vegetables are cut into wedges. The food is added to the hot oil (carefully), then stirred vigorously until done. Vegetables cooked this way remain crisp and retain their color.

Scalloped Corn Deluxe

4 ears fresh corn
1 tablespoon sugar
1 tablespoon lemon juice
1 gallon cold water
2 tablespoons butter or margarine
1 small onion, finely chopped
¼ cup finely chopped green pepper
2 tablespoons flour
1 teaspoon salt
½ teaspoon paprika
¼ teaspoon dry mustard
    Dash of pepper
½ cup dry red wine
¼ cup milk
½ cup shredded natural Cheddar cheese
1 egg, slightly beaten
1 tablespoon butter or margarine
⅓ cup cracker crumbs

Heat corn, sugar, lemon juice and water to boiling in Dutch oven or large kettle. Boil uncovered 2 minutes. Remove from heat; let stand 10 minutes. Cut enough kernels from ears to measure 2 cups.

Heat oven to 350°. Melt 2 tablespoons butter in 8-inch skillet. Cook and stir onion and green pepper in butter until onion is tender. Remove from heat. Stir in flour, salt, paprika, mustard and pepper. Cook over low heat, stirring constantly, until mixture is hot and bubbly. Remove from heat.

Gradually stir wine and milk into flour mixture. Heat to boiling, stirring constantly. Boil and stir 1 minute. Stir in cheese, egg and corn kernels. Pour into ungreased 1-quart casserole. Melt 1 tablespoon butter. Remove from heat. Stir in cracker crumbs. Sprinkle crumbs evenly over corn mixture. Bake uncovered until bubbly, 30 to 35 minutes. 4 SERVINGS.

Corn Sesame Sauté

1 package (10 ounces) frozen whole
    kernel corn
3 tablespoons butter or margarine
1 clove garlic, crushed
2 tablespoons sesame seed
2 tablespoons chopped green pepper
½ teaspoon salt
¼ teaspoon dried basil leaves
⅛ teaspoon pepper

Cook and stir corn and remaining ingredients over medium heat until butter is melted; reduce heat. Cover and cook, stirring occasionally, until corn is tender, about 7 minutes. 4 SERVINGS.

Tomatoed Corn

1 package (10 ounces) frozen whole kernel
    corn*
¼ cup butter or margarine
1 small onion, chopped (about ¼ cup)
½ small green pepper, chopped
2 teaspoons sugar
½ teaspoon salt
¼ teaspoon ground cumin
1 large tomato, cut up

Cook and stir all ingredients except tomato over medium heat until butter is melted. Cover and cook over low heat 10 minutes. Stir in tomato. Cover and cook 5 minutes longer. 4 SERVINGS.

*1 can (17 ounces) whole kernel corn can be substituted for the frozen corn. Decrease butter to 3 tablespoons and stir in drained corn with the tomato.

First dip the eggplant slices in the melted butter.

Dip in crumb mixture to coat both sides evenly.

Spread with the tomato sauce.

Sprinkle with grated cheese.

Eggplant Bake

½ cup fine dry bread crumbs
1 teaspoon dried oregano leaves
½ teaspoon garlic salt
1 medium eggplant (about 1½ pounds), pared and cut into ½-inch slices
½ cup butter or margarine, melted
1 can (8 ounces) tomato sauce
½ cup grated Parmesan cheese

Heat oven to 400°. Mix crumbs, oregano and garlic salt. Dip eggplant slices in butter, then in crumb mixture. Place in single layer in greased jelly roll pan, 15½x10½x1 inch. Spread evenly with tomato sauce. Sprinkle with cheese. Bake until tender, 20 to 30 minutes.   4 TO 6 SERVINGS.

Eggplant Combo

1 medium eggplant (about 1½ pounds), pared and cut into ½-inch pieces
1 medium onion, sliced
¼ cup butter or margarine
1 medium green pepper, cut into 1-inch pieces
8 to 10 cherry tomatoes, cut in half
1½ teaspoons seasoned salt
¼ teaspoon pepper
⅓ cup dairy sour cream

Cook and stir eggplant and onion in butter in 10-inch skillet until onion is tender, about 5 minutes. Stir in green pepper. Cover and simmer 5 minutes.

Add tomatoes; sprinkle with seasoned salt and pepper. Cover and simmer until eggplant is tender, about 5 minutes. Serve with sour cream and garnish with snipped chives.   4 SERVINGS.

Peas and Cucumbers

1 unpared medium cucumber
2 pounds fresh green peas, shelled
¼ cup water
½ small head lettuce, shredded (about
   2 cups)
2 tablespoons butter or margarine
1 teaspoon sugar
½ teaspoon salt
⅛ teaspoon pepper
¼ cup dairy sour cream or unflavored yogurt
1 teaspoon lemon juice
   Paprika

Cut cucumber lengthwise into fourths, then crosswise into 1-inch pieces. Heat cucumber pieces, peas and water to boiling; reduce heat. Cover and simmer until peas are tender, about 10 minutes; drain. Stir in lettuce, butter, sugar, salt and pepper; heat until lettuce is hot. Mix sour cream and lemon juice. Toss or serve with vegetables. Sprinkle with paprika.   4 SERVINGS.

Cut cucumber lengthwise into fourths, then cut crosswise.

Heat the cucumber pieces, peas and water to boiling.

Stir in the lettuce, butter, sugar, salt and pepper; heat.

Mix sour cream and lemon juice; serve with vegetables.

VEGETABLE SPARKLERS

Kids complaining about plain old vegetables? Out-maneuver them with simple, flavorful garnishes like crumbled bacon bits, grated cheese, croutons, chopped nuts, parsley or French fried onions. Or add sliced olives, chopped pimiento, snipped chives or diced green pepper. A little lemon juice, sour cream or instant minced onion will spark the flavor, and for eye appeal you can create vegetable combos. They'll know the difference, and like it!

Cut peppers into rings, removing seeds and membranes.

Layer cauliflowerets, peas, peppers and onion in skillet.

Pepper Medley

2 cups cauliflowerets, cut into ½-inch
  pieces
2 pounds fresh green peas, shelled
2 medium green or red peppers, cut into
  rings
1 small onion, sliced and separated into
  rings
¾ cup water
1½ teaspoons snipped fresh dill leaves or ½
  teaspoon dried dill weed
1 teaspoon salt

Layer cauliflowerets, peas, peppers and onion in 10-inch skillet; add water. Sprinkle with dill and salt. Heat to boiling; reduce heat. Cover and simmer over medium heat until vegetables are tender, about 10 minutes.   4 SERVINGS.

Okra Medley

1 medium onion, sliced
2 tablespoons butter or margarine
½ pound fresh okra, sliced (about 2 cups)
4 medium tomatoes, peeled and cut into
  eighths
1 cup fresh corn (2 to 3 ears)
1 teaspoon salt
⅛ teaspoon pepper

Cook and stir onion in butter in 10-inch skillet until tender. Add okra and cook over medium-high heat, stirring constantly, 3 minutes. Add tomatoes and corn. Cover and simmer over medium heat until corn is tender, 10 to 15 minutes. Stir in salt and pepper.   4 SERVINGS.

Potatoes Au Gratin

1 medium onion, chopped (about ½ cup)
2 tablespoons butter or margarine
1 tablespoon flour
1 teaspoon salt
¼ teaspoon pepper
2 cups half-and-half*
2 cups shredded natural sharp Cheddar
    cheese (about 8 ounces)
6 medium potatoes, sliced
¼ cup fine dry bread crumbs

Place potatoes in cold water to prevent discoloration.

Cut the potatoes into thin slices; place in casserole.

Heat oven to 375°. Cook and stir onion in butter in 2-quart saucepan until onion is tender. Stir in flour, salt and pepper. Cook over low heat, stirring constantly, until mixture is smooth and bubbly; remove from heat. Stir in half-and-half and 1½ cups of the cheese. Heat to boiling, stirring constantly. Boil and stir 1 minute. Place potatoes in ungreased 1½-quart casserole. Pour cheese sauce on potatoes. Bake uncovered until top is brown and bubbly, 1¼ to 1½ hours.

Pour cheese sauce on sliced potatoes and bake uncovered.

Sprinkle the baked casserole with crumb mixture and broil.

Mix remaining cheese and the bread crumbs; sprinkle over casserole. Set oven control to broil and/or 550°. Broil 3 to 4 inches from heat until top is crusty and light brown, about 4 minutes (see note).   6 SERVINGS.

*2 cups milk and 2 tablespoons butter or margarine can be substituted for the half-and-half.

Note: Broiling step can be omitted. Bake casserole uncovered 1 hour; sprinkle with cheese-crumb mixture. Bake until top is brown and bubbly, 15 to 30 minutes.

Chive-Potato Latkes

Blend half each of the potatoes, water and onion.

Drain; pour into bowl. Repeat with remaining half.

6 medium new potatoes, cut into 1-inch
  pieces
1 cup water
1 medium onion, cut into fourths
2 eggs, beaten
2 tablespoons chives
1 tablespoon flour
1½ teaspoons salt
½ teaspoon paprika
¼ teaspoon baking powder

Place half each of the potatoes, water and onion in blender container. Cover and blend on high speed until finely grated, about 20 seconds; drain. Pour potato mixture into large bowl. Repeat with remaining potatoes, water and onion. Stir in remaining ingredients.

Grease heated griddle generously. Pour batter by ¼ cupfuls onto hot griddle. Cook over medium heat, turning when edges begin to brown, about 3 minutes on each side. Latkes can be held on baking sheet in warm oven 5 minutes. 12 LATKES.

Potato Bake

1 egg
1 tablespoon milk
1 envelope (about 2½ ounces) seasoned
   coating mix for chicken, fish, pork or
   hamburger
1 tablespoon grated Parmesan cheese
2 cans (16 ounces each) whole new potatoes,
   drained

Heat oven to 350°. Beat egg and milk. Blend coating mix and cheese. Roll potatoes in egg mixture, then in coating mixture. Place potatoes in greased baking pan, 13x9x2 inches. Bake uncovered 30 minutes.   6 TO 8 SERVINGS.

For Potato Bake, roll the potatoes in the egg mixture.

Then roll in the seasoned coating mixture and bake.

Mandarin Sweets

¼ cup packed brown sugar
2 tablespoons butter or margarine
2 tablespoons orange marmalade
½ teaspoon salt
1 can (18 ounces) vacuum-pack sweet
   potatoes
1 can (11 ounces) mandarin orange
   segments, drained

Heat brown sugar, butter, marmalade and salt to boiling in 10-inch skillet over medium heat, stirring constantly. Add potatoes; cook, stirring occasionally, until potatoes are coated and hot. Stir in orange segments; reduce heat. Heat until oranges are hot.   3 OR 4 SERVINGS.

Citrus Sweet Potatoes

Heat the liqueur in a small, long-handled skillet or pan at the table or on range top.

Ignite the warm liqueur at the table with a long match, then pour on the potatoes.

6 cups water
2 pounds sweet potatoes (about 6 medium)*
1 orange, thinly sliced
¼ cup butter or margarine
½ cup packed brown sugar
¼ teaspoon salt
3 tablespoons orange-flavored liqueur or rum

Heat water to boiling; add potatoes. Heat to boiling; reduce heat. Cover and simmer until tender, 30 to 35 minutes. Drain; slip off skins. Cut potatoes lengthwise in half.

Cut fruit from orange slices, leaving orange peel rings intact. Heat butter until melted. Stir in brown sugar and salt. Cook, stirring constantly, until smooth and bubbly. Add sweet potatoes, orange peel rings and orange slices; cook and stir gently until glazed and hot.

Transfer sweet potato mixture to chafing dish or skillet. Heat liqueur in small skillet or saucepan just until warm. Ignite and pour on potatoes.   4 SERVINGS.

*1 can (18 ounces) vacuum-pack sweet potatoes can be substituted for fresh sweet potatoes. Add with orange peel rings.

Citrus Carrots: Substitute 2 cans (16 ounces each) whole carrots, drained, for the sweet potatoes.

Creamy Radishes

¾ pound red radishes, cut in half or sliced
  (about 3 cups)
3 tablespoons butter or margarine
1 tablespoon flour
½ teaspoon salt
  Dash of pepper
¼ cup milk
  Snipped chives or parsley

Heat radishes and enough water to cover to boiling in 2-quart saucepan; reduce heat. Cover and simmer until crisp-tender, 5 to 7 minutes. Drain, reserving ½ cup liquid. Heat butter over low heat until melted. Blend in flour, salt and pepper. Cook over low heat, stirring constantly, until mixture is smooth and bubbly; remove from heat. Stir in milk and reserved liquid. Heat to boiling, stirring constantly. Boil and stir 1 minute. Stir in radishes; heat 5 minutes. Sprinkle with chives. 4 TO 6 SERVINGS.

Cook the radishes just until crisp-tender to retain color.

Add the cooked radishes to the white sauce and heat.

SPICE FOR VARIETY

For extra appetite appeal without extra calories, experiment with herbs and spices when cooking vegetables. Try adding instant bouillon to your cooking liquid or substituting seasoned salt for regular. A dash of soy sauce will add new flavor to broccoli, while allspice, nutmeg, ginger, mint or mace will perk up your carrots. Basil, chili powder, dill and thyme go well with green beans—but remember, add only enough to impart a subtle flavor.

Rutabaga with Cheese Sauce

Drain the vegetables, reserving the liquid in saucepan.

Stir cheese into cornstarch mixture just until melted.

1 small rutabaga (about 1 pound), pared and
  cut into 2x½-inch strips
1 medium onion, sliced
2 medium stalks celery, thinly sliced (about
  1 cup)
1 teaspoon salt
⅛ teaspoon pepper
1 cup water
2 tablespoons cornstarch
¼ cup cold water
½ cup shredded Monterey Jack cheese (about
  2 ounces)
  Paprika

Heat rutabaga, onion, celery, salt, pepper and 1 cup water to boiling in 2-quart saucepan; reduce heat. Cover and simmer until rutabaga is tender, about 20 minutes.

Drain vegetables, reserving liquid in saucepan. Mix cornstarch and ¼ cup cold water; add to reserved liquid. Cook cornstarch mixture over medium heat, stirring constantly, until mixture thickens and boils. Boil and stir 1 minute; reduce heat. Stir in cheese just until melted. Pour sauce on hot vegetables; sprinkle with paprika.   4 TO 6 SERVINGS.

Spinach Puff

2 packages (10 ounces each) frozen
   chopped spinach, thawed
8 eggs
½ cup dairy sour cream
1½ teaspoons salt
1 teaspoon grated lemon peel
½ teaspoon garlic salt
½ cup grated Parmesan cheese

Heat oven to 350°. Drain spinach completely. Beat eggs, sour cream, salt, lemon peel and garlic salt until well blended. Stir in spinach; pour into ungreased baking dish, 8x8x2 inches. Sprinkle with cheese. Bake until knife inserted in center comes out clean, 35 to 40 minutes. 8 OR 9 SERVINGS.

Cider Squash

2 medium acorn squash
½ cup apple cider
¼ cup packed brown sugar
½ teaspoon salt
⅛ teaspoon ground cinnamon
⅛ teaspoon ground mace

Heat oven to 325°. Cut squash lengthwise in half; remove seeds and membrane. Then cut crosswise into 1-inch slices. Spread slices in ungreased jelly roll pan, 15½x10½x1 inch. Pour apple cider on slices. Mix remaining ingredients; sprinkle over squash. Cover with aluminum foil and bake until tender, 45 minutes to 1 hour. 6 SERVINGS.

Tomato Bake

9 medium tomatoes, cored
3 tablespoons butter or margarine, softened
1 tablespoon chopped onion
¼ teaspoon dried basil leaves
   Parsley

Heat oven to 350°. Place tomatoes in ungreased baking pan, 13x9x2 inches. Mix butter, onion and basil. Spoon about 1 teaspoon butter mixture into each tomato. Bake until tomatoes are hot, 20 to 25 minutes. Serve tomatoes on parsley. 9 SERVINGS.

Vegetable Bake

1 package (10 ounces) frozen creamed small
   onions
1 package (10 ounces) carrots frozen in
   butter sauce
½ cup shredded Cheddar cheese (about 2
   ounces)
1 can (1½ ounces) shoestring potatoes

Heat oven to 350°. Cook frozen onions and carrots as directed on packages; pour into ungreased 1-quart casserole. Stir in cheese; top with potatoes. Bake uncovered until bubbly, about 10 minutes. 4 SERVINGS.

Pour dressing on artichoke hearts, olives and mushrooms.

Add the marinated mixture to salad greens in plastic bag.

Artichoke-Mushroom Toss

1 package (about 1 ounce) Italian salad
    dressing mix
1 can (14 ounces) artichoke hearts, drained
¾ cup pitted ripe olives
½ pound fresh mushrooms, sliced
1 large head lettuce, torn into bite-size
    pieces
½ pound spinach, torn into bite-size pieces

Prepare salad dressing mix as directed on package; pour on artichoke hearts, olives and mushrooms. Cover and refrigerate up to 24 hours. Place greens in large plastic bag. Close bag and refrigerate up to 24 hours.

Just before serving, add marinated mixture to greens in bag. Close bag tightly; shake to coat greens. Sprinkle with salt and pepper.　8 TO 10 SERVINGS.

Spinach-Melon Toss

¼ cup vegetable oil
3 tablespoons lemon juice or vinegar
1 teaspoon sugar
½ teaspoon salt
    Dash of pepper
½ medium honeydew melon or 1 medium
    cantaloupe, cut up (about 2 cups)
2 small cucumbers, thinly sliced
3 ounces spinach or ½ medium head lettuce,
    torn into bite-size pieces (about 3 cups)

Mix oil, juice, sugar, salt and pepper. Toss with melon and cucumbers. Cover and refrigerate up to 24 hours.

Just before serving, toss with spinach.　6 SERVINGS.

Spinach-Bacon Flambé

6 slices bacon, cut into ½-inch pieces
2 tablespoons honey
2 tablespoons red wine vinegar
1½ teaspoons Worcestershire sauce
¼ teaspoon salt
10 ounces spinach, torn into bite-size pieces
5 ounces mushrooms, sliced
1 lemon, cut in half
¼ cup brandy

Fry bacon in skillet until crisp. Remove from skillet; drain on paper towel. Drain skillet, reserving 2 tablespoons bacon fat. Heat reserved bacon fat, honey, vinegar, Worcestershire sauce and salt just to boiling. Pour mixture on spinach and mushrooms; toss. Squeeze lemon over salad.

Heat bacon pieces and brandy in small skillet or saucepan just until warm. Ignite and pour on salad. Toss gently; serve immediately.　6 SERVINGS.

Heat bacon fat-honey-vinegar mixture; pour on spinach and mushrooms. Toss.

Squeeze lemon over the salad, then ignite bacon and brandy and pour on salad.

Cook and stir salami until light brown, about 5 minutes.

Stir in vinegar, oil, sugar and seasonings, then heat.

Add lettuce, romaine, apple and green pepper.

Toss gently until salad greens are well coated.

Wilted Lettuce and Salami

4 ounces sliced salami, cut into 8 wedges
¼ cup vinegar
3 tablespoons vegetable oil
2 teaspoons sugar
1 teaspoon dried oregano leaves
¼ teaspoon salt
⅛ teaspoon pepper
1 small head lettuce, torn into bite-size pieces (about 4 cups)
1 small bunch romaine, torn into bite-size pieces (about 4 cups)
1 medium apple, sliced
1 small green pepper, chopped (about ¼ cup)

Cook and stir salami in electric skillet or wok until light brown, about 5 minutes. Stir in vinegar, oil, sugar, oregano, salt and pepper. Heat just to boiling; turn off heat. Add lettuce, romaine, apple and green pepper; toss gently. Serve immediately.   8 SERVINGS.

Caesar Salad

1 clove garlic, cut in half
⅓ cup olive oil
1 teaspoon Worcestershire sauce
½ teaspoon salt
¼ teaspoon dry mustard
1 large bunch romaine, chilled and torn into
    bite-size pieces (about 12 cups)
    Coddled Egg (below)
1 lemon, cut in half
    Onion-Cheese Croutons (below)
¼ cup grated Parmesan cheese
    Freshly ground pepper
1 can (about 2 ounces) anchovy fillets,
    drained and cut up

Just before serving, rub large salad bowl with garlic. Place garlic in oil; let stand 5 minutes. Discard garlic. Mix oil, Worcestershire sauce, salt and mustard. Place romaine in salad bowl. Pour oil mixture on top; toss. Break Coddled Egg onto romaine; squeeze lemon over salad. Toss until leaves are well coated. Sprinkle with Onion-Cheese Croutons, cheese, pepper and anchovies; toss.   6 SERVINGS.

CODDLED EGG

To prevent cold egg from cracking, place in warm water. Heat enough water to completely cover egg to boiling. Transfer egg to boiling water. Remove from heat; cover and let stand 30 seconds. Immediately cool egg in cold water; refrigerate.

ONION-CHEESE CROUTONS

Heat oven to 400°. Trim crusts from 4 slices white bread; butter both sides. Mix ¼ teaspoon onion powder and 1½ tablespoons grated Parmesan cheese; sprinkle over bread. Cut bread into ½-inch cubes; place in ungreased shallow baking pan. Bake, stirring occasionally, until golden brown and crisp, 10 to 15 minutes.

Pour oil mixture on romaine in a large salad bowl.

Toss romaine with oil mixture until leaves glisten.

Break Coddled Egg onto the romaine; squeeze lemon over the salad and toss.

Sprinkle salad with croutons, cheese, freshly ground pepper and anchovies; toss.

Freezer Coleslaw

Shred 1 medium head cabbage.

Spoon mixture into containers.

1 medium head cabbage, shredded (about
   5 cups)
1 teaspoon salt
2 cups sugar
1 cup vinegar
½ cup water
1 teaspoon celery seed
4 medium stalks celery, chopped (about
   2 cups)
1 small green pepper, chopped (about ½
   cup)
1 medium carrot, cut lengthwise into fourths
   and thinly sliced (about ½ cup)
1 small onion, chopped (about ¼ cup)

Mix cabbage and salt; let stand 1 hour. Heat sugar, vinegar, water and celery seed to boiling in 1-quart saucepan. Boil and stir 1 minute. Cool to lukewarm.

Drain cabbage; stir in celery, green pepper, carrot and onion. Stir vinegar mixture into cabbage mixture. Spoon into three 1-pint freezer containers. Cover and label; freeze up to 1 month.

■8 hours before serving, place in refrigerator to thaw. Drain well before serving. Garnish with sliced pimiento-stuffed olives. 6 CUPS COLESLAW.

Garden Slaw

1 small onion, sliced and separated into
    rings
½ medium head cabbage, chopped
2 medium stalks celery, chopped (about 1
    cup)
1 medium carrot, shredded (about ½ cup)
1 medium zucchini, sliced
¼ cup sugar
¼ cup vinegar
¼ cup vegetable oil
1 teaspoon celery seed
½ teaspoon salt
½ teaspoon dry mustard
    Dash of pepper

Reserve a few onion rings. Toss remaining onion rings, the cabbage, celery, carrot and zucchini. Heat remaining ingredients to boiling; boil and stir 1 minute. Toss with vegetables. Refrigerate 3 hours, stirring occasionally. Garnish with reserved onion rings.　8 SERVINGS.

Toss remaining onion rings with the other vegetables.

Heat the dressing ingredients and toss with the slaw.

Tomato Plate

½ cup dairy sour cream
¼ teaspoon onion salt
¼ teaspoon garlic salt
    Leaf lettuce
2 medium tomatoes, thinly sliced
1 medium Bermuda onion, sliced
1 small cucumber, sliced

Mix sour cream, onion salt and garlic salt. Arrange lettuce on large platter. Alternate slices of tomatoes, onion and cucumber on lettuce. Spoon dressing onto vegetables.
3 OR 4 SERVINGS.

Garbanzo Bean Salad

1 can (15 ounces) garbanzo beans, drained
1 can (15 ounces) kidney beans, drained
1 can (16 ounces) cut green beans, drained
2 medium carrots, cut into 1½ x ¼-inch strips
1 medium stalk celery, thinly sliced (about ½ cup)
1 small onion, thinly sliced and separated into rings
1 cup wine vinegar
½ cup sugar
½ cup vegetable oil
1 teaspoon seasoned salt
½ teaspoon dry mustard

Mix beans, carrots, celery and onion. Mix remaining ingredients; pour on bean mixture and toss. Refrigerate at least 3 hours. Just before serving, toss and drain.
8 SERVINGS.

Brussels Sprouts-Tomato Salad

2 packages (10 ounces each) frozen Brussels sprouts
¾ cup oil-and-vinegar salad dressing
½ pint cherry tomatoes, cut in half

Cook Brussels sprouts as directed on package. Pour salad dressing over hot Brussels sprouts, turning each until well coated. Cool; cover and refrigerate at least 3 hours. Add tomatoes to Brussels sprouts and toss. Serve in lettuce cups if desired.   8 SERVINGS.

Sweet Potato Salad

5 cups water
1½ pounds sweet potatoes
2 medium stalks celery, thinly sliced (about 1 cup)
1 small onion, thinly sliced
1 medium orange, peeled and sectioned
½ cup mayonnaise or salad dressing
1 to 2 tablespoons orange or pineapple juice
½ teaspoon dry mustard
½ teaspoon grated orange peel
¼ teaspoon salt
¼ teaspoon ground ginger
⅛ teaspoon pepper
Lettuce leaves

Heat water to boiling; add potatoes. Heat to boiling; reduce heat. Cover and simmer until tender, 30 to 35 minutes.

Drain potatoes; slip off skins. Cut potatoes into ½-inch cubes. Add celery, onion and orange. Mix remaining ingredients except lettuce leaves; pour on vegetables and orange. Stir to blend. Refrigerate at least 2 hours. Serve in lettuce-lined salad bowl.   4 TO 6 SERVINGS.

Down Home Potato Salad

8 medium new potatoes, cooked, cut into
¼-inch cubes and chilled (about 5 cups)
3 large stalks celery, cut into diagonal slices
(about 2¼ cups)
1 jar (4 ounces) whole pimiento, drained and
sliced
¼ cup sweet pickle relish
½ small green pepper, chopped (about ¼
cup)
2 hard-cooked eggs, chopped
2 tablespoons sweet pickle juice
2 teaspoons instant minced onion
½ cup mayonnaise or salad dressing
1 to 2 tablespoons prepared mustard
1 teaspoon seasoned salt
2 hard-cooked eggs, sliced
Celery leaves

Toss potatoes, celery, pimiento, relish, green pepper and
chopped eggs. Mix pickle juice and onion; let stand 3
minutes. Stir in mayonnaise, mustard and seasoned salt;
toss with potato mixture. Garnish with egg slices and celery leaves.   12 SERVINGS.

Potatoes cut into small pieces
absorb flavors readily.

Ingredients tossed with a light
hand hold their shapes.

Pour ½ cup of gelatin mixture into mold. Stir the mayonnaise mixture into second gelatin mixture. Add half the vegetables.

Pour vegetable-mayonnaise mixture on first layer. Stir remaining vegetables into reserved gelatin. Pour into mold; refrigerate.

Cucumber Soufflé Salad

1 cup boiling water
2 packages (3 ounces each) lime-flavored
   gelatin
¾ cup cold water
1 cup boiling water
½ cup mayonnaise or salad dressing
¼ cup cold water
2 tablespoons vinegar
¼ teaspoon salt
1 medium cucumber, chopped (about 1 cup)
1 medium stalk celery, thinly sliced (about
   ½ cup)
7 medium radishes, sliced (about ½ cup)

For first layer, pour 1 cup boiling water on 1 package gelatin in bowl; stir until gelatin is dissolved. Stir in ¾ cup cold water. Pour ½ cup of the gelatin mixture into 5-cup mold; refrigerate. Reserve remaining gelatin mixture for third layer.

For second layer, pour 1 cup boiling water on second package gelatin in bowl; stir until gelatin is dissolved. Mix mayonnaise, ¼ cup cold water, the vinegar and salt; stir into gelatin mixture. Refrigerate until slightly thickened, about 1 hour. Stir in half of the cucumber, celery and radishes. Pour on the first layer in mold; refrigerate.

For third layer, refrigerate reserved gelatin until slightly thickened, about 1 hour. Stir in remaining vegetables; pour on second layer in mold. Refrigerate until firm, at least 5 hours.   8 SERVINGS.

Guacamole Salad

1 tablespoon plus 1 teaspoon unflavored
   gelatin
1½ cups cold water
2 medium avocados, mashed (about 1½
   cups)
¼ cup lemon juice
1 medium stalk celery, thinly sliced (about
   ½ cup)
1 small tomato, peeled and chopped (about
   ½ cup)
2 green onions, chopped (about 3
   tablespoons)
1 to 2 tablespoons chopped canned chilies
1 teaspoon salt
¼ teaspoon red pepper sauce
   Salad greens
   Ripe olives
   Cherry tomatoes

Sprinkle gelatin on ½ cup of the cold water in 1-quart saucepan; stir over low heat until gelatin is dissolved, about 3 minutes. Stir in remaining 1 cup cold water. Refrigerate until slightly thickened, about 40 minutes.

Mix avocados and lemon juice in large bowl. Stir in gelatin mixture, celery, tomato, onions, chilies, salt and pepper sauce. Pour into 4-cup mold. Refrigerate until firm, about 3 hours. Just before serving, unmold on salad greens and garnish with olives and tomatoes.　8 SERVINGS.

Sprinkle gelatin on the cold water in saucepan.

Stir over low heat until the gelatin is dissolved.

Mix the avocados and lemon juice in a large bowl.

Stir in gelatin mixture, vegetables and seasonings.

Fruit Salad Hawaiian

To prepare papaya, pare and cut in half; then remove the seeds and cut into slices.

To prepare the mango, score skin into sections; then peel back and cut into slices.

Banana Dressing (below)
Ginger Dressing (below)
1 pineapple
1 medium cantaloupe
1 medium honeydew melon
1 papaya, pared and sliced
1 mango, peeled and sliced
2 kiwi fruit, pared and sliced
1 cup green grapes
1 cup strawberries, cut in half
Leaf lettuce

Prepare Banana Dressing and Ginger Dressing. Remove top from pineapple. Cut pineapple in half, then into quarters; cut rind and eyes from quarters. Remove core. Slice quarters into 3x1-inch pieces. Cut balls from cantaloupe and honeydew. Arrange fruit on lettuce. Serve with Banana Dressing and Ginger Dressing.　8 TO 10 SERVINGS.

BANANA DRESSING

　1 banana, sliced
　½ cup dairy sour cream
　2 tablespoons packed brown sugar
1½ teaspoons lemon juice

Mix all ingredients in blender container. Cover and blend until smooth, 12 to 15 seconds. Refrigerate 1 hour.

GINGER DRESSING

⅓ cup mayonnaise or salad dressing
⅓ cup honey
　2 tablespoons chopped crystallized ginger
　1 tablespoon lime juice
　1 tablespoon vegetable oil
　½ teaspoon grated lime peel

Mix all ingredients; refrigerate 1 hour.

Sesame Fruit

½ cup vegetable oil
⅓ cup powdered sugar
2 tablespoons lemon juice
½ teaspoon dry mustard
½ teaspoon salt
½ teaspoon paprika
2 teaspoons sesame seed
1 can (15¼ ounces) pineapple chunks,
    drained
1 unpared medium apple, coarsely chopped
½ cup green or red grape halves
3 medium bananas
1 medium head lettuce, shredded

Blend oil, sugar, lemon juice, mustard, salt and paprika in small mixer bowl. Beat on medium speed until creamy, 3 to 4 minutes. Stir in sesame seed.

Toss pineapple, apple and grapes. Cut bananas lengthwise in half, then crosswise. Place 2 banana pieces on shredded lettuce on each of 6 salad plates. Spoon fruit into center of bananas. Spoon dressing onto each serving.   6 SERVINGS.

Beat dressing until creamy, scraping bowl occasionally.

Toss the pineapple chunks, apple and grape halves.

To shred lettuce, first cut the head lengthwise in half.

Place cut sides down, then cut into thin crosswise slices.

Tequila Salad

Shake dressing ingredients; refrigerate at least 1 hour.

Toss the fruit just before serving; place on greens.

1 can (15¼ ounces) sliced pineapple, drained (reserve ¼ cup syrup)
¼ cup lime juice
2 tablespoons powdered sugar
2 tablespoons tequila
2 tablespoons vegetable oil
¼ teaspoon salt
3 medium avocados
   Lime juice
2 large grapefruit
2 large oranges
   Salad greens
   Chopped walnuts
   Salt

Shake reserved pineapple syrup, ¼ cup lime juice, the sugar, tequila, oil and ¼ teaspoon salt in tightly covered container. Refrigerate at least 1 hour.

Cut avocados lengthwise in half; remove pits. Peel avocados; cut into ½-inch pieces. Sprinkle pieces with lime juice. Cut pineapple slices in half. Pare and section grapefruit and oranges; cut sections in half if desired.

Just before serving, toss avocado pieces with pineapple and grapefruit and orange sections; place on salad greens. Sprinkle walnuts and salt over salad. Serve with dressing. 8 SERVINGS.

Mallow Fruits

- 2 cans (11 ounces each) mandarin orange segments, drained
- 1 can (15¼ ounces) pineapple chunks, drained
- 1 jar (4 ounces) maraschino cherries, drained
- 2 cups miniature marshmallows
- 1 cup broken walnuts
- 1 teaspoon lemon juice
- 1 envelope (1.4 ounces) whipped topping mix
  Celery leaves

Toss orange segments, pineapple, cherries, marshmallows and walnuts; drizzle with lemon juice. Prepare topping mix as directed on package; fold into fruit. Cover and refrigerate 1 hour. Garnish with celery leaves.   8 TO 10 SERVINGS.

Cherry Mold

- 1 can (16½ ounces) pitted dark sweet cherries, drained (reserve ¾ cup liquid)
- ¾ cup water
- 1 package (6 ounces) raspberry-flavored gelatin
- 1¾ cups strawberry-flavored beverage
- ½ cup slivered almonds
  Celery leaves
- ½ cup mayonnaise or salad dressing

Heat reserved cherry liquid and water to boiling. Pour on gelatin in medium bowl; stir until gelatin is dissolved. Stir in beverage. Refrigerate until slightly thickened. Stir in cherries and almonds; pour into 6-cup mold. Refrigerate until firm, about 4 hours. Garnish with celery leaves and serve with mayonnaise.   10 SERVINGS.

One large marshmallow equals 10 miniature marshmallows.

One cup miniature marshmallows equals 11 or 12 large.

Apple Cider Salad

For the dressing, mix cream cheese and mayonnaise.

Add the crumbled blue cheese and apple cider; stir.

3½ cups apple cider or apple juice
 1 package (6 ounces) lemon-flavored gelatin
 1 to 2 tablespoons lemon juice
 ½ teaspoon salt
 1 cup Tokay grapes, cut in half and seeded
 1 medium stalk celery, chopped (about ½ cup)
 Salad greens
 Blue Cheese Mayonnaise (below)

Heat 2 cups of the apple cider to boiling. Pour on gelatin in bowl; stir until gelatin is dissolved. Stir in remaining apple cider, the lemon juice and salt. Refrigerate until slightly thickened, about 1 hour. Stir in grapes and celery. Pour into 6-cup mold. Refrigerate until firm, about 3 hours.

Unmold on salad greens. Serve with Blue Cheese Mayonnaise.   6 SERVINGS.

BLUE CHEESE MAYONNAISE
 1 package (3 ounces) cream cheese, softened
 ¼ cup mayonnaise or salad dressing
 2 tablespoons crumbled blue cheese (about 1 ounce)
 2 tablespoons apple cider or apple juice

Mix cream cheese and mayonnaise. Stir in blue cheese and apple cider.

Golden Apricot Salad

2 cups boiling water
1 package (6 ounces) orange-flavored gelatin
1 can (30 ounces) apricot halves, drained (reserve syrup)
1 can (15¼ ounces) crushed pineapple, drained (reserve syrup)
¾ cup miniature marshmallows
¼ cup sugar
1 tablespoon flour
1 egg, beaten
1 cup chilled whipping cream
   Toasted coconut

Pour boiling water on gelatin in large bowl; stir until gelatin is dissolved. Mix apricot and pineapple syrups; reserve 1 cup. Measure remaining syrup; add enough water to measure 1 cup. Stir syrup-water mixture into gelatin mixture. Refrigerate until slightly thickened, about 1 hour.

Stir apricots, pineapple and marshmallows into gelatin mixture; pour into baking dish, 11¾x7½x1¾ inches. Refrigerate until firm, about 3 hours.

Mix sugar and flour in 1-quart saucepan. Stir in reserved apricot-pineapple syrup and the egg. Heat to boiling over low heat, stirring constantly. Boil and stir 1 minute; cool.

Beat whipping cream in chilled small mixer bowl until soft peaks form. Fold into fruit syrup mixture. Spread evenly over gelatin layer. Sprinkle coconut over the top.
10 TO 12 SERVINGS.

To toast coconut, sprinkle the desired amount evenly in an ungreased jelly roll pan.

Toast coconut in 350° oven until golden brown, about 10 minutes, stirring frequently.

For quick setting, place the gelatin mixture in a container of ice and water; stir often.

Use a melon baller to scoop round uniform balls from the honeydew melon as shown.

Daiquiri Salad

1 cup boiling water
1 package (6 ounces) lime-flavored gelatin
1 can (6 ounces) frozen limeade concentrate
   About ½ cup ginger ale
1 can (20 ounces) pineapple chunks in juice,
   drained (reserve juice)
½ cup light rum
   Salad greens
   Honeydew melon balls

Pour boiling water on gelatin in 2-quart bowl; stir until gelatin is dissolved. Stir in frozen concentrate. Add enough ginger ale to reserved pineapple juice to measure 1¼ cups. Stir pineapple juice–ginger ale mixture and rum into gelatin mixture. Refrigerate until slightly thickened, about 1 hour.

Stir in pineapple. Pour into 5-cup mold. Refrigerate until firm, at least 3 hours. Unmold on salad greens. Garnish with melon balls. If desired, serve with whipped topping. 8 TO 10 SERVINGS.

Breads

To form loaf, flatten dough into rectangle, 18x9 inches. Fold dough into thirds.

Roll tightly and press with thumbs after each turn; pinch length of the roll.

Press each end to seal; fold ends under. Let rise in a greased loaf pan.

When done, loaves should sound hollow when tapped with wooden spoon.

Honey-Wheat Bread

2 packages active dry yeast
½ cup warm water (105 to 115°)
⅓ cup honey
1 tablespoon salt
¼ cup shortening
1¾ cups warm water
3 cups stone-ground whole wheat or
    graham flour
3 to 4 cups all-purpose* or unbleached flour
    Butter or margarine, softened
    Whole wheat flour

Dissolve yeast in ½ cup warm water in large mixer bowl. Stir in honey, salt, shortening, 1¾ cups warm water and 3 cups whole wheat flour. Beat until smooth. Stir in enough of the all-purpose flour to make dough easy to handle.

Turn dough onto lightly floured surface; knead until smooth and elastic, about 10 minutes. Place in greased bowl; turn greased side up. Cover; let rise in warm place until double, about 1 hour.

Grease 2 loaf pans, 9x5x3 or 8½x4½x2½ inches. Punch down dough. Divide in half; flatten each into a rectangle, 18x9 inches. Fold crosswise into thirds, overlapping the 2 sides. Roll dough tightly toward you, beginning at one of the open ends. Press with thumbs to seal after each turn. Pinch edge firmly to seal. Press each end with side of hand to seal; fold ends under.

Place loaves seam sides down in pans. Brush with butter; sprinkle with whole wheat flour. Let rise until double, about 1 hour.

Heat oven to 375°. Bake until loaves are deep golden brown and sound hollow when tapped, 40 to 45 minutes. Remove from pans; cool on wire rack.   2 LOAVES.

*If using self-rising flour, reduce salt to 1 teaspoon.

Peasant Rye Bread

3 packages active dry yeast
1½ cups warm potato water or warm water
   (105 to 115°)
½ cup light molasses
2 tablespoons shortening
1 tablespoon salt
1½ cups rye flour
1½ cups whole wheat flour
2 to 2¼ cups all-purpose flour*
   Cornmeal
   Flour

Baking sheet is sprinkled with cornmeal for this bread.

Loaves are shaped, rolled in flour and allowed to rise.

Dissolve yeast in warm potato water in 3-quart bowl. Stir in molasses, shortening, salt, rye flour and whole wheat flour. Beat until smooth. Stir in enough all-purpose flour to make dough easy to handle.

Turn dough onto lightly floured surface. Cover; let rest 10 to 15 minutes. Knead until smooth, 5 to 10 minutes. Place in greased bowl; turn greased side up. Cover; let rise in warm place until double, about 1 hour. Punch down dough. Cover; let rise until double, about 40 minutes.

Grease baking sheet; sprinkle with cornmeal. Punch down dough; divide in half. Shape each half into round, slightly flat loaf. Roll in flour. Place loaves in opposite corners of baking sheet. Let rise 1 hour.

Heat oven to 375°. Bake until loaves sound hollow when tapped, 30 to 35 minutes. Remove from baking sheet; cool on wire rack.   2 LOAVES.

*If using self-rising flour, omit salt.

Egg Bread

2 packages active dry yeast
¾ cup warm water (105 to 115°)
1¾ cups lukewarm milk (scalded then cooled)
2 eggs
3 tablespoons sugar
3 tablespoons shortening
1 tablespoon salt
7 to 8 cups all-purpose flour*
   Butter or margarine, softened

Dissolve yeast in warm water in large bowl. Stir in milk, eggs, sugar, shortening, salt and 4 cups of the flour. Beat until smooth. Mix in enough remaining flour to make dough easy to handle.

Turn dough onto lightly floured surface; knead until smooth and elastic, about 10 minutes. Place in greased bowl; turn greased side up. Cover; let rise in warm place until double, about 1 hour. (Dough is ready if indentation remains when touched.)

Punch down dough; divide into halves. Roll each half into rectangle, 18x9 inches. Fold 9-inch sides crosswise into thirds, overlapping ends. Roll up tightly, beginning at narrow end. Pinch edge of dough into roll to seal well; press in ends of roll. Press each end with side of hand to seal; fold ends under.

Place loaves seam sides down in 2 greased loaf pans, 9x5x3 or 8½x4½x2½ inches. Brush lightly with butter. Let rise until double, about 1 hour.

Heat oven to 425°. Bake until loaves are deep golden brown and sound hollow when tapped, 25 to 30 minutes. Immediately remove from pans. Brush tops of loaves with butter; cool on wire racks.   2 LOAVES.

*If using self-rising flour, omit salt.

Pocket Bread

1 package active dry yeast
1⅓ cups warm water (105 to 115°)
1 tablespoon vegetable oil
1 teaspoon salt
¼ teaspoon sugar
1½ cups whole wheat flour
1½ to 2 cups all-purpose flour*
   Cornmeal

Dissolve yeast in warm water in large bowl; stir in oil, salt, sugar and whole wheat flour. Beat until smooth. Mix in enough all-purpose flour to make dough easy to handle. Knead on lightly floured surface until smooth and elastic, about 10 minutes. Place in greased bowl; turn greased side up. Cover and let rise in warm place until double, about 1 hour.

Punch down dough; divide into 6 parts. Shape each part into a ball. Cover and let rise 30 minutes. Sprinkle 3 ungreased baking sheets with cornmeal. Roll each ball into a 6½-inch circle on lightly floured surface. Place 2 circles on each baking sheet. Cover and let rise 30 minutes.

Heat oven to 450°. Bake circles until puffed and light brown, about 12 minutes.   6 POCKET BREADS.

*If using self-rising flour, omit salt.

Swiss Cheese Casserole Bread

½ cup dairy sour cream
1 package active dry yeast
1 cup warm water (105 to 115°)
2 tablespoons sugar
2 tablespoons shortening
2 teaspoons salt
3 cups all-purpose flour*
1 cup shredded Swiss cheese (about
  4 ounces)
  Soft butter or margarine

Heat sour cream over low heat just until lukewarm. Dissolve yeast in warm water in large mixer bowl. Add sour cream, sugar, shortening, salt and 2 cups of the flour. Blend 30 seconds on low speed, scraping bowl constantly. Beat 2 minutes on medium speed, scraping bowl occasionally. (Or beat by hand 300 strokes.) Stir in remaining flour and the cheese until smooth. Scrape batter from side of bowl. Cover and let rise in warm place until double, about 45 minutes.

Grease round layer pan, 9x1½ inches. Stir down batter by beating about 25 strokes. Spread evenly in pan. Smooth top of loaf by patting with floured hand. Cover and let rise until double, about 40 minutes.

Heat oven to 375°. Bake until loaf sounds hollow when tapped, 45 minutes. Remove loaf from pan; brush top with butter. Cool on wire rack.

*If using self-rising flour, omit salt.

Dissolve the yeast in warm water in a large mixer bowl.

Beat batter on medium speed, scraping bowl occasionally.

Stir in remaining flour and the cheese until smooth.

Smooth top of loaf in pan by patting with floured hand.

To mash bananas easily, slice ripe bananas and beat with mixer, rotary beater or fork.

Knead the dough on a lightly floured surface until smooth and elastic, about 5 minutes.

Let rise in warm place until double. (Indentation will remain when dough is touched.)

Roll rectangle up tightly, beginning at narrow side; pinch edge into the roll to seal it well.

Banana Swirl Bread

1 package active dry yeast
½ cup warm water (105 to 115°)
1 cup mashed bananas (2 large)
¼ cup sugar
1 teaspoon salt
1 egg
¼ cup shortening
3½ to 3¾ cups all-purpose flour*
¼ cup sugar
2 teaspoons ground cinnamon
   Butter or margarine, softened
   Vanilla-Cream Frosting (below)

Dissolve yeast in warm water. Stir in bananas, ¼ cup sugar, the salt, egg, shortening and 1¾ cups of the flour. Beat until smooth. Stir in enough remaining flour to make dough easy to handle. Turn dough onto lightly floured surface; knead until smooth and elastic, about 5 minutes. Place in greased bowl; turn greased side up. Cover; let rise in warm place until double, about 1½ hours. (Dough is ready if indentation remains when touched.)

Grease generously loaf pan, 9x5x3 inches. Punch down dough. Roll into rectangle, 16x8 inches. Mix ¼ cup sugar and the cinnamon and sprinkle over rectangle. Roll up tightly, beginning at narrow side. Pinch edge of dough into roll to seal well. Place seam side down in pan. Cover; let rise until double, about 1 hour.

Heat oven to 375°. Bake until golden brown, about 35 minutes. Remove from pan. Brush loaf with butter; cool. Frost with Vanilla-Cream Frosting.

*If using self-rising flour, omit salt.

VANILLA-CREAM FROSTING

Mix ¾ cup powdered sugar, ¼ teaspoon vanilla and 1 to 2 teaspoons milk until of spreading consistency.

Braided Lemon-Raisin Loaves

2 packages active dry yeast
½ cup warm water (105 to 115°)
1½ cups lukewarm milk (scalded, then cooled)
¼ cup sugar
¼ cup shortening
1 tablespoon salt
3 eggs
7¼ to 7½ cups all-purpose flour*
2 cups raisins
2 tablespoons grated lemon peel
Butter or margarine, softened

Dissolve yeast in warm water. Stir in milk, sugar, shortening, salt, eggs and 3½ cups of the flour. Beat until smooth. Stir in raisins, lemon peel and enough of the remaining flour to make dough easy to handle.

Turn dough onto lightly floured board; knead until smooth and elastic, about 5 minutes. Place in greased bowl; turn greased side up. Cover and let rise in warm place until double, 1½ to 2 hours.

Grease 2 loaf pans, 9x5x3 inches. Punch down dough; divide into 4 parts. Roll 1 part into 9-inch square; roll up. Press each end to seal; fold ends under loaf. Place loaf seam side down in 1 pan.

Divide 1 part dough into thirds. Roll each third into a strip 10 inches long. Pinch ends of strips together and braid; seal end. Place braid on loaf in pan. Repeat with remaining 2 parts dough to make second loaf. Let rise until double, about 1 hour.

Heat oven to 400°. Bake until golden brown, about 30 minutes. Immediately remove from pans and cool. Brush with butter.   2 LOAVES.

*Do not use self-rising flour in this recipe.

Divide dough into 4 parts; roll 1 part into square. Roll up; seal ends and fold under. Place seam side down in 1 loaf pan.

Divide 1 part of dough into thirds. Roll into strips, pinch ends together and braid. Place braid on the loaf in pan. Repeat.

Light Cornmeal Crescents

Grease 2 baking sheets; sprinkle with cornmeal.

Roll each half of dough into a 12-inch circle.

Spread each circle of dough with softened butter.

Roll up each wedge, beginning at the rounded side.

1 package active dry yeast
½ cup warm water (105 to 115°)
1½ cups lukewarm milk (scalded then cooled)
1 cup cornmeal
½ cup sugar
½ cup butter or margarine, softened
2 eggs, slightly beaten
2 teaspoons salt
5¾ to 6¼ cups all-purpose flour*
Cornmeal
Butter or margarine, softened
Butter or margarine, melted

Dissolve yeast in warm water. Stir in milk, 1 cup cornmeal, the sugar, ½ cup butter, the eggs, salt and 2 cups of the flour. Beat until smooth. Stir in enough remaining flour to make dough easy to handle.

Turn dough onto lightly floured surface; knead until smooth and elastic, about 5 minutes. Place in greased bowl; turn greased side up. Cover; let rise in warm place until double, about 1½ hours. (Dough is ready if indentation remains when touched.)

Grease 2 baking sheets; sprinkle with cornmeal. Punch down dough; divide in half. Roll each half into 12-inch circle. Spread with softened butter; cut each circle into 16 wedges. Roll up each wedge, beginning at rounded side. Place crescents with points down on baking sheets. Cover; let rise until double, about 40 minutes.

Heat oven to 400°. Brush crescents lightly with melted butter; sprinkle with cornmeal. Bake until golden brown, 15 to 20 minutes.   32 CRESCENTS.

*If using self-rising flour, omit salt.

Petite Dinner Braids

1 package active dry yeast
½ cup warm water (105 to 115°)
2 tablespoons sugar
1 teaspoon salt
2 eggs
2 tablespoons shortening
2½ to 2¾ cups all-purpose flour*
   Shortening
1 egg yolk
1 tablespoon cold water
¾ teaspoon poppy seed
¾ teaspoon sesame seed

Dissolve yeast in warm water in large mixing bowl. Stir in sugar, salt, 2 eggs, 2 tablespoons shortening and 1¼ cups of the flour. Beat until smooth. Stir in enough remaining flour to make dough easy to handle.

Turn dough onto lightly floured surface; knead until smooth and elastic, about 5 minutes. Place in greased bowl; turn greased side up. Cover; let rise in warm place until double, 1½ to 2 hours.

Punch down dough; divide into 18 parts. Roll each part into a rope 7 inches long. Place groups of 3 ropes each close together on lightly greased baking sheet. Braid ropes gently and loosely. Do not stretch. Pinch ends to fasten; tuck under securely. Brush with shortening; let rise until double, about 20 minutes.

Heat oven to 375°. Beat egg yolk and cold water slightly; brush over braids. Sprinkle 3 braids with ¼ teaspoon poppy seed each and 3 remaining braids with ¼ teaspoon sesame seed each. Bake until braids are golden brown and sound hollow when tapped, about 15 minutes.   6 BRAIDS.

*If using self-rising flour, omit salt.

For butter balls, scald paddles in boiling water 30 seconds; chill in ice water.

Cut ¼-pound stick of firm butter into 1-inch pieces; cut each piece in half.

Stand one half butter pat upright on paddle; then smack butter between paddles.

Holding the bottom paddle steady, rotate top paddle quickly to form butter ball.

Knead dough until smooth and elastic, about 5 minutes.

Shape dough into balls; place on baking sheet and flatten.

Brush buns with egg yolk mixture, using pastry brush.

Top each bun with about ¼ teaspoon chopped onion.

Whole Wheat-Onion Buns

2 packages active dry yeast
2 cups warm water (105 to 115°)
½ cup sugar
¼ cup shortening
1 egg
2 teaspoons salt
1 teaspoon onion powder
2 cups whole wheat flour
4 to 5 cups all-purpose flour*
1 egg yolk
1 tablespoon water
1 medium onion, finely chopped (about ½ cup)

Dissolve yeast in 2 cups warm water. Stir in sugar, shortening, egg, salt, onion powder, whole wheat flour and 1½ cups of the all-purpose flour. Beat until smooth. Mix in enough remaining flour to make dough easy to handle. Knead until smooth and elastic, about 5 minutes. Place dough in greased bowl; turn greased side up. Cover and refrigerate at least 2 hours or until ready to use. (Dough can be stored covered in refrigerator up to 4 days.)

Shape dough into 1¼- to 1½-inch balls; place 2 inches apart on lightly greased baking sheet. Flatten balls. Cover; let rise until double, 1 to 1½ hours.

Heat oven to 400°. Blend egg yolk and 1 tablespoon water; brush buns with egg yolk mixture. Cook and stir chopped onion in butter until tender; drain. Top each bun with about ¼ teaspoon onion. Bake until golden brown, about 10 minutes. Cool.   4 TO 5 DOZEN BUNS.

*If using self-rising flour, omit salt.

Onion-Cheese Breadsticks

1 package active dry yeast
⅓ cup warm water (105 to 115°)
1 cup all-purpose flour*
1 tablespoon dried parsley flakes
1 tablespoon shortening
1 teaspoon sugar
¾ teaspoon salt
⅛ teaspoon garlic powder
1 egg
1 tablespoon instant minced onion
¼ cup grated Parmesan cheese
1 tablespoon butter or margarine, melted
2 tablespoons sesame seed

Grease baking pan, 13x9x2 inches. Dissolve yeast in warm water in small mixer bowl. Add flour, parsley flakes, shortening, sugar, salt, garlic powder and egg. Beat on medium speed 30 seconds, scraping bowl constantly. Beat on medium speed 2 minutes, scraping bowl occasionally.

Stir in onion and cheese. Pat dough evenly in pan with floured hands. Let rise in warm place until almost double, about 20 minutes.

Heat oven to 450°. Cut dough into 3x1-inch sticks; brush with butter. Sprinkle with sesame seed; bake until edges are brown, 12 to 15 minutes.   3 DOZEN BREADSTICKS.

*If using self-rising flour, omit salt.

Stir onion and cheese into seasoned yeast dough.

Pat dough evenly in pan with floured hands. Let rise.

Cut dough into sticks in the pan. Brush with butter.

Sprinkle with sesame seed; bake 12 to 15 minutes.

Strawberry Braid

Roll each half of dough into a rectangle, 15x9 inches.

Make 2-inch cuts at 1-inch intervals on long sides.

Reserve 2 tablespoons jam; spread rest down centers.

Crisscross strips over jam. Let rise for 40 minutes.

2 packages active dry yeast
½ cup warm water (105 to 115°)
½ cup granulated sugar
½ cup lukewarm milk (scalded then cooled)
½ cup butter or margarine, softened
2 eggs
1 teaspoon salt
1½ cups whole wheat flour
3½ cups all-purpose flour*
1 jar (12 ounces) strawberry jam
1½ cups powdered sugar
2 tablespoons milk

Dissolve yeast in warm water in large bowl. Stir in granulated sugar, ½ cup milk, the butter, eggs, salt, whole wheat flour and 1 cup of the all-purpose flour. Beat until smooth. Stir in enough of the remaining flour to make dough easy to handle.

Turn dough onto lightly floured surface; knead until smooth and elastic, about 5 minutes. Place in greased bowl; turn greased side up. Cover; let rise in warm place until double, about 1½ hours.

Grease 2 baking sheets. Punch down dough; divide in half. Roll each half into rectangle, 15x9 inches; place each on baking sheet. Make 2-inch cuts at 1-inch intervals on long sides of rectangles with scissors. Reserve ·2 tablespoons jam; spread remaining jam lengthwise down centers of rectangles. Crisscross strips over jam. Let rise 40 minutes.

Heat oven to 375°. Bake until light brown, 20 to 25 minutes. Mix powdered sugar, 2 tablespoons milk and the reserved jam. Drizzle over braids while warm.   2 BRAIDS.

*Do not use self-rising flour in this recipe.

Apricot Braid: Substitute 1 jar (12 ounces) apricot preserves for the strawberry jam.

Almond-Cream Coffee Cake

1 package active dry yeast
¼ cup warm water (105 to 115°)
½ cup butter or margarine, softened
1 egg, slightly beaten
1 tablespoon granulated sugar
¼ teaspoon salt
1¾ to 2 cups all-purpose flour*
1 package (8 ounces) cream cheese, softened
1 egg
½ cup granulated or packed brown sugar
½ teaspoon almond extract
1 tablespoon butter or margarine, softened
¼ cup sliced almonds

Spread cream cheese mixture evenly over the dough in pan.

Top with second dough square, easing carefully to fit pan.

Dissolve yeast in warm water in large bowl. Add ½ cup butter, the beaten egg, 1 tablespoon sugar, the salt and 1 cup of the flour. Beat until smooth. Stir in enough remaining flour to make dough easy to handle. Turn onto well-floured surface. Knead until smooth and elastic, about 5 minutes.

Divide dough in half. Roll each half into a 9-inch square on lightly floured surface. Ease 1 square into ungreased baking pan, 9x9x2 inches.

Beat cheese, 1 egg, ½ cup sugar and the extract in small mixer bowl on medium speed until thick and fluffy. Spread evenly over dough in pan; top with second dough square. Brush with 1 tablespoon butter; press almonds into dough. Cover and let rise until almost double, 1 to 1½ hours.

Heat oven to 350°. Bake until golden brown, 25 to 30 minutes.   9 TO 12 SERVINGS.

*If using self-rising flour, omit salt.

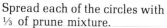

Spread each of the circles with ⅓ of prune mixture.

Cut each of the circles into 12 wedges with knife.

Roll up each wedge, beginning at the rounded side.

Place on a baking sheet and curve to form crescents.

Glazed Pumpkin Crescents

1 package active dry yeast
1 cup warm water (105 to 115°)
1 cup canned pumpkin
½ cup shortening
1 egg
⅓ cup packed brown sugar
1½ teaspoons salt
5 to 6 cups all-purpose flour*
1 cup pitted prunes, chopped
¼ cup water
   Butter or margarine, softened
   Spice Glaze (below)

Dissolve yeast in 1 cup warm water in large bowl. Stir in pumpkin, shortening, egg, brown sugar, salt and 3 cups of the flour; beat thoroughly. Stir in enough remaining flour to make dough easy to handle. Turn dough onto lightly floured surface; knead until smooth and elastic, about 5 minutes. Place in greased bowl; turn greased side up. Cover; let rise in warm place until double, about 1½ hours.

Heat prunes and ¼ cup water until thickened, about 5 minutes. Punch down dough; divide into 3 parts. Roll each part into 12-inch circle. Spread with prune mixture. Cut into 12 wedges. Roll up each wedge, beginning at rounded side. Place with points underneath on greased baking sheet; curve to form crescents. Brush with butter. Let rise until double, about 1 hour. Heat oven to 400°. Bake until golden brown, 15 to 20 minutes. Spread with Spice Glaze. 3 DOZEN CRESCENTS.

*If using self-rising flour, omit salt.

SPICE GLAZE

Mix 1½ cups powdered sugar, ½ teaspoon pumpkin pie spice and 1 to 2 tablespoons orange juice until smooth and of desired consistency.

Sweet Potato Doughnuts

1 cup mashed vacuum-pack sweet potatoes
1 cup water
¾ cup shortening
½ cup granulated sugar
1 tablespoon salt
1 package active dry yeast
¾ cup warm water (105 to 115°)
2 eggs
2 tablespoons grated orange peel
1 teaspoon ground nutmeg
6 to 7 cups all-purpose flour*
    Vegetable oil
4 cups powdered sugar
⅔ cup boiling water

Mix potatoes, 1 cup water, the shortening, granulated sugar and salt in large bowl. Dissolve yeast in ¾ cup warm water; stir into potato mixture. Stir in eggs, peel, nutmeg and enough flour to make dough easy to handle. Turn dough onto floured surface; knead until smooth and elastic, 5 to 8 minutes (see note). Place in greased bowl; turn greased side up. Cover; let rise until double, 1 to 1½ hours.

Divide dough in half. Pat each half ¾ inch thick. Cut with floured 2½-inch doughnut cutter; let rise until double, about 1 hour. Heat oil (2 to 3 inches) to 375°. Fry doughnuts until golden, 1½ to 2½ minutes on each side; drain.

Mix powdered sugar and ⅔ cup water. Dip doughnuts into sugar mixture 2 times. Store covered at room temperature.
ABOUT 2½ DOZEN DOUGHNUTS.

*If using self-rising flour, omit salt.

Note: Dough can be stored in refrigerator up to 3 days. Refrigerate in greased bowl immediately after kneading. Grease top of dough generously and cover with damp towel. If dough rises in refrigerator, punch down and re-cover with damp towel.

Turn dough greased side up in bowl. Cover and let rise.

Divide dough in half and pat each half ¾ inch thick.

Cut with floured doughnut cutter, then let rise again.

Fry until golden, 1½ to 2½ minutes on each side.

Fruited Lemon Loaf

Beat in flour, baking powder and salt alternately with milk on low speed until smooth.

Stir in the candied cherries, pineapple and pecans. Pour into loaf pan and bake.

⅔ cup granulated sugar
½ cup butter or margarine, softened
¼ cup shortening
2 eggs
1 tablespoon grated lemon peel
½ teaspoon vanilla
2 cups all-purpose flour*
1½ teaspoons baking powder
½ teaspoon salt
⅔ cup milk
1 cup candied red and green cherries, cut in half
1 cup cut-up glazed pineapple
¾ cup pecan or walnut halves
½ cup powdered sugar
1 to 2 tablespoons lemon juice

Heat oven to 350°. Grease and flour loaf pan, 9x5x3 inches. Beat granulated sugar, butter, shortening, eggs, lemon peel and vanilla in large mixer bowl on low speed 30 seconds, scraping bowl constantly. Beat on high speed until light and fluffy, about 2 minutes, scraping bowl occasionally.

Beat in flour, baking powder and salt alternately with milk on low speed until smooth, about 2 minutes. Stir in cherries, pineapple and pecans. Pour into pan. Bake until wooden pick inserted in center comes out clean, 1 hour 5 minutes to 1 hour 15 minutes.

Remove cake from pan; cool on wire rack. Wrap and refrigerate at least 24 hours. Mix powdered sugar and lemon juice until smooth and of desired consistency; spread over top of loaf.

*If using self-rising flour, omit baking powder and salt.

Orange-Pecan Tea Loaf

⅔ cup water
    Peel of 3 medium oranges, cut into ½-inch
        pieces (about 1½ cups)
¾ cup sugar
2 cups all-purpose flour
⅔ cup sugar
⅔ cup milk
1 tablespoon plus 1 teaspoon vegetable oil
2 teaspoons baking powder
1 egg
½ teaspoon salt
⅔ cup finely chopped pecans

Heat oven to 325°. Grease loaf pan, 9x5x3 inches. Place water and orange peel in blender container. Cover and blend on medium speed until finely chopped, about 1 minute. Mix orange peel mixture and ¾ cup sugar in 1-quart saucepan. Heat to boiling. Boil and stir until consistency of thick applesauce, 10 to 12 minutes. (Mixture should measure about ¾ cup after cooking.) Cool.

Beat orange mixture and remaining ingredients in large mixer bowl on medium speed, scraping bowl constantly, 1 minute; pour into pan. Bake until wooden pick inserted in center comes out clean, 50 to 60 minutes. Cool in pan 10 minutes; remove from pan. Cool completely before slicing.

Blend water and cut-up peel until finely chopped, 1 minute.

Stir peel mixture and sugar in saucepan and heat to boiling.

Boil and stir until it is the consistency of thick applesauce.

Beat orange mixture and remaining ingredients 1 minute.

Zucchini Bread

Coarsely shred enough zucchini to measure 4 cups.

Grease generously the bottoms only of 2 loaf pans.

Divide batter evenly between pans; level with spatula.

Bake until pick inserted in center comes out clean.

  4 **cups coarsely shredded zucchini (see note)**
  3 **cups all-purpose flour***
2½ **cups sugar**
1¼ **cups vegetable oil**
  4 **eggs, beaten**
  1 **tablespoon plus 1 teaspoon vanilla**
  1 **tablespoon ground cinnamon**
1½ **teaspoons salt**
1½ **teaspoons baking soda**
  ½ **teaspoon baking powder**
  1 **cup chopped nuts (optional)**

Heat oven to 325°. Grease generously bottoms only of 2 loaf pans, 9x5x3 inches. Blend all ingredients on low speed 1 minute, scraping bowl constantly. Beat on medium speed 1 minute. Pour into pans. Bake until wooden pick inserted in center comes out clean, 50 minutes to 1 hour. Cool 10 minutes; remove from pans. Cool completely.   2 LOAVES.

*If using self-rising flour, omit salt, baking soda and baking powder.

Note: Do not shred zucchini in blender.

Nut Bread Mix

9 cups all-purpose flour*
¼ cup baking powder
1 tablespoon salt
1 cup shortening

Mix flour, baking powder and salt. Cut in shortening completely until particles are size of coarse cornmeal. Refrigerate in airtight container up to 1 month.   **10 CUPS MIX.**

*If using self-rising flour, omit baking powder and salt.

Nut Bread

3 cups Nut Bread Mix (above)
1½ cups milk
1 cup sugar
1 egg
1 cup chopped walnuts

Heat oven to 350°. Grease bottom of loaf pan, 9x5x3 inches. Stir Nut Bread Mix, milk, sugar and egg until mix is moistened. Stir in walnuts; pour into pan. Bake until wooden pick inserted in center comes out clean, 55 minutes to 1 hour. Remove from pan; cool completely. Wrap in plastic wrap or aluminum foil; let stand at room temperature or refrigerate at least 8 hours for easier cutting.

Peanut Bread

3 cups Nut Bread Mix (left)
1¾ cups milk
1 cup sugar
1 cup peanut butter
1 egg
1 cup chopped salted peanuts

Heat oven to 350°. Grease bottom of loaf pan, 9x5x3 inches. Stir Nut Bread Mix, milk, sugar, peanut butter and egg until mix is moistened. Stir in peanuts; pour into pan. Bake until wooden pick inserted in center comes out clean, 1 hour to 1 hour 10 minutes. Remove from pan; cool completely. Wrap in plastic wrap or aluminum foil; let stand at least 8 hours for easier cutting.

Banana Bread

3 cups Nut Bread Mix (left)
1 cup sugar
1 cup mashed ripe bananas (2 to 3 medium)
1 cup milk
1 egg
1 cup chopped walnuts

Heat oven to 350°. Grease bottom of loaf pan, 9x5x3 inches. Stir Nut Bread Mix, sugar, bananas, milk and egg until mix is moistened. Stir in walnuts; pour into pan. Bake until wooden pick inserted in center comes out clean, 1 hour to 1 hour 5 minutes. Remove from pan; cool completely. Wrap in plastic wrap or aluminum foil; let stand at least 8 hours for easier cutting.

Molasses Corn Bread

Grease bundt cake pan generously with pastry brush.

Place all ingredients except Lemon Whip in bowl; beat.

Bake until a pick inserted in center comes out clean.

Cool on rack 10 minutes before removing from pan.

  2 cups all-purpose flour*
1¼ cups beer or water
  1 cup cornmeal
  ½ cup sugar
  ½ cup dark molasses
  3 tablespoons vegetable oil
  1 teaspoon salt
  1 teaspoon baking soda
     Lemon Whip or Cream Cheese Topping
     (below)

Heat oven to 350°. Grease generously 6-cup bundt cake pan or 6½-cup ring mold. Beat all ingredients except Lemon Whip in large mixer bowl on low speed until blended. Beat 2 minutes on medium speed, scraping bowl occasionally. Pour batter into pan. Bake until wooden pick inserted in center comes out clean, 45 to 50 minutes.

Cool corn bread 10 minutes. Remove from pan. Serve warm with Lemon Whip. (Or cool completely and spread slices with Cream Cheese Topping.)

*If using self-rising flour, omit salt and reduce baking soda to ½ teaspoon.

LEMON WHIP
Mix 2 cups frozen whipped topping, thawed, and ¼ cup frozen lemonade concentrate, thawed.

CREAM CHEESE TOPPING
  1 package (8 ounces) cream cheese, softened
  ⅓ cup dairy sour cream
  3 tablespoons sugar
  1 tablespoon grated orange peel

Mix cheese, sour cream, sugar and orange peel until blended. Refrigerate.

Mexican Corn Bread

1 egg
⅔ cup milk
¼ cup vegetable oil
1 can (4 ounces) chopped chilies, rinsed and
    drained
1 can (8¾ ounces) whole kernel corn
1 cup shredded sharp Cheddar cheese (about
    4 ounces)
1 cup cornmeal
1 cup all-purpose flour*
1 tablespoon plus 1 teaspoon baking powder
1 tablespoon sugar (optional)
1 teaspoon salt

Heat oven to 400°. Grease baking pan, 9x9x2 inches. Mix egg, milk and oil in medium bowl. Add chilies, corn (with liquid) and remaining ingredients to egg mixture; beat 1 minute. Spread evenly in pan.

Bake until golden brown, 35 to 40 minutes. Serve warm. 9 TO 12 SERVINGS.

*If using self-rising flour, reduce baking powder to 2 teaspoons and omit salt.

Add the rinsed and drained chilies to the egg mixture.

Spread the corn bread batter evenly in a greased pan.

Corn Bread Mix

4 cups all-purpose flour*
4 cups yellow cornmeal
1¾ cups nonfat dry milk
⅓ cup baking powder
2 teaspoons salt
1¾ cups shortening

Mix flour, cornmeal, dry milk, baking powder and salt. Cut in shortening completely. Refrigerate in airtight container up to 1 month.　**12** CUPS MIX.

*If using self-rising flour, reduce baking powder to 2 tablespoons plus 1½ teaspoons and omit salt.

Corn Bread

4 cups Corn Bread Mix (above)
1⅓ cups water
⅓ cup sugar
1 egg

Heat oven to 425°. Grease baking pan, 9x9x2 inches. Stir Corn Bread Mix, water, sugar and egg just until mix is moistened. (Batter will be lumpy.) Pour batter into pan. Bake until wooden pick inserted in center comes out clean, 20 to 25 minutes.　**9** SERVINGS.

Whole Wheat Corn Bread

2 cups Corn Bread Mix (left)
1 cup whole wheat flour
⅓ cup sugar
1 teaspoon baking powder
1¼ cups water
⅓ cup dark molasses
1 egg
　Orange Butter (below)

Heat oven to 350°. Grease bottom of loaf pan, 9x5x3 inches. Stir all ingredients except Orange Butter until mix and flour are moistened; pour into pan. Bake until wooden pick inserted in center comes out clean, 50 minutes to 1 hour. Remove from pan; cool slightly on wire rack. Serve warm with Orange Butter.

ORANGE BUTTER
½ cup butter or margarine, softened
2 tablespoons powdered sugar
¼ cup light corn syrup
2 teaspoons grated orange peel

Beat butter and sugar in small mixer bowl until light and fluffy. Beat in corn syrup gradually. Stir in orange peel.

Boston Brown Bread

2 cups Corn Bread Mix (page 232)
2 cups buttermilk
1 cup graham flour
1 cup seedless raisins or currants
¾ cup dark molasses
1½ teaspoons baking soda
   Whipped Cream Sauce (below)

Grease and flour four 1-pound cans. Mix all ingredients except Whipped Cream Sauce; divide batter among cans. Cover with double thickness aluminum foil; secure foil with string.

Place cans on rack in Dutch oven; pour boiling water into Dutch oven to depth of 1 inch. Cover Dutch oven; keep water boiling over low heat to steam bread until wooden pick inserted in center comes out clean, about 2 hours. (If necessary, add boiling water during steaming.)

Remove foil; cool bread in cans on wire rack 20 minutes. Remove bottoms of cans; push bread through. Serve with Whipped Cream Sauce.   4 LOAVES.

WHIPPED CREAM SAUCE
1 cup chilled whipping cream
1 cup powdered sugar
1 teaspoon vanilla

Beat whipping cream, sugar and vanilla in chilled bowl until stiff. Serve immediately or refrigerate up to 2 hours.

You can use 1-pound fruit or vegetable (not coffee) cans.

After cooling, remove bottoms of cans; push bread through.

Pear Coffee Cake

Cut the unpared pears into fourths; core and chop.

Toss the pears, nuts, sugar and pumpkin pie spice.

Spread pear mixture to within ½ inch of edges; roll up.

Place roll seam side down in greased loaf pan and bake.

2 medium pears, cored and chopped (about 1½ cups)
½ cup chopped nuts
⅓ cup granulated sugar
1 teaspoon pumpkin pie spice
3 cups biscuit baking mix
2 eggs, beaten
¼ cup butter or margarine, melted
¼ cup milk
½ cup powdered sugar
2 to 3 teaspoons milk

Heat oven to 350°. Grease loaf pan, 9x5x3 inches. Toss pears, nuts, granulated sugar and pumpkin pie spice. Mix baking mix, eggs, butter and ¼ cup milk. Beat 20 strokes. Turn onto lightly floured surface; knead 8 to 10 times.

Roll into rectangle, 13x9 inches. Spread pear mixture to within ½ inch of edges of rectangle. Beginning at narrow side, roll up as for jelly roll. Pinch edges into roll. Place roll seam side down in pan. Bake 1 hour.

Remove from pan immediately. Cool slightly. Mix powdered sugar and 2 to 3 teaspoons milk until smooth and of desired consistency; drizzle over warm loaf.

Easy Valentine Strudels

½ cup butter or margarine, softened
2 cups all-purpose flour*
½ teaspoon salt
1 cup dairy sour cream
3 tablespoons butter or margarine, melted
Cherry Filling (below)
Pink Glaze (below)

Cut butter into flour and salt with pastry blender. Stir in sour cream until a soft dough forms. Wrap and refrigerate at least 2 hours.

Heat oven to 350°. Divide dough into 3 parts. Roll 1 part dough into rectangle, 15x10 inches, on lightly floured cloth-covered board. (Refrigerate remaining dough.)

Brush butter lengthwise over about ⅔ of rectangle. Gently spread ⅓ of the Cherry Filling over butter. Roll up tightly, beginning with fruit side. Place on greased baking sheet, bringing ends together to make heart shape as pictured. Repeat with remaining 2 parts dough.

Bake until light golden brown, about 40 minutes. Cool 15 minutes; drizzle with Pink Glaze.   3 STRUDELS.

*Do not use self-rising flour in this recipe.

CHERRY FILLING

Mix 1 jar (12 ounces) cherry preserves, ¼ cup orange marmalade, 2 cups thinly sliced almonds and 1 cup golden raisins.

PINK GLAZE

Mix 1 cup powdered sugar, 1 to 2 tablespoons milk, 1 tablespoon butter or margarine, softened, ½ teaspoon almond extract and 1 drop red food color.

Divide dough into 3 equal portions.

Roll out each part into a rectangle.

Brush butter over ⅔ of rolled dough.

Spread the strudel filling over butter.

Roll dough, beginning at fruit side.

Pinch the ends and shape into hearts.

Cherry Brunch Muffins

To make 24 muffins, beat the eggs in separate bowls.

Add milk, oil and the cherry syrup to each bowl; stir.

Measure the dry ingredients in two separate portions.

Stir in dry ingredients and cherries just before baking.

1 egg
¾ cup milk
¼ cup vegetable oil
3 tablespoons maraschino cherry syrup
2 cups all-purpose flour*
¼ cup sugar
¼ cup chopped maraschino cherries
3 teaspoons baking powder
1 teaspoon salt
2 tablespoons sugar
2 tablespoons chopped almonds

Heat oven to 375°. Grease bottoms of 12 medium muffin cups or line with paper baking cups. Beat egg; stir in milk, oil and cherry syrup. Mix in flour, ¼ cup sugar, the cherries, baking powder and salt just until flour is moistened.

Fill muffin cups ⅔ full. Mix 2 tablespoons sugar and the almonds; sprinkle over batter in cups. Bake 25 minutes. 12 MUFFINS.

*If using self-rising flour, omit baking powder and salt.

Three-Day Bran Muffins

2 cups whole bran cereal
2 cups buttermilk
2 eggs
½ cup vegetable oil
2 cups all-purpose flour*
⅔ cup packed brown sugar
2 teaspoons baking powder
2 teaspoons baking soda
1 teaspoon salt

Grease bottoms only of the desired number of muffin cups.

Use an ice-cream scoop to fill the muffin cups ⅔ full.

Mix cereal and buttermilk; let stand until buttermilk is absorbed, about 3 minutes. Beat in eggs and oil. Add remaining ingredients; mix until flour is moistened. Cover tightly and refrigerate up to 3 days. (When you want hot muffins, bake as many as you need.)

■**30 minutes before serving**, heat oven to 400°. Grease bottoms of medium muffin cups. Fill muffin cups ⅔ full. Bake until light brown, 15 to 20 minutes. Remove from muffin pan immediately.   24 MUFFINS.

*If using self-rising flour, omit baking powder and salt.

Raisin Muffins: Fill muffin cups ½ full. Sprinkle 1 teaspoon raisins over batter in each cup; add enough batter to fill cups ⅔ full.

Sugar Crunch Muffins: Fill muffin cups ⅔ full. Mix 2 tablespoons granulated sugar and 1 teaspoon finely grated orange or lemon peel. Sprinkle over batter.

Surprise Muffins: Fill muffin cups ½ full. Drop 1 teaspoon apricot preserves or orange marmalade in center of each; add batter to fill cups ⅔ full.

Cut butter into flour-sugar mixture; stir in milk and egg until the dough forms a ball.

Roll half of dough into rectangle; place on baking sheet. Repeat with remaining dough.

Spread the sugar-raisin filling down centers of rectangles.

Bring long edges of dough together; seal securely.

Sugar-Nut Sticks

2 cups all-purpose flour*
1 tablespoon sugar
¾ cup butter or margarine, softened
¼ cup milk
1 egg, beaten
½ cup sugar
¼ cup butter or margarine, softened
¼ cup raisins
¼ cup chopped nuts
1 teaspoon almond extract
   Glaze (below)

Mix flour and 1 tablespoon sugar. Cut in ¾ cup butter until particles are the size of small peas. Stir in milk and egg until dough forms a ball and cleans side of bowl. Divide dough in half. Roll half of dough into rectangle, 12x4 inches, on lightly floured board. Place on ungreased baking sheet. Repeat with remaining dough.

Heat oven to 350°. Mix ½ cup sugar, ¼ cup butter, the raisins, nuts and extract. Spread half of the sugar mixture lengthwise down center of each rectangle. Bring long edges of dough together; seal securely. Bake 30 minutes. Cool slightly; drizzle with Glaze. Cut crosswise into 1-inch sticks.   24 STICKS.

*Do not use self-rising flour in this recipe.

GLAZE

Mix ½ cup powdered sugar and 1 tablespoon water until smooth.

Doughnut Triangles

Vegetable oil
1½ cups Nut Bread Mix (page 229)
½ cup granulated sugar
¼ cup milk
1 egg
¼ teaspoon ground cinnamon
⅛ teaspoon ground nutmeg
Vanilla Glaze (below)

Heat oil (2 to 3 inches) to 400° in 2-quart saucepan or deep fat fryer. Stir all ingredients except Vanilla Glaze until mix is moistened and dough almost cleans side of bowl. Turn dough onto well-floured cloth-covered board; roll around lightly to coat with flour. Roll dough into a 10-inch square; cut into 2½-inch squares with floured knife. Cut squares diagonally in half.

Fry triangles, about 3 at a time, in hot oil until golden brown on both sides, about 1 minute. Remove with slotted spoon; drain on paper towels. Cool; drizzle with Vanilla Glaze.   32 TRIANGLES.

VANILLA GLAZE

Mix 1 cup powdered sugar and ½ teaspoon vanilla. Stir in 1 to 2 tablespoons hot water, 1 tablespoon at a time, until smooth and of desired consistency.

Roll dough around lightly to coat with flour.

Cut into squares; cut squares diagonally in half.

Maple-Coconut Bread

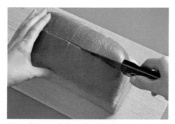

Cut bread loaf almost to bottom in 2-inch squares.

Heat butter, honey and syrup until butter is melted.

Pour ¼ cup of the honey mixture between cuts.

Add coconut mixture, then the remaining honey mixture.

1 loaf (1 pound) unsliced white bread
½ cup butter or margarine
¼ cup honey
¼ cup maple-flavored syrup
⅓ cup flaked coconut
⅓ cup slightly crushed whole wheat flake
    cereal
⅓ cup packed brown sugar

Heat oven to 350°. Cut bread almost to bottom in 2-inch squares; place on aluminum foil on baking sheet. Turn up edges of foil.

Heat butter, honey and syrup over low heat, stirring constantly, until butter is melted. Pour ¼ cup of the honey mixture between cuts in loaf. Mix coconut, cereal and brown sugar; sprinkle between cuts and over loaf. Drizzle with remaining honey mixture. Bake until top is light brown, about 20 minutes. Serve warm.

Desserts

Stuffed Baked Apples

Remove core from blossom end of each apple, leaving about ¼ inch at the stem end.

Pare the upper half of each apple to prevent the peel from splitting while apples bake.

6 medium baking apples
6 tablespoons cut-up dates or raisins
6 tablespoons honey
  Whipped Brandy Sauce (below)

Heat oven to 375°. Remove core from blossom end of each apple, leaving about ¼ inch at stem end. Remove 1-inch strip of peel around middle of each apple or pare upper half as pictured to prevent peel from splitting. Place apples stem ends down in ungreased baking dish, 9x9x2 inches. Spoon about 1 tablespoon dates and 1 tablespoon honey into center of each apple. Pour ¼ inch water into baking dish.

Bake uncovered until apples are tender when pierced with fork, 45 to 50 minutes, spooning syrup in baking dish onto apples several times during baking. (Baking time will vary with size and variety of apples.) Serve warm or cool with Whipped Brandy Sauce.   6 SERVINGS.

WHIPPED BRANDY SAUCE
  1 cup chilled whipping cream
¼ cup sugar
  1 teaspoon brandy flavoring

Beat whipping cream, sugar and flavoring in chilled small mixer bowl until stiff.

Cinnamon-Apple Tart

¾ cup cinnamon candies
2 tablespoons water
2 tablespoons light corn syrup
2 tablespoons packed brown sugar
2 tablespoons butter or margarine
5 medium apples (such as Rhode Island, Greening or Winesap), pared and thinly sliced (about 5 cups)
1 package (11 ounces) pie crust mix or sticks
½ cup chilled whipping cream (optional)

Heat cinnamon candies, water and corn syrup to boiling; reduce heat. Simmer uncovered, stirring occasionally, until candies are partially dissolved, about 10 minutes. Pour cinnamon mixture into ungreased round layer pan, 9x1½ inches. Cool.

Heat brown sugar and butter in 10-inch skillet, stirring constantly, until sugar is dissolved. Add apples. Cook and stir until apples are crisp-tender, 3 to 4 minutes. Cool.

Heat oven to 425°. Arrange apples on cinnamon mixture in pan. Prepare pastry for One-Crust Pie as directed on pie crust mix package. Roll pastry into 9-inch circle on floured cloth-covered board. Place pastry circle on apples. Bake until pastry is light golden brown, 40 to 45 minutes.

Cool about 1 hour. Invert on serving plate. Beat whipping cream in chilled small mixer bowl until stiff. Cut tart into wedges; top with whipped cream.   8 TO 10 SERVINGS.

Simmer candy mixture until the candies are partially dissolved; pour into pan. Cook and stir the apples just until crisp-tender.

Arrange apples on cinnamon mixture, placing outer edges down. Place pastry circle on apples. After baking, cool and invert.

Banana Roll-Ups

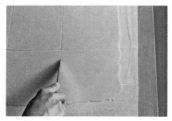

Roll pastry into a rectangle; cut rectangle into 6 squares.

Place banana half 1 inch from end of each square.

Sprinkle brown sugar mixture evenly over banana halves.

Roll up pastry; moisten edges and press to seal securely.

1 package (11 ounces) pie crust sticks
½ cup packed brown sugar
½ teaspoon ground mace
3 medium bananas
   Orange Topping (below)

Heat oven to 450°. Prepare 1 pie crust stick as directed on package except—roll pastry into rectangle, 15x10 inches, on floured cloth-covered board. Cut rectangle into 6 squares.

Mix brown sugar and mace. Cut bananas crosswise in half. Place 1 banana half 1 inch from end of each square; sprinkle brown sugar mixture evenly over bananas. Roll up pastry; moisten edges and press to seal. Place on ungreased baking sheet. Bake until golden brown, 10 to 12 minutes. Serve warm with Orange Topping.   6 SERVINGS.

ORANGE TOPPING
½ cup chilled whipping cream
2 tablespoons packed brown sugar
¼ teaspoon orange flavoring
1 can (11 ounces) mandarin orange
   segments, drained

Beat whipping cream, brown sugar and flavoring in chilled small mixer bowl until soft peaks form. Fold in orange segments.

Flaming Blueberry Sundaes

Homemade Ice Milk (below)
½ cup sugar-free cherry-flavored carbonated
    beverage
¼ cup low-calorie cherry jelly
2 cups blueberries
1 teaspoon lemon juice
¼ cup rum

Prepare Homemade Ice Milk; freeze until firm, at least 8 hours.

Heat carbonated beverage and jelly in 2-quart saucepan, stirring constantly, until jelly is melted and mixture is smooth. Remove from heat. Stir in blueberries and lemon juice; pour into fondue pot.

Heat rum just until warm. Ignite rum and pour on blueberries. Serve over scoops of Homemade Ice Milk.
8 SERVINGS.

HOMEMADE ICE MILK
2 teaspoons unflavored gelatin
2 tablespoons cold water
⅔ cup evaporated skim milk, chilled
¼ cup sugar
1 teaspoon vanilla

Sprinkle gelatin on cold water in saucepan to soften; stir over low heat until gelatin is dissolved. Beat milk, sugar and vanilla in chilled small mixer bowl on high speed until very thick and fluffy, about 2 minutes. Beat in gelatin gradually until mixture is very stiff, about 3 minutes; pour into ice cube tray.

Stir blueberries and lemon juice into the hot sauce.

Heat rum just until warm. Ignite; pour on blueberries.

Arrange split ladyfingers in serving bowl, using as many as needed to line bowl.

Layer vanilla pudding, the blueberries and the remaining ladyfingers in bowl.

Fresh Berry Trifle

1 package (3⅛ ounces) vanilla pudding
  and pie filling
1 teaspoon rum flavoring
12 ladyfingers*
2 cups fresh blueberries or strawberries
1 cup chilled whipping cream
¼ cup packed brown sugar
2 tablespoons toasted sliced almonds

Prepare pudding and pie filling as directed on package for pudding. Cover surface of pudding with plastic wrap to prevent skin from forming. Cool to room temperature; stir in flavoring. Split ladyfingers lengthwise; arrange in 2-quart glass serving bowl, using as many as needed to line bowl. Layer pudding, blueberries and remaining ladyfingers in bowl.

Beat whipping cream and brown sugar in chilled small mixer bowl until stiff. Spread over trifle; sprinkle with almonds. Refrigerate at least 1 hour. To serve, spoon into dessert dishes.   8 TO 10 SERVINGS.

* ½ lemon chiffon or angel food cake, torn into 1-inch pieces (4 to 5 cups), or eight ½-inch slices pound cake can be substituted for the ladyfingers.

Berry Shortcakes

1 pint strawberries, cut in half
1 pint blueberries
¼ cup sugar
2⅓ cups biscuit baking mix
3 tablespoons sugar
⅔ cup half-and-half
Half-and-half
Vanilla ice cream, slightly softened

Heat oven to 450°. Mix strawberries, blueberries and ¼ cup sugar; cover and refrigerate.

Stir baking mix, 3 tablespoons sugar and ⅔ cup half-and-half until a soft dough forms. Gently smooth dough into ball on floured cloth-covered board. Knead 8 to 10 times. Roll dough ½ inch thick. Cut with floured 3-inch round or 4-inch star-shaped cutter or sharp knife; place on un-greased baking sheet. Brush tops with half-and-half. Bake until light brown, about 10 minutes.

Split shortcakes. Mound ice cream on bottom halves. Spoon half of the berry mixture onto ice cream. Top with remaining shortcake halves and berry mixture.

8 SERVINGS.

Mound softened ice cream, then fruit on the bottom half of each split shortcake.

Top the assembled shortcakes with additional spoonfuls of the sweetened berries.

Raspberry Revel Meringue

Meringue Shell (below)
2 packages (10 ounces each) frozen
   raspberries, thawed and drained (reserve
   syrup)
3 tablespoons cornstarch
1 cup chilled whipping cream
1 package (3 ounces) cream cheese, softened
½ cup sugar
½ teaspoon vanilla
1 cup miniature marshmallows

Spread half (about 2 cups) of the meringue mixture in 8-inch circle, building up the side.

Drop remaining meringue mixture by rounded teaspoonfuls on edge, making small peaks.

Bake Meringue Shell. Mix ¼ cup of the reserved raspberry syrup and the cornstarch in saucepan. Add raspberries and remaining syrup. Heat to boiling, stirring constantly. Boil and stir 1 minute. Cool to room temperature.

Beat whipping cream in chilled bowl until stiff. Blend cheese, sugar and vanilla. Fold cheese mixture and marshmallows into whipped cream. Spread ⅓ of the raspberry mixture in Meringue Shell. Spread ½ of the cheese mixture over raspberry layer. Repeat, using ½ of the remaining raspberry mixture, the remaining cheese mixture and remaining raspberry mixture. Refrigerate at least 2 hours but no longer than 24 hours.   8 TO 10 SERVINGS.

MERINGUE SHELL

Heat oven to 250°. Cover baking sheet with brown paper. Beat 4 egg whites and ¼ teaspoon cream of tartar in small mixer bowl until foamy. Beat in 1 cup sugar, 1 tablespoon at a time; continue beating until stiff and glossy, about 4 minutes. Spread half of the meringue mixture in 8-inch circle on brown paper, building up side. Drop remaining meringue mixture by rounded teaspoonfuls on edge of circle, making small peaks. Bake 1½ hours. Turn off oven; leave meringue in oven with door closed 1 hour. Remove from oven; cool.

French Strawberry Dessert

1¼ cups biscuit baking mix
¼ cup sugar
1 tablespoon grated orange peel
¼ cup butter or margarine, softened
1 pint fresh strawberries, cut in half
½ cup orange juice
¼ cup water
2 tablespoons sugar
1 tablespoon cornstarch
½ cup chilled whipping cream
2 tablespoons sugar

Heat oven to 400°. Mix baking mix, ¼ cup sugar and the orange peel. Cut in butter until mixture resembles coarse cornmeal. Press mixture in ungreased round layer pan, 9x1½ inches. Bake until light brown, 10 to 12 minutes. Cool about 30 minutes.

Invert crust on serving plate. Arrange strawberries on crust. Mix orange juice, water, 2 tablespoons sugar and the cornstarch in saucepan. Heat to boiling, stirring constantly. Boil and stir 1 minute. Cool completely. Pour orange glaze on strawberries. Refrigerate 1 hour.

Beat whipping cream and 2 tablespoons sugar until stiff. Garnish with whipped cream.   8 TO 10 SERVINGS.

Cut in butter until mixture resembles coarse cornmeal.

Press mixture in an ungreased round layer pan and bake.

Arrange the strawberry halves on the cooled baked crust.

Pour the orange glaze evenly on the strawberry halves.

Sprinkle brown sugar over the buttered baking sheet.

Remove broiled and cooled praline crunch with spatula.

Alternate layers of fruit, rum custard sauce and crunch.

For the children, top fruit with plain custard sauce.

Fruit Praline Parfaits

1 package (3⅛ ounces) vanilla pudding and pie filling
1 cup half-and-half
¾ to 1 teaspoon rum flavoring
1 tablespoon butter or margarine, softened
⅓ cup packed brown sugar
2½ to 3 cups fruit (blueberries, strawberries, peaches or grapes)

Prepare pudding and pie filling as directed on package for pudding except—reduce milk to 1¼ cups and add half-and-half. Stir rum flavoring into pudding; cool as directed.

Spread butter on baking sheet, leaving 1½-inch margin on all sides. Sprinkle brown sugar over buttered area. Set oven control to broil and/or 550°. Broil sugar 3 to 4 inches from heat 1 to 2 minutes. (Watch closely—mixture burns easily.) Cool 2 to 3 minutes; remove with spatula and break into pieces. Alternate layers of fruit, rum custard sauce and praline crunch in 8 parfait glasses.   8 SERVINGS.

Especially For The Kids: Reserve ½ cup of the pudding and omit the rum. Alternate layers of fruit, reserved pudding and praline crunch in dessert dishes.

Fruit Parfaits

For each parfait, layer ⅓ cup sliced strawberries, ½ teaspoon orange-flavored liqueur, 1 spoonful frozen whipped topping, thawed, a few mandarin orange segments, ½ teaspoon orange-flavored liqueur and additional whipped topping in each parfait glass. Repeat if desired. Top with a strawberry.

Sparkling Fruit

¾ cup boiling water
1 package (3 ounces) peach- or
   orange-flavored gelatin
1¼ cups sweet white wine (sauterne,
   muscatel, Tokay)
1 medium banana, sliced
4 medium peaches, cut into eighths
1 pint strawberries or raspberries
1½ cups seedless green grapes
   Whipped topping
   Ground nutmeg

Pour boiling water on gelatin in bowl; stir until gelatin is dissolved. Stir in wine. Refrigerate until slightly thickened, about 1¼ hours.

Mound fruit in attractive arrangement in compote, shallow glass bowl or 9-inch pie plate. Pour gelatin mixture on fruit. Refrigerate until chilled. Spoon ring of whipped topping around edge; sprinkle topping with nutmeg.   8 SERVINGS.

Honey Grapes

1 pound seedless green grapes
¼ cup honey
3 tablespoons rum
3 small cantaloupes, chilled
½ cup dairy sour cream

Remove stems from grapes. Mix honey and rum; toss with grapes. Refrigerate 2 hours, stirring occasionally.

Cut cantaloupes lengthwise in half, using scalloped cut. Scoop out seeds. Toss grapes with sour cream; spoon into cantaloupes. Drizzle with remaining honey-rum mixture.
6 SERVINGS.

Mound the fruit attractively in a pretty compote.

Pour thickened gelatin-wine mixture on fruit.

Melon Parfaits

1 cup boiling water
1 envelope low-calorie lime-flavored gelatin
⅓ cup cold water
⅓ cup sweet white wine (sauterne or Tokay)
½ medium honeydew melon or cantaloupe,
   cut into balls (about 2 cups)
½ medium pineapple, cut into cubes (about
   2 cups)
1 medium orange, sectioned and membrane
   removed
1 cup strawberries, cut in half

Pour boiling water on gelatin in bowl; stir until gelatin is dissolved. Stir in cold water and wine. Pour into baking pan, 8x8x2 inches. Refrigerate until firm, about 2 hours.

Mix melon balls, pineapple cubes, orange sections and strawberry halves. Cover and refrigerate at least 1 hour. Beat gelatin with fork until frothy. Layer gelatin and fruit in 6 parfait glasses.   6 SERVINGS.

Stir water and wine into the gelatin mixture; refrigerate.

Mix the fruit for parfaits; cover. Refrigerate 1 hour.

Beat the chilled gelatin mixture with a fork until frothy.

Layer the gelatin and fruit in each of 6 parfait glasses.

Melon Ring

1 slice watermelon, 1½ inches thick
1 can (11 ounces) mandarin orange segments,
   chilled and drained
1 medium apple, cored and thinly sliced
   Mint leaves

Cut melon from watermelon slice, leaving 1-inch rim. Cut melon into bite-size pieces; remove seeds. Place melon ring on serving plate. Mix melon pieces, orange segments and apple slices. Mound fruit in melon ring and on plate around ring. Garnish with mint leaves.   6 SERVINGS.

Peach-Plum Cobbler

1 cup sugar
3 tablespoons cornstarch
½ teaspoon ground cinnamon
3 cups sliced fresh red plums (about 10 to 12 large)
4 medium peaches or nectarines, peeled and sliced (about 3 cups)
1 cup all-purpose flour*
⅓ cup shortening
2 tablespoons sugar
1½ teaspoons baking powder
½ teaspoon salt
¼ cup milk
1 egg, slightly beaten
1 tablespoon sugar
Ice cream (optional)

Heat oven to 375°. Mix 1 cup sugar, the cornstarch and cinnamon in 3-quart saucepan. Stir in plums and peaches. Cook, stirring constantly, until mixture thickens and boils. Boil and stir 1 minute. Pour into ungreased baking dish, 8x8x2 inches, or 1½-quart casserole.

Mix flour, shortening, 2 tablespoons sugar, the baking powder and salt with pastry blender or fork until crumbly. Stir in milk and egg. Drop dough by spoonfuls onto hot fruit mixture; sprinkle with 1 tablespoon sugar. Bake until topping is golden brown, 25 to 30 minutes. Serve warm with ice cream.   9 SERVINGS.

*If using self-rising flour, omit baking powder and salt.

To peel peaches, dip into boiling water 20 to 30 seconds, then into cold water.

The peach skins will loosen and can be pulled off easily with a paring knife.

Dip hot rosette iron in batter just to top edge, being careful not to go over top.

Fry rosette until golden brown; immediately remove and invert on paper towel.

Peach Rosettes

Vegetable oil
1 egg
1 tablespoon sugar
½ teaspoon salt
½ cup all-purpose flour*
½ cup water or milk
1 tablespoon vegetable oil
⅓ cup sugar
½ teaspoon ground cinnamon
9 peaches, sliced
¼ cup sugar
Coffee Whipped Cream (below)

Heat oil (2 to 3 inches) to 400° in small deep saucepan. Beat egg, 1 tablespoon sugar and the salt in small deep bowl. Beat in flour, water and 1 tablespoon oil until smooth.

Heat rosette iron by placing in hot oil 1 minute. Tap excess oil from iron; dip hot iron in batter just to top edge, being careful not to go over top. Fry until golden brown, about 30 seconds. Immediately remove rosette, using fork if necessary; invert on paper towel to cool. (If rosette is not crisp, batter is too thick. Stir in small amount of water or milk.) Heat iron in hot oil before making each rosette. (If iron is not heated, batter will not stick to iron.)

Mix ⅓ cup sugar and the cinnamon. Dip rosettes in sugar mixture. Mix peaches and ¼ cup sugar. Serve rosettes with sweetened peaches and Coffee Whipped Cream. 18 ROSETTES.

*If using self-rising flour, omit salt.

COFFEE WHIPPED CREAM

Beat 1 cup chilled whipping cream, ¼ cup powdered sugar, 1 teaspoon instant coffee, ½ teaspoon vanilla and ⅛ teaspoon ground cardamom or ground cinnamon in chilled small mixer bowl.

Ruby Peaches

6 canned peach halves
1 cup sugar-free strawberry-flavored
   carbonated beverage
¼ cup low-calorie raspberry preserves
1 tablespoon cornstarch
6 tablespoons low-calorie whipped topping

Place 1 peach half cut side up in each of 6 dessert dishes. Heat remaining ingredients except topping to boiling, stirring constantly. Boil and stir 1 minute. Cool; top each peach half with 1 tablespoon whipped topping. Pour sauce on peach halves. Refrigerate 2 hours.   6 SERVINGS.

Meringue Pears

6 medium pears, pared
½ cup sugar-free strawberry-flavored
   carbonated beverage
3 egg whites
¼ teaspoon cream of tartar
¼ cup powdered sugar
2 teaspoons grated lemon peel
12 teaspoons low-calorie strawberry-flavored
   syrup

Heat oven to 350°. Cut pears lengthwise in half; place cut sides down in ungreased baking dish, 11¾x7½x1¾ inches. Pour beverage on pears. Bake uncovered 25 minutes.

Beat egg whites and cream of tartar in small mixer bowl until foamy. Beat in sugar and lemon peel; beat until stiff and glossy. Spoon meringue around pears; pour 1 teaspoon syrup on each. Reduce oven temperature to 300°. Bake until light brown, 16 minutes.   12 SERVINGS.

Pour the strawberry beverage around the pears; bake in a 350° oven.

Spoon the meringue around the pears. Add the syrup; bake in a 300° oven.

Spiced Pears

Cut pears lengthwise in half; insert cloves in halves.

Simmer pears in orange syrup, turning occasionally.

3 large pears, pared
12 whole cloves
½ cup sugar
⅔ cup orange juice
2 tablespoons lemon juice
1 stick cinnamon
1 large orange, peeled and thinly sliced
1 cup seedless green grapes

Cut pears lengthwise in half; insert 2 cloves in broad end of each pear half. Heat sugar, orange juice, lemon juice and cinnamon stick to boiling in 3-quart saucepan, stirring until sugar is dissolved; place pears in orange syrup. Simmer uncovered, turning occasionally, until tender, 10 to 15 minutes. Remove pears to serving dish; add orange slices and grapes. Pour orange syrup on fruit.   6 SERVINGS.

Rum Pineapple

1 medium pineapple, pared and cut into
    chunks
1 large orange, peeled, sectioned and cut up
⅓ cup packed brown sugar
¼ cup rum
2 tablespoons butter or margarine

Heat oven to 350°. Mix all ingredients in ungreased 1½-quart casserole. Cover and bake until hot and bubbly, about 30 minutes.   4 SERVINGS.

Pineapple Polynesian

1 quart vanilla ice cream
1½ cups flaked coconut
⅔ cup packed brown sugar
1 tablespoon cornstarch
½ cup butter or margarine
1 tablespoon lemon juice
2 teaspoons finely shredded orange peel
4 cups cut-up fresh pineapple (about 1 medium)
¼ cup rum or apricot brandy

Ahead of time, shape the ice cream into balls; roll balls in the coconut and freeze.

At the table, stir pineapple into the brown sugar mixture and heat until fruit is hot.

Shape ice cream into 6 to 8 balls as pictured and roll in coconut. Place on waxed paper-covered baking sheet and freeze.

Mix brown sugar and cornstarch in chafing dish or skillet; add butter, lemon juice and orange peel. Cook over medium heat, stirring constantly, until mixture thickens and boils. Boil and stir 1 minute. Stir in pineapple; heat until fruit is hot, about 2 minutes. Heat rum in small saucepan just until warm; ignite and pour flaming rum on pineapple. Stir; spoon over each serving of ice cream.
6 TO 8 SERVINGS.

Fresh Fruit Polynesian: Omit coconut. Substitute 4 cups cut-up or sliced fresh fruit for the pineapple. Choose from the following: strawberries and peaches, bananas and raspberries or pears and blueberries.

Pineapple Shortcake

Cut 1 pineapple slice into 4 pieces. Dip the pieces and the remaining slices in sugar.

Press the pineapple and cherries into shortcake dough. Sprinkle with nuts and bake.

2⅓ cups biscuit baking mix
½ cup milk
3 tablespoons sugar
3 tablespoons butter or margarine, melted
½ teaspoon ground nutmeg
1 can (20 ounces) pineapple slices, drained
⅓ cup sugar*
9 large maraschino cherries
½ cup chopped nuts
1 envelope (about 2 ounces) whipped topping mix

Heat oven to 400°. Grease baking sheet. Stir baking mix, milk, 3 tablespoons sugar, the butter and nutmeg until a soft dough forms. Turn dough onto baking sheet. Pat dough into rectangle, 12x9 inches, with floured hands. (Dough will be sticky.)

Cut 1 pineapple slice into 4 pieces. Dip pieces and remaining slices in ⅓ cup sugar. Press pineapple and cherries into shortcake dough as pictured. Sprinkle with nuts. Bake until light brown, about 20 minutes.

Prepare whipped topping as directed on package. Cut shortcake into rectangles. Top each rectangle with whipped topping.   9 SERVINGS.

*1 package (3 ounces) lemon- or lime-flavored gelatin can be substituted for ⅓ cup sugar.

Plum Pudding Cake

1 cup all-purpose flour*
¾ cup granulated sugar
2 teaspoons baking powder
¼ teaspoon salt
½ cup milk
3 tablespoons vegetable oil
2 cups sliced fresh red plums (7 to 8 large)
1 cup packed brown sugar
1 teaspoon ground cinnamon
1 cup boiling water
   Whipped cream (optional)

Heat oven to 350°. Mix flour, granulated sugar, baking powder and salt. Beat in milk and oil until smooth. Pour into ungreased baking pan, 8x8x2 inches. Top with plums. Mix brown sugar and cinnamon; sprinkle over plums. Pour boiling water on plums. Bake until wooden pick inserted in center comes out clean, 1 hour to 1 hour 10 minutes. Serve warm with whipped cream.   6 SERVINGS.

*If using self-rising flour, omit baking powder and salt.

Pour batter into baking pan.

Top batter with sliced plums.

Sprinkle with sugar mixture.

Pour boiling water on plums.

FRESH FRUIT PREPARATION

When paring apples and pears, pare as thinly as possible. (You don't want to cut away valuable nutrients.)

To loosen the skin of ripe peaches or apricots, first dip them in boiling water for 20 to 30 seconds, then into cold water—the skin will pucker and pull off easily.

You can prevent fruit from discoloring after it has been cut by dipping it in lemon, lime, orange or pineapple juice.

Spicy Pumpkin Squares

Press graham cracker crust in an ungreased baking pan.

Pour filling into crust; bake and cool. Spread with topping.

Graham Cracker Nut Crust (below)
1 can (16 ounces) pumpkin
1 can (13 ounces) evaporated milk
¾ cup sugar
2 eggs
1¾ teaspoons pumpkin pie spice*
1½ cups whipped topping
¾ cup miniature marshmallows
1 teaspoon grated orange peel

Heat oven to 350°. Prepare Graham Cracker Nut Crust. Beat pumpkin, milk, sugar, eggs and pumpkin pie spice until blended; pour into crust. Bake until knife inserted near center comes out clean, about 1 hour. Cool.

Mix whipped topping, marshmallows and orange peel; spread over filling. Refrigerate until serving time.
9 SERVINGS.

*1 teaspoon ground cinnamon, ½ teaspoon ground ginger and ¼ teaspoon ground cloves can be substituted for the pumpkin pie spice.

GRAHAM CRACKER NUT CRUST
½ cup graham cracker crumbs
¼ cup chopped nuts
¼ cup butter or margarine, softened
2 tablespoons sugar

Mix all ingredients; press in ungreased baking pan, 9x9x2 inches. Bake 15 minutes. Cool.

Deluxe Pumpkin Custards

2 eggs
1 can (16 ounces) pumpkin
1 cup half-and-half
¾ cup packed brown sugar
1 teaspoon pumpkin pie spice
½ teaspoon salt
   Crunchy Pecan Topping (below)
⅛ teaspoon rum flavoring
¼ cup frozen whipped topping, thawed

Heat oven to 350°. Beat eggs, pumpkin, half-and-half, brown sugar, pumpkin pie spice and salt until smooth. Pour into six 6-ounce custard cups. Place cups in baking pan, 13x9x2 inches; pour very hot water into pan to within ½ inch of tops of cups. Bake 20 minutes.

Prepare Crunchy Pecan Topping; sprinkle over custards. Bake until knife inserted halfway between center and edge comes out clean, 30 to 40 minutes. Remove custards from hot water immediately after baking. Just before serving, stir rum flavoring into whipped topping; serve over pecan-topped custards.   6 SERVINGS.

CRUNCHY PECAN TOPPING

Mix ¼ cup chopped pecans, ¼ cup packed brown sugar and 1 tablespoon butter or margarine, softened.

After filling the custard cups, carefully place them in a 13x9x2-inch baking pan.

To prevent spilling, pour hot water into the pan after placing it on the oven rack.

Pour cheesecake mixture into a 9-inch springform pan.

Remove the side of springform pan from the cheesecake.

Do-Ahead Lemon Cheesecake

1¼ cups graham cracker crumbs (about 16 squares)
  3 tablespoons butter or margarine, softened
  2 tablespoons sugar
  5 packages (8 ounces each) cream cheese, softened
1¾ cups sugar
  3 tablespoons flour
  2 to 3 teaspoons finely grated lemon peel
 ¼ teaspoon salt
  5 eggs
  2 egg yolks
 ¼ cup whipping cream

Heat oven to 350°. Mix crumbs, butter and 2 tablespoons sugar. Press mixture firmly and evenly in bottom of ungreased 9-inch springform pan. Bake 10 minutes. Cool.

Heat oven to 475°. Beat cream cheese, 1¾ cups sugar, the flour, lemon peel, salt and 2 of the eggs in large mixer bowl until smooth. Continue beating, adding remaining 3 eggs and the egg yolks, one at a time, until blended. Blend in whipping cream on low speed. Pour into pan. Bake 15 minutes. Reduce oven temperature to 200°. Bake 1 hour.

Turn off oven; leave cheesecake in oven 15 minutes. Remove from oven and cool completely. Loosen cheesecake from side of pan; remove side. Cover and refrigerate up to 10 days. For longer storage, wrap and label; freeze up to 3 weeks.

■1 hour before serving, unwrap cheesecake; thaw uncovered at room temperature. Serve with sweetened sliced strawberries.   20 TO 22 SERVINGS.

Butter Praline Cheesecake

1¼ cups graham cracker crumbs or chocolate
   wafer crumbs (about 16 square crackers
   or 18 wafers)
2 tablespoons granulated sugar
3 tablespoons butter or margarine, melted
3 packages (8 ounces each) cream cheese,
   softened
1 teaspoon vanilla
1 cup packed brown sugar
3 eggs
½ cup chilled whipping cream or 1 cup
   frozen whipped topping, thawed
   Chopped pecans or grated chocolate

To crush crackers easily, place them in a plastic bag and crush with a rolling pin.

Or use a blender: Break about 6 crackers at a time into container; cover and blend.

Heat oven to 350°. Mix crumbs and granulated sugar; stir in butter thoroughly. Press crumb mixture evenly in bottom of ungreased 9-inch springform pan or baking pan, 9x9x2 inches. Bake 10 minutes. Cool.

Reduce oven temperature to 325°. Beat cheese and vanilla in large mixer bowl. Beat in brown sugar gradually until fluffy. Beat in eggs, one at a time. Pour onto crumb mixture. Bake until center is firm, 1 to 1¼ hours. (A crack in top is typical.) Cool to room temperature.

Beat whipping cream in chilled small mixer bowl. Spread over cheesecake and sprinkle with pecans. Refrigerate until ready to serve. Loosen edge of cheesecake with knife before removing side of springform pan.   16 SERVINGS.

Chocolate Alaska Supreme

Spread 1 quart ice cream in each layer pan; freeze.

Alternate cake and ice-cream layers; return to freezer.

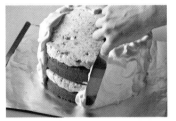

Quickly cover layers with meringue, sealing to foil.

Bake until meringue is light brown, 3 to 5 minutes.

1 package (18.5 ounces) devils food cake
   mix
2 quarts chocolate chip, chocolate revel or
   peppermint ice cream, slightly softened
6 egg whites
½ teaspoon cream of tartar
1 cup sugar
1 cup chocolate ice-cream topping
2 tablespoons coffee-flavored liqueur

Bake cake as directed on package for round layer pans, 9x1½ inches. Line 2 round layer pans, 9x1½ inches, with aluminum foil. Spread 1 quart ice cream in each pan. Freeze until very firm, at least 6 hours.

Cover baking sheet with aluminum foil. Place 1 cake layer on baking sheet. Place 1 ice-cream layer on cake. Top with second cake layer and second ice-cream layer; place in freezer while preparing meringue. (Ice cream must be very firm before it is covered with meringue.)

Move oven rack to lowest position. Heat oven to 500°. Beat egg whites and cream of tartar until foamy. Beat in sugar, 1 tablespoon at a time; continue beating until stiff and glossy. Do not underbeat. Completely cover cake and ice cream with meringue, sealing it to foil. Bake until meringue is light brown, 3 to 5 minutes.

Trim foil to edge of meringue; transfer cake to serving plate. Let stand 10 to 15 minutes before serving to make cutting easier.

Just before serving, heat topping and liqueur until warm, about 3 minutes; pour over each serving of Chocolate Alaska Supreme. Store any remaining dessert in freezer up to 24 hours.　16 SERVINGS.

Carnival Ice-Cream Cake

One 10-inch round angel food cake
1 envelope (.20 ounce) strawberry-flavored
   unsweetened soft drink mix
1 envelope (.21 ounce) orange-flavored
   unsweetened soft drink mix
1 envelope (.24 ounce) raspberry-flavored
   unsweetened soft drink mix
1 package (10 ounces) frozen sliced
   strawberries, thawed
½ gallon vanilla ice cream, slightly softened
1 package (10 ounces) frozen sliced peaches,
   thawed and cut up
1 package (10 ounces) frozen raspberries,
   thawed

Toss cake pieces with drink mix. Place layer of strawberry cake pieces, strawberries and ice cream in pan.

Repeat with orange cake pieces, peaches, ice cream, then raspberry cake pieces, raspberries and remaining ice cream.

Tear cake into bite-size pieces. Divide among 3 bowls. Sprinkle strawberry drink mix over cake in 1 bowl, orange over the second and raspberry over the third. Toss each lightly with fork until cake pieces are well coated with drink mix.

Line 10-inch tube pan with aluminum foil. Place strawberry cake pieces in pan; spoon strawberries (with liquid) onto cake. Spread ⅓ of the ice cream over strawberries. Repeat layers with orange cake pieces, peaches (with liquid), half of the remaining ice cream, the raspberry cake pieces, raspberries (with liquid) and remaining ice cream. Cover and freeze 24 hours.

About 2 hours before serving, place cake in refrigerator. About 30 minutes before serving, unmold on chilled plate; remove aluminum foil. Refrigerate until serving time.
16 TO 20 SERVINGS.

For frosting, stir milk into cooked butter-sugar mixture.

Beat powdered sugar into the cooled frosting; add cashews.

Butterscotch Nut Cake

1 cup all-purpose flour*
1 cup whole wheat flour
1 cup packed brown sugar
½ cup granulated sugar
3½ teaspoons baking powder
1 teaspoon salt
½ cup shortening
1 cup milk
1 teaspoon vanilla
3 eggs
Cashew Frosting (below)

Heat oven to 350°. Grease and flour baking pan, 13x9x2 inches. Blend all ingredients except Cashew Frosting on low speed 30 seconds, scraping bowl constantly. Beat on high speed 3 minutes, scraping bowl occasionally; pour into pan. Bake until pick inserted in center comes out clean, 40 to 45 minutes. Cool. Frost with Cashew Frosting.

*If using self-rising flour, omit baking powder and salt.

CASHEW FROSTING

½ cup butter or margarine
¾ cup packed brown sugar
¼ cup milk
2 cups powdered sugar
½ cup broken cashews

Heat butter in 2-quart saucepan until melted. Stir in brown sugar. Heat to boiling, stirring constantly; reduce heat. Boil and stir 2 minutes. Stir in milk; heat to boiling. Cool. Beat in powdered sugar gradually; continue beating until of spreading consistency. Stir in cashews.

Fudgy Chocolate Cake

1 cup butter or margarine
1 cup water
½ cup cocoa
2 cups all-purpose flour*
2 cups sugar
½ cup dairy sour cream
2 eggs
1 teaspoon baking soda
½ teaspoon salt
   Butter Frosting (below)

Heat oven to 350°. Grease and flour baking pan, 13x9x2 inches. Heat butter, water and cocoa to boiling in 3-quart saucepan, stirring occasionally. Remove from heat. Add flour, sugar, sour cream, eggs, baking soda and salt. Beat on medium speed or with hand beater until smooth, about 2 minutes. Pour into pan. Bake until wooden pick inserted in center comes out clean, 35 to 40 minutes. Cool completely. Frost with Butter Frosting.

*If using self-rising flour, omit baking soda and salt.

BUTTER FROSTING

⅓ cup butter or margarine, softened
3 cups powdered sugar
1 teaspoon orange flavoring or allspice
2 to 3 tablespoons milk

Mix butter, sugar and flavoring until thoroughly blended. Stir in milk; beat until frosting is smooth and of spreading consistency.

Irish Chocolate Cake: Substitute 2 teaspoons Irish whiskey and 1 to 2 teaspoons instant coffee for the orange flavoring in the frosting.

Heat butter, water and cocoa to boiling in 3-quart saucepan, stirring occasionally.

Remove from heat. Add flour, sugar, sour cream, eggs, soda and salt; beat until smooth.

Cherry-Fudge Cake

Arrange chopped cherries on top of the cooled cake.

Pour frosting on cherries; spread to cover the cake.

2 cups all-purpose flour*
2 cups sugar
1 cup water
¾ cup dairy sour cream
¼ cup shortening
1¼ teaspoons baking soda
1 teaspoon salt
1 teaspoon almond extract
½ teaspoon baking powder
2 eggs
4 squares (1 ounce each) unsweetened chocolate, melted and cooled
Chocolate-Cherry Frosting (below)

Heat oven to 350°. Grease and flour baking pan, 13x9x2 inches. Mix all ingredients except Chocolate-Cherry Frosting on low speed 30 seconds, scraping bowl constantly. Beat on high speed 3 minutes, scraping bowl occasionally; pour into pan. Bake until top springs back when touched lightly, 40 to 45 minutes. Cool. Frost with Chocolate-Cherry Frosting.

*If using self-rising flour, reduce baking soda to ¼ teaspoon and omit salt and baking powder.

CHOCOLATE-CHERRY FROSTING

Drain 1 jar (10 ounces) maraschino cherries, reserving ½ cup syrup. Chop cherries; drain on paper towels. Arrange cherries on cake. Mix reserved syrup and 2 envelopes (1 ounce each) premelted unsweetened chocolate in small mixer bowl. Beat in 3 cups powdered sugar until smooth. Pour frosting on cherries carefully; spread frosting to cover cake.

Do-Ahead Coconut Pound Cake

2¾ cups sugar
1¼ cups butter or margarine, softened
5 eggs
1 teaspoon vanilla
3 cups all-purpose flour*
1 teaspoon baking powder
¼ teaspoon salt
1 cup evaporated milk
1 can (3½ ounces) flaked coconut
2 to 3 tablespoons shredded orange peel

Heat oven to 350°. Grease and flour tube pan, 10x4 inches, or 12-cup bundt cake pan. Blend sugar, butter, eggs and vanilla in large mixer bowl ½ minute on low speed, scraping bowl constantly. Beat 5 minutes on high speed, scraping bowl occasionally. On low speed, mix in flour, baking powder and salt alternately with milk. Fold in coconut and orange peel. Pour into pan. Bake until wooden pick inserted in center comes out clean, 1 to 1¼ hours.

Cool 20 minutes; remove from pan. Cool completely. Wrap and refrigerate or freeze. Store in refrigerator up to 1 week, in freezer up to 4 months.

■2 hours before serving, remove cake from freezer and loosen wrapper so that it does not touch cake. Thaw at room temperature.

*Do not use self-rising flour in this recipe.

Almond Pound Cake: Substitute almond extract for the vanilla and sprinkle 1 package (1½ ounces) sliced almonds (about ¼ cup) on batter before baking; omit coconut.

Lemon Pound Cake: Substitute lemon extract for the vanilla and 2 to 3 teaspoons finely grated lemon peel for the orange peel. Omit coconut.

Tap and shake flour in the pan to cover it completely.

Mix in the milk alternately with the dry ingredients.

Oven rack should be placed below the center of oven.

Bake until pick inserted in the center comes out clean.

Grease foil-lined pan. Beat eggs until thick and lemon colored. After beating in remaining ingredients, spread batter in the pan.

Remove the foil from the inverted cake. Roll up the cake with a towel; cool. Spread ice cream almost to edges of cake; roll up.

Chocolate Ice-Cream Roll

¾ cup all-purpose flour*
¼ cup cocoa
1 teaspoon baking powder
¼ teaspoon salt
3 eggs (½ to ⅔ cup)
1 cup granulated sugar
⅓ cup water
1 teaspoon vanilla
　Powdered sugar
1 pint ice cream

Heat oven to 375°. Line jelly roll pan, 15½x10½x1 inch, with aluminum foil or waxed paper; grease. Mix flour, cocoa, baking powder and salt; reserve.

Beat eggs in small mixer bowl on high speed until very thick and lemon colored, 3 to 5 minutes. Pour eggs into large mixer bowl; gradually beat in granulated sugar. On low speed, blend in water and vanilla. Gradually add flour mixture, beating until batter is smooth. Pour into pan, spreading batter to corners. Bake until wooden pick inserted in center comes out clean, 12 to 15 minutes.

Loosen cake from edges of pan; invert on towel sprinkled with powdered sugar. Carefully remove foil; trim stiff edges from cake if necessary. While hot, roll cake and towel from narrow end as pictured. Cool. Unroll cake and remove towel. Soften ice cream slightly. Quickly spread over cake. Roll up and place seam side down on piece of aluminum foil. Wrap and freeze at least 4 hours. For longer storage, wrap and label; freeze up to 1 month.

■15 minutes before serving, remove roll from freezer and sprinkle with powdered sugar.　　10 TO 12 SERVINGS.

*If using self-rising flour, omit baking powder and salt.

Caramel-Orange Angel Cake

1¼ cups cake flour
1 cup packed brown sugar
12 egg whites (about 1½ cups)
1½ teaspoons cream of tartar
1 teaspoon salt
1 cup packed brown sugar
3 teaspoons shredded orange peel
1½ teaspoons vanilla
3 cups frozen whipped topping, thawed

Heat oven to 375°. Mix flour and 1 cup brown sugar. Beat egg whites, cream of tartar and salt in large bowl until foamy. Beat in 1 cup brown sugar, 2 tablespoons at a time, on high speed until stiff peaks form; sprinkle with 2 teaspoons of the orange peel and the vanilla.

Fold flour mixture, ¼ cup at a time, into meringue as pictured just until flour mixture disappears. Spread batter in ungreased tube pan, 10x4 inches. Gently cut through batter with knife. Bake until top springs back when touched lightly and cracks are dry, 30 to 35 minutes.

Invert pan on funnel as pictured; let hang until cake is cool. Frost cake with whipped topping. Sprinkle with remaining orange peel. Refrigerate until serving time.

Fold flour mixture ¼ cup at a time into the meringue, turning the bowl as you fold.

Gently cut through batter to break any air pockets and seal the batter to pan.

Bake until top of cake springs back when touched lightly and the cracks feel dry.

Invert pan to let cake cool. (If cake falls out of pan, it has been underbaked.)

HOW TO FOLD ANGEL CAKES

Sprinkle flour mixture over egg white meringue. Fold by cutting down through the center of meringue, along the bottom and up the side. Rotate bowl ¼ turn; repeat. Not all of the flour mixture disappears with each folding motion. Continue folding just until the flour mixture disappears. Too much folding breaks down the cake.

Blueberry Grenadine Pie

Stir ¼ cup grenadine syrup and 2 teaspoons lemon juice into cornstarch mixture.

Pour the grenadine mixture evenly on the blueberries in pie shell; refrigerate.

1 package (11 ounces) pie crust mix
2 cups fresh blueberries
½ cup sugar
1 tablespoon plus 2 teaspoons cornstarch
¼ teaspoon salt
¼ teaspoon ground cinnamon
¾ cup water
¼ cup grenadine syrup
2 teaspoons lemon juice
½ cup chilled whipping cream
1 tablespoon sugar

Bake 9-inch pie shell as directed on pie crust mix package. Cool. Place blueberries in pie shell. Blend ½ cup sugar, the cornstarch, salt and cinnamon in saucepan. Stir in water. Heat to boiling, stirring constantly. Boil and stir 1 minute. Stir in grenadine syrup and lemon juice. Pour on blueberries in pie shell. Refrigerate.

Beat whipping cream and 1 tablespoon sugar in chilled small mixer bowl until stiff. Cut pie into wedges; top with whipped cream.

Prune Whip Pie

Cinnamon Pie Shell (below)
2 cups miniature marshmallows
½ cup hot water
½ teaspoon instant coffee
1½ cups chopped cooked prunes
1 tablespoon lemon juice
⅛ teaspoon salt
2 envelopes (1¼ ounces each) low-calorie
  whipped topping mix

Prepare Cinnamon Pie Shell. Heat marshmallows, water and coffee over low heat, stirring constantly, until marshmallows are melted, about 3 minutes. Refrigerate 30 minutes.

Reserve ¼ cup of the prunes. Stir remaining prunes, the lemon juice and salt into marshmallow mixture. Prepare 1 envelope whipped topping mix as directed on package; fold into prune mixture. Spread in pie shell. Refrigerate until set, about 5 hours. Prepare remaining envelope whipped topping mix as directed on package; swirl over pie. Garnish with reserved prunes.

CINNAMON PIE SHELL

Bake pastry for 9-inch One-Crust Pie as directed on 1 package (11 ounces) pie crust sticks except—stir 1 teaspoon ground cinnamon into crumbled stick before adding water. Cool.

Ease the cinnamon pastry into pie plate to avoid stretching. Trim edge, leaving a 1-inch rim. Roll pastry under around edge.

Pinch to form rim. Press a rope edge at an angle to rim; repeat to make sharp edges. Prick the pastry with a fork; bake. Cool.

Mix the granola, butter and sugar; press into pie plate.

Pour the cream cheese mixture into the baked pie crust.

Tangy Mince Cream Pie

2 cups regular granola, crushed
¼ cup butter or margarine, melted
2 tablespoons sugar
2 packages (8 ounces each) cream cheese, softened
2 eggs
¾ cup sugar
2 teaspoons vanilla
½ teaspoon grated lemon peel
Mincemeat Topping (below)

Heat oven to 350°. Mix granola, butter and 2 tablespoons sugar. Press mixture firmly and evenly against bottom and side of 9-inch pie plate. Bake until golden brown, 6 to 8 minutes.

Beat cream cheese slightly. Add eggs, ¾ cup sugar, the vanilla and lemon peel; beat until light and fluffy. Pour into crust. Bake until center is firm, about 25 minutes. Cool to room temperature. Refrigerate at least 4 hours. Serve with Mincemeat Topping.

MINCEMEAT TOPPING
Blend 2 teaspoons cornstarch and 1 cup cranberry juice or port in 1-quart saucepan. Heat to boiling. Boil and stir 1 minute; remove from heat. Stir in 1 cup prepared mincemeat. Serve warm or cool.

Frosty Pumpkin Pie

Gingersnap Crust (below)
1 cup mashed cooked pumpkin
¼ cup packed brown sugar
1 teaspoon aromatic bitters
½ teaspoon salt
½ teaspoon ground ginger
¼ teaspoon ground nutmeg
¼ teaspoon ground cinnamon
1 carton (4 ounces) frozen whipped
   topping, thawed
1 pint butter pecan ice cream, slightly
   softened
2 tablespoons chopped pecans

Spread ice cream to edge of the Gingersnap Crust.

Swirl pumpkin mixture over the ice cream layer.

Bake Gingersnap Crust; cool. Mix pumpkin, brown sugar, bitters, salt, ginger, nutmeg and cinnamon. Fold whipped topping into pumpkin mixture. Spoon ice cream into Gingersnap Crust; spread to edge of crust. Swirl pumpkin mixture over ice cream. Freeze uncovered at least 3 hours.

Let stand at room temperature 15 minutes before serving. Sprinkle pecans in circle on pie.

GINGERSNAP CRUST

Heat oven to 350°. Mix 1½ cups gingersnap crumbs and ¼ cup butter or margarine, melted. Press firmly and evenly against bottom and side of 9-inch pie plate. Bake 10 minutes.

Do-Ahead Ice-Cream Pie

An 8-inch pie plate can be used to press the chocolate crumb mixture in a 9-inch pie plate.

Quickly stir the rum, ginger and instant coffee into the slightly softened ice cream.

1½ cups chocolate wafer crumbs (about 25 wafers)
¼ cup butter or margarine, melted
¼ cup rum or 1 teaspoon rum flavoring
2 tablespoons chopped crystallized ginger or ¼ teaspoon ground ginger
2 teaspoons instant coffee
1 quart vanilla ice cream, slightly softened

Heat oven to 350°. Mix crumbs and butter; reserve 1 to 2 tablespoons crumb mixture for topping. Press remaining mixture firmly and evenly against bottom and side of 9-inch pie plate. Bake until set, 8 to 10 minutes. Cool.

Stir rum, ginger and instant coffee into softened ice cream; pour into pie shell. Freeze uncovered until firm, about 4 hours. Wrap and label; freeze up to 3 weeks.

■**15 minutes before serving,** unwrap pie and let stand at room temperature for easier cutting.

Apricot-Almond Ice-Cream Pie: Substitute ½ cup diced roasted almonds and ½ cup apricot preserves for the ginger and coffee.

Banana Ice-Cream Pie: Substitute 2 bananas, mashed, and ¼ cup frozen orange juice concentrate, thawed, for the rum, ginger and coffee.

Melon Alaska Pie

1 package (11 ounces) pie crust mix
1 quart vanilla or peach ice cream, slightly
   softened
4 egg whites
¼ teaspoon cream of tartar
½ cup sugar
2 cups honeydew and/or cantaloupe balls*

Bake 9-inch pie shell as directed on pie crust mix package. Cool. Pack ice cream carefully into pie shell. Freeze until firm, at least 8 hours.

Ten minutes before serving, heat oven to 500°. Beat egg whites and cream of tartar until foamy. Beat in sugar gradually until meringue is stiff and glossy. Arrange fruit on ice cream; top with meringue, sealing to edge of crust. Bake until meringue is light brown, about 3 minutes.

*2 cups sliced nectarines, peaches, strawberries or blueberries can be substituted for the honeydew and cantaloupe balls.

Pack the slightly softened ice cream into the pie shell.

Use a melon baller to scoop uniform balls from melons.

Arrange melon balls on the ice-cream layer in pie shell.

Top with meringue, carefully sealing to edge of crust.

Apricot-Banana Bars

For the Apricot Glaze, mix powdered sugar, the reserved preserves and water.

Spread baked layer with Apricot Glaze while slightly warm. Cool and cut into bars.

¾ cup packed brown sugar
½ cup butter or margarine, softened
1 jar (12 ounces) apricot or pineapple-apricot preserves
2 eggs
1 teaspoon vanilla
2 cups all-purpose flour*
1 teaspoon baking powder
½ teaspoon baking soda
¼ teaspoon salt
¾ cup mashed bananas (about 2 medium)
½ cup chopped pecans
Apricot Glaze (below)

Heat oven to 350°. Grease and flour jelly roll pan, 15½x10½x1 inch. Mix brown sugar and butter. Reserve 2 tablespoons of the preserves for Apricot Glaze. Stir remaining preserves, the eggs and vanilla into sugar-butter mixture. Stir in remaining ingredients except Apricot Glaze; mix until dry ingredients are moistened. Spread in pan. Bake until golden brown, about 30 minutes.

Spread with Apricot Glaze while slightly warm. Cool completely before cutting. Cut into bars, 3x1 inch.   ABOUT 4 DOZEN BARS.

*If using self-rising flour, omit baking powder and salt.

APRICOT GLAZE

Mix 1½ cups powdered sugar, 2 tablespoons reserved preserves and 1 tablespoon water until smooth and of desired consistency.

Chip and Granola Bars

⅓ cup shortening
⅓ cup butter or margarine
½ cup granulated sugar
½ cup packed brown sugar
1 egg
1 teaspoon vanilla
1½ cups all-purpose flour*
½ teaspoon baking soda
½ teaspoon salt
1 package (6 ounces) semisweet chocolate chips
1 cup granola (any flavor)

Heat oven to 375°. Grease baking pan, 13x9x2 inches. Mix shortening, butter, sugars, egg and vanilla thoroughly. Stir in remaining ingredients. Spread dough in pan. Bake until light brown, 20 to 25 minutes. Cut into 3x1½-inch bars. 2 DOZEN BARS.

*If using self-rising flour, omit baking soda and salt.

Chip and Nut Bars: Substitute 1 package (4 ounces) shelled sunflower nuts for the granola.

Add the chocolate chips and granola to shortening mixture.

Spread the dough evenly in a greased baking pan.

Slice the almond paste; chop the slices into small pieces.

With knife point down, move handle in circle to chop nuts.

Almond Brownies

4 squares (1 ounce each) unsweetened chocolate
⅔ cup shortening
2 cups sugar
4 eggs
1¼ cups all-purpose flour*
1 teaspoon baking powder
1 teaspoon salt
1 cup chopped nuts
1 cup chopped almond paste

Heat oven to 350°. Grease baking pan, 13x9x2 inches. Heat chocolate and shortening in 3-quart saucepan over low heat until melted; remove from heat. Stir in remaining ingredients. Spread in pan.

Bake until brownies begin to pull away from sides of pan, about 30 minutes. Do not overbake. Cool slightly; cut into bars, about 2x1½ inches.   ABOUT 3 DOZEN BARS.

*If using self-rising flour, omit baking powder and salt.

Sesame Bars

4 packages (2⅜ ounces each) sesame seed
1 cup butter or margarine, softened
2 cups packed brown sugar
2 eggs, beaten
1 cup all-purpose flour*
2 tablespoons hot water
¾ teaspoon salt

Heat oven to 325°. Mix all ingredients. Spread in greased jelly roll pan, 15½x10½x1 inch. Bake until center is set, 45 minutes. Cool; cut into bars, 2x1 inch.   6 DOZEN BARS.

*Do not use self-rising flour in this recipe.

Frosted Lemon Bars

½ cup butter or margarine, softened
½ cup packed brown sugar
1 cup all-purpose flour
2 eggs
1 cup packed brown sugar
1 teaspoon vanilla
¼ cup all-purpose flour*
1 teaspoon baking powder
1 teaspoon grated lemon peel
½ teaspoon salt
1 cup flaked coconut
½ cup chopped almonds
Lemon Frosting (below)

Heat oven to 350°. Mix butter and ½ cup brown sugar; stir in 1 cup flour. Press mixture firmly and evenly in ungreased baking pan, 13x9x2 inches. Bake 10 minutes.

Beat eggs, 1 cup brown sugar and the vanilla until foamy. Beat in ¼ cup flour, the baking powder, lemon peel and salt on low speed. Stir in coconut and almonds; spread over crust. Bake 25 minutes. Cool completely. Frost with Lemon Frosting. Cut into bars, 3x1 inch.   3 DOZEN BARS.

*If using self-rising flour, omit baking powder and salt.

LEMON FROSTING

Mix 2 cups powdered sugar, 1 teaspoon grated lemon peel, 2 teaspoons lemon juice and about 2 tablespoons milk until smooth and of spreading consistency.

Press butter mixture firmly and evenly in baking pan.

Beat the eggs, brown sugar and vanilla until foamy.

Stir the coconut and almonds into the flour mixture.

Spread mixture evenly over crust; bake 25 minutes.

Lemon-Spice Oatmeal Cookies

Shape the dough into balls.   Press down balls with fork.

1 cup packed brown sugar
1 cup butter or margarine, softened
1 egg
1½ cups quick-cooking oats
1½ cups all-purpose flour*
1 cup chopped nuts
2 tablespoons grated lemon peel
½ teaspoon baking soda
½ teaspoon salt
½ teaspoon ground cinnamon
¼ teaspoon ground cloves
¼ teaspoon ground allspice
   Lemon Glaze (below)

Heat oven to 375°. Mix brown sugar, butter and egg thoroughly. Stir in oats, flour, nuts, lemon peel, baking soda, salt, cinnamon, cloves and allspice. Shape dough by tablespoonfuls into 1½-inch balls. Place 1 inch apart on ungreased baking sheet; press down with fork. Bake until almost no indentation remains when touched, 8 to 10 minutes. Cool slightly; remove from baking sheet. Spread Lemon Glaze over cookies. Cool completely.   ABOUT 2½ DOZEN COOKIES.

*If using self-rising flour, omit baking soda and salt.

LEMON GLAZE
Mix 1 cup powdered sugar, 2 tablespoons lemon juice and 2 teaspoons butter or margarine, softened, until smooth.

Oatmeal Drops

1½ cups quick-cooking oats
½ cup sugar
3 tablespoons butter or margarine, softened
1 teaspoon vanilla
½ teaspoon baking powder
½ teaspoon ground cinnamon
¼ teaspoon salt
1 egg

Heat oven to 350°. Mix all ingredients. Drop dough by teaspoonfuls 2 inches apart onto greased baking sheet. Bake until tops are dry and edges are light brown, 8 to 10 minutes. Cool slightly; remove from baking sheet.
3 DOZEN COOKIES.

Use a shiny baking sheet at least 2 inches smaller than your oven for best results.

When baking a second batch, be sure baking sheet is cool to keep dough from spreading.

Cereal Crisps

2 eggs
1 cup sugar
2 cups chocolate-flavored corn puff cereal
1 cup all-purpose flour
1½ teaspoons vanilla
½ teaspoon ground nutmeg
¼ teaspoon ground cardamom
⅛ teaspoon salt

Heat oven to 375°. Beat eggs until very thick. Beat in sugar until well mixed. Stir in remaining ingredients. Refrigerate until dough is stiff, about 15 minutes.

Drop dough by teaspoonfuls 2 inches apart onto greased baking sheet. Bake until edges are light brown, 10 to 12 minutes. Immediately remove from baking sheet. Cool on wire rack.   4 DOZEN COOKIES.

Beat dry ingredients alternately with liquid into egg yolk mixture. Make meringue.

After folding yolk mixture into meringue, drop by tablespoonfuls onto baking sheets.

Soft Cocoa Drops

⅓ cup sugar
¼ cup cocoa
 3 eggs, separated
¾ cup all-purpose flour*
¼ teaspoon baking powder
¼ teaspoon ground cinnamon
⅛ teaspoon salt
¼ cup water
 1 teaspoon vanilla
¼ teaspoon lemon extract
¼ teaspoon cream of tartar
¼ cup sugar

Heat oven to 350°. Grease and flour 2 baking sheets. Beat ⅓ cup sugar, the cocoa and egg yolks in small mixer bowl on medium speed until very thick, about 3 minutes. Beat in flour, baking powder, cinnamon and salt alternately with water, vanilla and lemon extract on low speed.

Beat egg whites and cream of tartar in large mixer bowl until foamy. Beat in ¼ cup sugar gradually; continue beating until stiff and glossy. Fold egg yolk mixture into egg whites. Drop by rounded tablespoonfuls 2 inches apart onto baking sheets. Bake until set, 10 to 12 minutes.
30 COOKIES.

*If using self-rising flour, omit baking powder and salt.

Appetizers
and Beverages

Cut dough into squares.

Dot with beef mixture.

Moisten, fold and pinch.

Fry until golden brown.

Beef Wrap-ups

½ pound ground beef
1 small onion, chopped (about ¼ cup)
2 tablespoons grated American cheese food
¼ teaspoon salt
¼ teaspoon garlic salt
1 egg, separated
1 cup all-purpose flour*
⅓ cup water
½ teaspoon salt
¼ teaspoon paprika
Vegetable oil or shortening

Mix ground beef, onion, cheese, ¼ teaspoon salt, the garlic salt and egg white; reserve. Mix flour, egg yolk, water, ½ teaspoon salt and the paprika until a soft dough forms. Knead on floured surface until dough is elastic, about 2 minutes. Divide dough in half. Roll half into 12-inch square about 1/16 inch thick; cut into 2-inch squares.

Fill each square with scant teaspoon beef mixture. Moisten edges of squares; fold into triangles. Pinch edges together. Repeat with remaining dough. Heat oil (1 inch) to 400° in 10-inch skillet. Fry wrap-ups until golden, about 45 seconds; drain. Serve hot or cold.   6 DOZEN APPETIZERS.

*Do not use self-rising flour in this recipe.

Tomato Cooler

Mix 2 cans (15 ounces each) tomato sauce, 1 quart buttermilk and 3 tablespoons lemon juice. Stir in ½ teaspoon each dill seed and seasoned salt, and ¼ teaspoon each garlic salt and onion salt. Serve over crushed ice, using green onions as swizzle sticks.   7 SERVINGS (½ CUP EACH).

Runzas

1 pound ground beef
4 cups shredded cabbage
¼ cup water
1 small onion, chopped (about ¼ cup)
1 teaspoon salt
½ teaspoon caraway seed
⅛ teaspoon pepper
   Yeast Roll Dough (below)

Cook and stir ground beef until light brown; drain. Stir in cabbage, water, onion, salt, caraway seed and pepper. Heat to boiling; reduce heat. Cover and simmer until cabbage is tender, about 10 minutes. Prepare Yeast Roll Dough; roll into rectangle, 20x15 inches, about ¼ inch thick. Cut into 3-inch circles; spoon beef mixture onto center of each circle. Bring side to center and pinch dough to seal as pictured. Place on greased baking sheet. Let rise in warm place until double, about 1 hour. Heat oven to 375°. Bake until golden, about 18 minutes.   2½ DOZEN RUNZAS.

YEAST ROLL DOUGH

  2 packages active dry yeast
  ¾ cup warm water (105 to 115°)
1¼ cups buttermilk
  ¼ cup shortening
  2 tablespoons sugar
  2 teaspoons baking powder
  2 teaspoons salt
4½ to 5 cups all-purpose flour

Dissolve yeast in warm water in large mixer bowl. Add buttermilk, shortening, sugar, baking powder, salt and 2½ cups of the flour. Blend on low speed, scraping bowl constantly, 30 seconds. Beat on medium speed, scraping bowl occasionally, 2 minutes. Stir in enough remaining flour to make dough easy to handle. Turn dough onto well-floured surface; knead 5 minutes.

Roll dough into a rectangle and cut into 3-inch circles.

Spoon rounded tablespoon of beef mixture onto centers.

Bring edge to center, stretching to cover; pinch to seal and place on baking sheet.

For last minute reheating of baked Runzas, cover and heat in 350° oven 20 minutes.

Meat Turnovers

Place 3 tablespoons filling in center of each circle.

Bring 2 edges of circle together; pinch edges to seal.

1 package active dry yeast
1 cup warm water (105 to 115°)
1 tablespoon sugar
1 tablespoon vegetable oil
½ teaspoon salt
2 to 2½ cups all-purpose flour
  Chopped Liver Filling (below)

Dissolve yeast in warm water. Stir in sugar, oil, salt and enough flour to make dough easy to handle; turn onto floured surface. Knead until smooth and elastic, about 5 minutes. Place in greased bowl; turn greased side up. Cover; let rise until double, about 1 hour. Prepare filling.

Punch down dough; divide into 10 parts. Roll into 5-inch circles. Fill circles as pictured. Place seam sides down on greased baking sheets. Cover with damp towel. Let rise until double, about 1 hour. Heat oven to 375°. Bake until light brown, 20 to 23 minutes.   10 TURNOVERS.

CHOPPED LIVER FILLING

5 ounces mushrooms, chopped
1 small onion, chopped (about ¼ cup)
1 clove garlic, crushed
¼ cup vegetable oil
½ pound chicken livers
1 tablespoon snipped parsley
1 teaspoon salt
½ teaspoon dried dill weed
⅛ teaspoon pepper
1 hard-cooked egg, finely chopped

Cook and stir mushrooms, onion and garlic in half of the oil until onion is tender; remove from pan. Cook and stir livers in remaining oil 10 minutes. Chop livers; mix with mushroom mixture and remaining ingredients.

Beef Empanadas

1 pound ground beef
1 small onion, chopped (about ¼ cup)
1 medium potato, finely chopped (about ½ cup)
1 can (8½ ounces) peas and carrots, drained (reserve liquid)
1 package (about 1 ounce) mushroom gravy mix
1 package (22 ounces) pie crust mix
Paprika

Simmer beef mixture, stirring occasionally, 1 minute.

Fold pastry rounds over beef mixture; seal with fork.

Cook and stir ground beef and onion in 10-inch skillet until beef is light brown and onion is tender; drain. Stir in potato, peas and carrots and gravy mix. Add enough water to reserved vegetable liquid to measure 1 cup; stir into beef mixture in skillet. Heat to boiling; reduce heat. Simmer uncovered, stirring occasionally, 1 minute. Cool.

Heat oven to 400°. Prepare pastry for 2 Two-Crust Pies as directed on pie crust mix package except—after rolling pastry, cut into 3-inch rounds. Place rounds on ungreased baking sheets.

Spoon scant tablespoon beef mixture onto half of each round. Fold pastry over filling as pictured; seal with fork. Sprinkle with paprika. Bake until light brown, about 15 minutes. (Empanadas can be baked ahead and frozen up to 3 weeks. Fifteen minutes before serving, place frozen empanadas on ungreased baking sheet and heat in 400° oven 15 minutes.)   ABOUT 5 DOZEN APPETIZERS.

Tarts Alsace

Ease the pastry rounds into un-greased muffin cups.

Fill pastry-lined muffin cups ½ full with beef mixture.

Spoon about 2 tablespoons of egg mixture into each cup.

Remove baked tarts from muffin cups with a spatula.

    1 package (11 ounces) pie crust mix
    ½ pound ground beef or pork bulk sausage
  1⅓ cups shredded natural Swiss cheese
    6 green onions, sliced (about ⅓ cup)
    4 eggs, slightly beaten
  1⅓ cups dairy sour cream
    1 teaspoon salt
    1 teaspoon Worcestershire sauce
    ¼ teaspoon pepper
      Paprika

Prepare pastry for Two-Crust Pie as directed on pie crust mix package except—roll half of the pastry 1/16 inch thick on lightly floured cloth-covered board. Cut into nine 4-inch rounds. Repeat with remaining half. Ease rounds into un-greased medium muffin cups.

Heat oven to 375°. Cook and stir ground beef until light brown; drain. Mix beef, cheese and onions. Fill pastry-lined muffin cups ½ full with beef mixture. Mix eggs, sour cream, salt, Worcestershire sauce and pepper. Spoon about 2 tablespoons of the egg-sour cream mixture into each muffin cup; sprinkle with paprika. Bake until golden brown, about 30 minutes. Cool 5 minutes; remove tarts from muffin cups. Serve warm.   1½ DOZEN TARTS.

Pork Egg Rolls

3 tablespoons soy sauce
2 tablespoons dry sherry
1 teaspoon salt
1 teaspoon sugar
¼ teaspoon pepper
1 pound pork boneless steak, cut into
   1x¼-inch pieces
   Vegetable oil
3 cups finely shredded cabbage
1 can (8 ounces) bamboo shoots, drained
   and chopped
1 can (4 ounces) mushrooms stems and
   pieces, drained
6 medium green onions, sliced
¼ teaspoon salt
1 tablespoon cornstarch
1 pound egg roll wrapper skins (16 to 18)

Mix soy sauce, sherry, 1 teaspoon salt, the sugar and pepper; pour on pork pieces. Let stand, stirring occasionally, 5 minutes. Drain well, reserving marinade. Cook and stir pork in 1 tablespoon oil in 10-inch skillet until light brown, about 4 minutes. Remove pork to large bowl.

Stir-fry cabbage, bamboo shoots, mushrooms and onions in 1 tablespoon oil in same skillet 2 minutes. Sprinkle with ¼ teaspoon salt. Add to pork. Heat cornstarch and marinade to boiling in skillet, stirring constantly. Boil and stir 1 minute. Return pork and vegetables to skillet. Boil and stir 1 minute; cool 5 minutes.

Heat oil (1½ to 1¾ inches) to 400° in deep fat fryer or electric skillet. Place filling on each wrapper; fold as pictured. Fry 4 at a time, sealed sides down first, until brown, 2 minutes on each side; drain.   16 TO 18 EGG ROLLS.

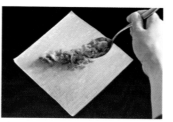

Place 3 tablespoons filling on each egg roll wrapper.

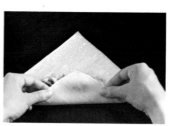

Fold the lower corner of the wrapper up over the filling.

Fold in sides, forming an envelope; moisten top corner.

Roll up from bottom; seal. Fry sealed sides down first.

Teriyaki Chicken Wings

To separate chicken wing at joint, first cut skin to bone.

Bend the wing back at joint, then separate with scissors.

Pour teriyaki sauce on the chicken; cover and refrigerate.

Place the chicken on rack in a foil-lined broiler pan; bake.

3 to 3½ pounds chicken wings (about 20)
½ cup catsup
¼ cup dry white wine
¼ cup soy sauce
2 tablespoons sugar
1 teaspoon salt
½ teaspoon ground ginger
1 clove garlic, crushed

Cut ½ inch from tip of each chicken wing; separate at joint. Place chicken in ungreased baking dish, 13½x8¾x1¼ inches. Mix remaining ingredients; pour on chicken. Cover and refrigerate, turning chicken occasionally, at least 1 hour.

Heat oven to 375°. Remove chicken from baking dish, reserving sauce. Place chicken on rack in aluminum foil-lined broiler pan. Bake 30 minutes. Brush with reserved sauce. Turn chicken; bake, brushing occasionally with sauce, until chicken is glazed, 30 to 40 minutes.
8 TO 12 SERVINGS.

PARTY TIPS

For a walk-about party, remember to serve a variety of foods that are spill-proof, do not require knives and forks and are easy to handle. A quick sampling: sandwiches of any kind, quiches, bite-size appetizers, cookies, tea breads, cheeses, dips, crackers and nuts. To complement these, provide serve-yourself beverages and coffee from easily accessible containers. It's informal fun and less work for you.

Chicken Bites

- 4 chicken breasts, boned, split and skin removed
- 1 cup finely crushed round buttery crackers (about 24)
- ½ cup grated Parmesan cheese
- ¼ cup finely chopped walnuts
- ½ teaspoon seasoned salt
- 1 teaspoon dried thyme leaves
- 1 teaspoon dried basil leaves
- ¼ teaspoon pepper
- ½ cup butter or margarine, melted

Cover 2 baking sheets with aluminum foil. Cut chicken into 1-inch pieces. Mix cracker crumbs, cheese, walnuts, seasoned salt, thyme, basil and pepper.

Heat oven to 400°. Dip chicken pieces into melted butter, then into crumb mixture. Place chicken pieces about ½ inch apart on baking sheets. Bake uncovered until golden brown, 20 to 25 minutes.   ABOUT 6 DOZEN APPETIZERS.

Garnet Punch

- 2 cans (6 ounces each) frozen grape juice concentrate, thawed
- 2 cans (6 ounces each) frozen apple juice concentrate, thawed
- 2 bottles (25.6 ounces each) sparkling catawba grape juice, chilled
- 1 bottle (10 ounces) club soda, chilled
- 1 pint pineapple sherbet

Mix grape juice concentrate, apple juice concentrate, catawba grape juice and club soda in punch bowl. Float scoops of sherbet on punch. Serve immediately.
22 SERVINGS (ABOUT ½ CUP EACH).

To bone chicken breast, cut only through white gristle at neck end. Bend back to pop keel bone. Loosen keel; pull from chicken.

Cut rib cages away, cutting through shoulder joint. Cut wishbone from chicken. Split breast after pulling and cutting the tendons.

Mini Hot Dog Roast

After wieners are toasted, they are placed in buns.

Relishes are removed from base of cabbage halves.

1 large head red cabbage (about 3 pounds)
2 cans (about 2½ ounces each) cooking fuel
  Assorted relishes
  Mini Buns (below)
3 packages (5½ ounces each) little wieners

Cut cabbage in half; place each half cut side down on a tray. Hollow out center of each cabbage half; insert 1 can of cooking fuel in each hollow. Spear relishes with wooden picks; insert in base of cabbage halves. Prepare Mini Buns.

Heat wieners in boiling water 5 minutes; drain. Ignite cooking fuel. Toast wieners over the flaming cabbage.
6 TO 8 SERVINGS.

MINI BUNS
2¼ cups biscuit baking mix
 ½ cup shredded Cheddar cheese (about
     2 ounces)
 ½ cup cold water
 1 tablespoon prepared mustard
 1 tablespoon catsup
   Catsup
   Prepared mustard

Heat oven to 450°. Stir baking mix, cheese, water, 1 tablespoon mustard and 1 tablespoon catsup to a soft dough; beat vigorously 20 strokes. Gently smooth into a ball on floured cloth-covered board. Knead 5 times. Roll into rectangle, 14x10 inches, about ¼ inch thick. Cut into 2-inch squares.

Spread about ½ teaspoon catsup or mustard on half of each square; fold in half. Place on ungreased baking sheet. Bake until brown, 8 to 10 minutes. Serve warm.

Oysters Rumaki

12 slices bacon, cut in half
24 large fresh or frozen (thawed) oysters
½ teaspoon salt
¼ teaspoon pepper

Fry bacon 2 minutes on each side. Drain oysters; dry on paper towels. Sprinkle oysters with salt and pepper. Wrap each oyster with 1 bacon slice as pictured; secure with wooden pick. (At this point, rumakis can be covered and refrigerated up to 24 hours.) Heat oven to 400°. Place rumakis on rack in broiler pan. Bake 10 minutes; turn. Bake 10 minutes longer.   2 DOZEN APPETIZERS.

Pineapple Ale

2 pineapples*
1 bottle (28 ounces) ginger ale, chilled
  Strawberries
  Mint leaves

Remove tops from pineapples. Cut 3 thin slices from 1 pineapple. Core and cut rind and eyes from slices; reserve slices. Cut remaining pineapple into wedges; cut rind and eyes from wedges. Remove core and cut pineapple into 1-inch pieces. Place 8 pineapple pieces in blender container. Cover and blend until liquified, about 15 seconds. Add half of the remaining pineapple pieces, a few at a time, blending until liquified. Strain out pulp. Repeat with remaining pineapple. Refrigerate.

Mix pineapple juice and ginger ale in punch bowl. Float reserved pineapple slices on punch; garnish with strawberries and mint leaves.   22 SERVINGS (ABOUT ½ CUP EACH).

*5½ cups chilled unsweetened pineapple juice can be substituted for the pineapples.

Drain the oysters and place on paper towels to dry.

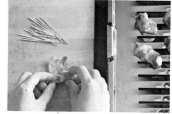
Wrap each oyster with bacon slice; secure with pick.

For pineapple garnish, core and cut eyes from 3 slices.

Cut rind and eyes from pineapple wedges; remove core.

Alternate the fruit and cucumber on 5-inch skewers.

Heat jelly until melted; stir in water and poppy seed.

Fruit Kabobs

2 cans (11 ounces each) mandarin orange
    segments and pineapple tidbits, drained
1 pound green grapes
1 large cucumber, cut up
½ cup mint-flavored apple jelly
3 tablespoons water
½ teaspoon poppy seed

Alternate fruit and cucumber on 5-inch skewers. Heat jelly until melted; stir in water and poppy seed. Refrigerate kabobs and sauce separately.   12 TO 16 SERVINGS.

Meat Kabobs

2 pounds pork tenderloin, cut into 1-inch
    pieces
2-pound frozen turkey roast, thawed and cut
    into 1-inch pieces
1 medium onion, finely chopped
½ cup soy sauce
¼ cup packed brown sugar
¼ cup lemon juice
1 teaspoon garlic salt
¾ to 1 teaspoon pepper
½ teaspoon ground coriander
⅛ teaspoon cayenne red pepper
    Dash of crushed red peppers

Place pork tenderloin pieces and turkey pieces in glass bowl. Mix remaining ingredients; pour on pork and turkey. Cover and refrigerate, stirring occasionally, 2 hours.

Set oven control to broil and/or 550°. Drain pork and turkey. Arrange pork and turkey on skewers. Place on rack in broiler pan. Broil 3 inches from heat until brown, about 8 minutes; turn. Broil 5 minutes.   12 TO 16 SERVINGS.

Sauerkraut Surprises

1 cup sauerkraut, drained and cut up
1 package (3 ounces) sliced corned beef,
    finely cut up (about 1 cup)
1 cup dry bread crumbs
1 egg, slightly beaten
1 small onion, finely chopped (about ¼ cup)
¼ cup water
2 tablespoons snipped parsley
1 teaspoon prepared horseradish
1 clove garlic, crushed
½ teaspoon salt
2 eggs, beaten
½ cup dry bread crumbs
    Prepared mustard

Mix sauerkraut, corned beef, 1 cup bread crumbs, 1 egg, the onion, water, parsley, horseradish, garlic and salt; refrigerate at least 1 hour.

Heat oven to 400°. Shape sauerkraut mixture into 1-inch balls. Dip balls in 2 beaten eggs, then roll in ½ cup bread crumbs. Bake on ungreased baking sheet until light brown, about 20 minutes. Serve hot with mustard.   2 TO 3 DOZEN APPETIZERS.

First dip the 1-inch sauerkraut balls in 2 beaten eggs.

Then roll balls in ½ cup dry bread crumbs and bake.

Fold the cheese mixture into the beaten egg whites.

Fill potato chips; place on ungreased baking sheet.

Hot Orange Cider

Heat equal amounts orange juice and apple cider just to boiling over low heat; pour into mugs. Stir in rum to taste (about 2 teaspoons per mug). Garnish with orange peel.

Cheese Chips

2 eggs, separated
½ teaspoon Worcestershire sauce
¼ teaspoon cayenne red pepper
1½ cups shredded Cheddar cheese (about 6 ounces)
½ cup finely crushed potato chips
Potato chips

Heat oven to 400°. Beat egg yolks, Worcestershire sauce and red pepper. Stir in cheese. Beat egg whites until stiff peaks form. Fold cheese mixture into egg whites; fold crushed potato chips into cheese-egg white mixture.

Drop filling by teaspoonfuls onto whole potato chips. Place on ungreased baking sheet. Bake until filling is puffed and brown, 5 to 6 minutes. Serve with eggplant centerpiece as pictured.   ABOUT 30 APPETIZERS.

Peach Punch

2 packages (10 ounces each) frozen sliced
   peaches
2 cups dry white wine, chilled (optional)
1 cup lemon juice, chilled
1 can (6 ounces) frozen red fruit punch
   concentrate, thawed
2 quarts ginger ale, chilled
   Mint sprigs

Thaw 1 package frozen peaches. Mix thawed peaches, wine, lemon juice and fruit punch concentrate; pour on frozen peaches in chilled punch bowl. Just before serving, stir in ginger ale; garnish with mint sprigs. (To keep punch cold, another package of frozen peaches can be added.) ABOUT 24 SERVINGS (½ CUP EACH).

Cheesy Buttons

1 cup biscuit baking mix
¼ cup butter or margarine, softened
3 tablespoons boiling water
3 tablespoons sesame seed
¼ cup grated Parmesan cheese

Heat oven to 450°. Mix baking mix and butter. Stir in water and sesame seed until dough forms ball. Drop by scant teaspoonfuls into cheese (shape half into ovals if desired); coat dough with cheese. Place about 1 inch apart on ungreased baking sheet. Bake until golden, 7 to 10 minutes. Serve warm. ABOUT 3 DOZEN APPETIZERS.

Drop dough by scant teaspoonfuls into the cheese.

Or shape dough into ovals and coat with the cheese.

Tropical Punch

6 medium bananas
2 cans (6 ounces each) frozen lemonade
   concentrate, thawed
6¾ cups water
1 can (6 ounces) frozen orange juice
   concentrate, thawed
3 cups light rum
½ cup honey
2 quarts ginger ale, chilled
4 cups assorted melon balls or pieces
1 lime, cut into thin slices

Slice bananas into blender container; add lemonade concentrate. Cover and blend on high speed until smooth, about 15 seconds; pour into large bowl. Stir in water, orange juice concentrate, rum and honey; pour into freezer containers or shallow pans. Freeze uncovered until slushy, 1½ to 2 hours.

Pour banana mixture into chilled punch bowl. Just before serving, stir in ginger ale and melon balls. Garnish with lime slices.   ABOUT 50 SERVINGS (½ CUP EACH).

Cool Canapés

Beat ¼ cup butter or margarine, softened, 1 teaspoon finely shredded lemon peel, 1 tablespoon lemon juice, ½ teaspoon sugar and dash of red pepper sauce until fluffy. Cut 24 slices day-old white sandwich bread into circles with 2-inch biscuit cutter; spread butter mixture over bread circles. Cut 1 medium cucumber or zucchini into thin slices. Top each bread circle with cucumber slice; sprinkle with salt.   ABOUT 4 DOZEN CANAPES.

Onion-Cheese Puffs

1 cup water
⅓ cup butter or margarine
1 cup all-purpose flour
1 teaspoon salt
¼ teaspoon garlic powder
4 eggs
¾ cup shredded Swiss or pizza cheese
   (about 3 ounces)
1 small Bermuda onion, chopped (about
   ¼ cup)

Heat oven to 400°. Heat water and butter to rolling boil. Stir in flour, salt and garlic powder. Stir vigorously over low heat 1 minute or until mixture forms a ball; remove from heat. Beat in eggs until smooth. Stir in cheese and onion. Drop dough by scant teaspoonfuls 1 inch apart onto lightly greased baking sheet. Bake until puffed and golden, 20 to 25 minutes.   ABOUT 6 DOZEN PUFFS.

Tip-Top Puffs: Place pimiento-stuffed olive or ½-inch-square cheese slice (⅛ inch thick) on each puff. Bake as directed.

Filled Puffs: Place salted peanut, ½-inch ham or bologna cube or half of pimiento-stuffed olive on each puff. Top with enough dough to cover. Bake as directed.

Lemony Bouillon and Snacks

6 cans (13¾ ounces each) chicken broth
2 tablespoons grated lemon peel
  Juice of 2 medium lemons (4 to 6
    tablespoons)
2 bay leaves
½ cup snipped parsley
2 lemons, each cut into 10 wedges

Heat broth, lemon peel, lemon juice and bay leaves to boiling in 3-quart saucepan over medium heat; remove from heat. Stir in parsley; garnish with lemon wedges.
ABOUT 20 SERVINGS (½ CUP EACH).

SHRIMP-CHEESE SPREAD

Place 3 packages (8 ounces each) cream cheese on serving tray. Pour ½ cup shrimp cocktail sauce on each block of cheese. Top each block with 1 can (4¼ ounces) deveined tiny shrimp, rinsed and drained. Serve with crackers.
18 TO 20 SERVINGS.

AVOCADO SANDWICHES

1 medium avocado, pared and pitted
1 package (3 ounces) cream cheese, softened
1 teaspoon anchovy paste
1 teaspoon lemon juice
1 teaspoon onion juice
1 jar (2 ounces) broken pimiento-stuffed
    olives, chopped
21 slices day-old white sandwich bread

Mash avocado. Stir in cream cheese, anchovy paste, lemon juice, onion juice and olives. Trim crusts from bread; spread avocado mixture over bread. Cut each bread slice into 4 fingers or squares. Cover and refrigerate no longer than 2 hours.   ABOUT 7 DOZEN SANDWICHES.

Cut avocado in half against seed. Twist to separate parts.

To remove seed, strike with knife. Twist seed gently; lift.

Corn Bread Canapés

Spread the bean mixture over cooled Corn Bread in pan.

Cut Corn Bread into rectangles; place on serving tray.

Layer the lettuce and ham rectangles on Corn Bread.

Cut the cheese with 1¾-inch canapé cutters or knife.

Corn Bread (below)
1 can (16 ounces) pork and beans, drained
2 green onions, chopped (about 2
   tablespoons)
2 tablespoons catsup
1 teaspoon Worcestershire sauce
½ teaspoon prepared mustard
¼ teaspoon liquid smoke
5 or 6 medium lettuce leaves
½ pound thinly sliced ham
8 slices American cheese

Bake Corn Bread. Mash pork and beans thoroughly. Stir in onions, catsup, Worcestershire sauce, mustard and liquid smoke. Spread over Corn Bread. Cut into 30 rectangles, about 2½x2 inches. Place on serving tray. Cut lettuce and ham slices into 30 rectangles each, about 2½x2 inches; layer on Corn Bread. Cut cheese with 1¾-inch canapé cutters or knife; place cheese cutouts on ham. Refrigerate until serving time.　2½ DOZEN CANAPES.

CORN BREAD
1 cup all-purpose flour*
1 cup yellow cornmeal
1 cup milk
¼ cup shortening
1 egg
2 tablespoons sugar
4 teaspoons baking powder
½ teaspoon salt

Heat oven to 400°. Grease jelly roll pan, 15½x10½x1 inch. Blend all ingredients about 20 seconds. Beat vigorously 1 minute. Pour into pan. Bake until golden brown, 10 to 12 minutes. Cool.

*If using self-rising flour, reduce baking powder to 2 teaspoons and omit salt.

Freezer Canapés

Trim crust from day-old unsliced loaf whole wheat, rye or white sandwich bread. Cut loaf horizontally into ½-inch slices. Spread softened butter or margarine lightly over each slice; cut into desired shapes. Spread about ½ teaspoonful of spread (below) to edge of each canapé.

Place canapés on cardboard tray; cover with plastic wrap. Wrap with aluminum foil and label; freeze up to 2 months.

■**1 hour before serving,** remove aluminum foil from tray and let stand at room temperature covered with plastic wrap. Garnish canapés with thinly sliced radishes, sliced pitted ripe olives, sliced pimiento-stuffed olives, celery leaves or snipped parsley.   6 to 8 DOZEN CANAPES.

Cut unsliced loaf horizontally into ½-inch slices.

Cut slices into 1- to 1½-inch shapes with a cutter.

SHRIMP SPREAD

Mix 1 can (4¼ ounces) broken shrimp, drained and finely chopped, 3 tablespoons mayonnaise or salad dressing, 2 tablespoons finely chopped celery, 1 tablespoon chili sauce and ¼ teaspoon instant minced onion.
¾ CUP SPREAD (ENOUGH FOR 3 DOZEN 1-INCH CANAPES).

TUNA SPREAD

Mix 1 can (6½ ounces) tuna, drained, 1 package (3 ounces) cream cheese, softened, and ¼ teaspoon red pepper sauce.
1 CUP SPREAD (ENOUGH FOR 4 DOZEN 1-INCH CANAPES).

HAM AND CHEESE SPREAD

Mix 1 can (4½ ounces) deviled ham, ½ cup shredded sharp Cheddar cheese, 3 tablespoons mayonnaise or salad dressing and ¼ teaspoon onion juice.
1 CUP SPREAD (ENOUGH FOR 4 DOZEN 1-INCH CANAPES).

Stir cheese, bacon, peanuts and sliced green onions into the mayonnaise mixture.

Spread about 3 tablespoons of the bacon mixture over each slice of bread; bake.

Bacon Squares

1 cup mayonnaise or salad dressing
2 teaspoons Worcestershire sauce
½ teaspoon salad seasoning
¼ teaspoon paprika
2 cups shredded Cheddar cheese (about 8 ounces)
8 slices bacon, crisply fried and crumbled
⅓ cup chopped peanuts
4 green onions, sliced (about ¼ cup)
14 slices white bread

Heat oven to 400°. Mix mayonnaise, Worcestershire sauce, salad seasoning and paprika. Stir in cheese, bacon, peanuts and onions. Spread about 3 tablespoons bacon mixture over each slice of bread. Bake on ungreased baking sheet 10 minutes. Cut each slice into 4 pieces. Serve hot. 56 APPETIZERS.

Golden Nectar

2 cans (6 ounces each) frozen orange juice concentrate
1 can (46 ounces) pineapple juice
7 cups apricot nectar
1 cup lemon juice
2 bottles (28 ounces each) ginger ale, chilled

Prepare orange juice as directed on cans. Add pineapple juice, apricot nectar and lemon juice. Refrigerate until chilled. Just before serving, stir in ginger ale.   50 SERVINGS (ABOUT ½ CUP EACH).

Do-Ahead Mushroom Rounds

6 slices white or whole wheat bread
2 tablespoons butter or margarine, melted
10 medium mushrooms, very finely chopped
   (about 1¼ cups)*
1 tablespoon butter or margarine
½ teaspoon garlic salt
2 tablespoons cut-up pimiento, drained

Heat oven to 400°. Cut each bread slice into four 1½-inch circles; brush one side of bread circles with 2 tablespoons melted butter. Place buttered sides down on ungreased baking sheet. Bake bread circles until bottoms are light brown, about 5 minutes.

Cook and stir mushrooms in 1 tablespoon butter over low heat until mushrooms are brown, about 5 minutes. Stir in garlic salt. Spread about ½ teaspoon mushroom mixture on unbuttered side of each bread circle. Cover and refrigerate up to 24 hours.

■15 minutes before serving, heat oven to 350°. Garnish each round with small piece pimento. Bake about 4 minutes. 24 ROUNDS.

*1 can (8 ounces) mushroom stems and pieces, drained and finely chopped, can be substituted for the fresh mushrooms.

Cut each of the bread slices into four 1½-inch circles.

To save time, use two French knives to chop mushrooms.

Chive-Cheese Rolls

Cut hard rolls or sourdough French rolls in half.

Spread each cut side with cheese mixture; broil.

1½ cups shredded mozzarella cheese (about
    6 ounces)
⅓ cup green goddess salad dressing
¼ cup butter or margarine, softened
3 tablespoons snipped chives
8 hard rolls or sourdough French rolls

Mix cheese, salad dressing, butter and chives. Cut rolls horizontally in half. If necessary, cut small slice from rounded bottom of each roll to avoid tipping. Spread each cut side with cheese mixture.

Just before serving, set oven control to broil and/or 550°. Broil with tops 4 to 5 inches from heat until topping is bubbly.   16 SERVINGS.

BREADS AND SPREADS

When you're in a party mood, but your budget isn't, think about an easy, inexpensive bread-fest. You can bake or buy an assortment of crunchy, soft, sweet and sour breads in a variety of shapes and sizes. Serve them on boards accompanied by seasoned or flavored butters that you have molded ahead in fanciful butter molds or placed in butter crocks. If your budget can stretch, add cheese, cold meats, raw vegetables and fruits. It's old-fashioned and it's fun!

Dill Yogurt Cup

1 can (10¾ ounces) condensed tomato soup, chilled
1 carton (8 ounces) unflavored yogurt
¼ cup water
1 unpared medium cucumber, cut into thick slices
1 medium tomato, chopped (about ¾ cup)
1 teaspoon Worcestershire sauce
¼ teaspoon salt
¼ teaspoon dried dill weed

Place all ingredients in blender container. Cover and blend on high speed until smooth, about 30 seconds. Serve over ice.   6 SERVINGS (ABOUT ⅔ CUP EACH).

Curry Tomato Cup: Substitute ½ teaspoon curry powder for the dried dill weed.

Snack Thins

1 cup biscuit baking mix
½ cup shredded sharp Cheddar cheese (about 2 ounces)
¼ cup cold water
1½ teaspoons instant minced onion
1 can (5 ounces) Vienna sausages, drained

Heat oven to 400°. Stir baking mix, cheese, water and onion until a soft dough forms. Pat dough with floured hands or roll with floured rolling pin into oblong, 14x11 inches, on greased baking sheet, 15½x12 inches.

Cut each of 3 sausages lengthwise into 4 strips. Cut each of remaining 4 sausages crosswise into 6 slices. Press into dough. Bake until golden brown, 8 to 10 minutes. Cut into strips; serve warm.   6 SERVINGS.

Pat dough with floured hands into oblong on baking sheet.

Press the sausage strips and slices into dough, then bake.

Stir beans, tomato sauce, seasonings, onion and green pepper into the ground beef.

Spread beef mixture in pie plate. Spread with Sour Cream Topping, lettuce and cheese.

Cranberry Sparkle

Fill wine glasses or cups ½ to ⅔ full with chilled cranberry juice cocktail. Pour chilled sparkling white wine or champagne almost to top of each glass.

Mexi-Dip

½ pound ground beef
1 can (16 ounces) mashed refried beans
1 can (8 ounces) tomato sauce
1 package (1¼ ounces) taco seasoning mix
1 small onion, finely chopped (about ¼ cup)
½ medium green pepper, finely chopped (about ¼ cup)
½ teaspoon dry mustard
¼ to ½ teaspoon chili powder
Sour Cream Topping (below)
Finely shredded lettuce
Shredded Cheddar cheese
Corn chips

Cook and stir ground beef in skillet until brown; drain. Stir in beans, tomato sauce, seasoning mix, onion, green pepper, mustard and chili powder. Heat to boiling, stirring constantly. Spread in ungreased 9-inch pie plate. Spread Sour Cream Topping over ground beef mixture; sprinkle with shredded lettuce and cheese. Serve with corn chips. 3½ CUPS DIP.

SOUR CREAM TOPPING
Mix 1 cup dairy sour cream, 2 tablespoons grated American cheese food and ¼ teaspoon chili powder.

Meatballs and Jalapeño Dip

2 pounds ground beef
2 eggs
⅔ cup dry bread crumbs
1 medium onion, chopped (about ½ cup)
½ cup milk
¼ cup toasted sesame seed
¼ cup snipped parsley
2 teaspoons Worcestershire sauce
1½ teaspoons salt
1 teaspoon prepared horseradish
¼ teaspoon pepper
    Jalapeño Dip (below)

Heat oven to 400°. Mix all ingredients except Jalapeño Dip. Shape ground beef mixture by spoonfuls into 1¼-inch balls. (For easy shaping, dip hands in cold water from time to time.) Place meatballs in 2 ungreased baking pans, 13x9x2 or 15½x10½x1 inch. Bake uncovered until light brown, about 20 minutes; drain. Serve with Jalapeño Dip.
7 TO 9 DOZEN MEATBALLS.

JALAPEÑO DIP

2 jalapeño chili peppers, drained
2 tablespoons butter or margarine
1 package (16 ounces) pasteurized process
    cheese spread, cut up
1 medium tomato, peeled and chopped (about
    ¾ cup)

Remove stems, seeds and membrane from peppers; chop peppers. Heat butter in 1-quart saucepan over low heat until melted. Stir in cheese; cook and stir until cheese is melted. Stir peppers and tomato into cheese mixture; heat until tomato is hot.

Toast the sesame seed in 350° oven until golden, about 10 minutes, stirring occasionally.

Remove stems, seeds and membrane from the jalapeño chili peppers; chop peppers.

Cut up cheese spread; cook and stir until melted.

Stir the peppers and tomato into cheese mixture.

Pizza Fondue

2 tablespoons cornstarch
2 cans (10½ ounces each) pizza sauce with cheese
¼ pound pepperoni, finely chopped
1 tablespoon instant minced onion
1 teaspoon dried oregano leaves
1 package (16 ounces) pasteurized process cheese food, cut into ½-inch cubes
1 tablespoon snipped parsley
3 or 4 drops red pepper sauce
Vegetable Dippers (below)

Mix cornstarch and ½ cup of the pizza sauce; stir in the remaining pizza sauce.

Stir the cheese cubes into hot mixture, ½ cup at a time, until the cheese is melted.

Mix cornstarch and ½ cup of the pizza sauce in 2-quart saucepan; stir in remaining pizza sauce. Add pepperoni, onion and oregano. Heat to boiling, stirring constantly. Boil and stir 1 minute; remove from heat. Stir in cheese, ½ cup at a time, until melted. Stir in parsley and pepper sauce. Pour into fondue pot to keep warm. Spear Vegetable Dippers and swirl them in fondue.   8 SERVINGS.

VEGETABLE DIPPERS
Serve the following in small bowls: 1 cup cherry tomatoes, 1 green pepper, cut into pieces, 8 breadsticks, cut into 1-inch pieces, and ½ cup fresh mushroom halves or 1 can (4 ounces) button mushrooms, drained.

Cheese Mound

1 jar (5 ounces) pasteurized process sharp
   cheese spread
1 cup finely crushed soda crackers
¼ cup butter or margarine
1 teaspoon instant minced onion
¼ teaspoon liquid smoke
½ cup snipped parsley
   Cucumber slices
   Snack crackers

Mix cheese, cracker crumbs, butter, onion and liquid smoke in small mixer bowl on medium speed until smooth, about 3 minutes; shape into a mound and roll in parsley. Cover and refrigerate 12 hours. Garnish with cucumber slices. Serve with crackers. 8 TO 12 SERVINGS.

Shape mixture into a mound.

Roll mound in snipped parsley.

Antipasto-Bobs

½ pound summer sausage or pepperoni,
   sliced and cut into wedges
2 large stalks celery, cut diagonally into
   1-inch slices (about 1½ cups)
1 can (14 ounces) artichoke hearts, drained
   and cut into fourths
1 cup cherry tomatoes, cut in half
1 cup pitted ripe olives
½ cup mayonnaise or salad dressing
1 tablespoon milk
¼ teaspoon garlic powder

Alternate sausage, celery, artichoke hearts, tomatoes and olives on 6-inch skewers. Arrange on serving tray. Mix mayonnaise, milk and garlic powder; serve with kabobs. 8 TO 12 SERVINGS.

Garden Cheesecake

For best results, crush only about ⅓ of the cheese snack crackers at a time in blender.

Add seasonings to the cheese mixture and vegetables in blender; blend on low speed.

Pour vegetable mixture over crumb base in springform pan.

Sprinkle with the reserved crumbs; refrigerate 24 hours.

2½ cups crushed cheese snack crackers
½ cup butter or margarine, melted
1 package (8 ounces) cream cheese, softened
1 carton (8 ounces) unflavored yogurt
½ cup pimiento-stuffed olives
1 medium green pepper, cut into large pieces
1 small onion, cut into fourths
1 medium stalk celery, cut into 1-inch pieces
1 teaspoon salt
1 teaspoon Worcestershire sauce
¼ teaspoon paprika
Dash of red pepper sauce
Assorted raw vegetables

Mix cracker crumbs and butter. Reserve half of the crumb mixture. Press remaining crumb mixture firmly and evenly in bottom of ungreased 9-inch springform pan.

Place cheese and yogurt in blender container. Cover and blend on low speed just until smooth. Add olives, green pepper pieces, onion, celery pieces, salt, Worcestershire sauce, paprika and pepper sauce. Blend on low speed just until vegetables are finely chopped. Pour over crumb base. Sprinkle with reserved crumbs. Refrigerate 24 hours before serving. Serve with raw vegetables.   16 SERVINGS.

Graham Wafers with Spreads

1 cup graham or whole wheat flour
1 cup all-purpose flour*
1 cup yellow cornmeal
3 tablespoons sugar
1¼ teaspoons baking soda
1 teaspoon salt
1 cup buttermilk
¼ cup vegetable oil
Deviled Ham Spread, Honey Spread and
Sesame Spread (below)

Heat oven to 350°. Mix flours, cornmeal, sugar, baking soda and salt. Stir in buttermilk and oil. Shape dough into 6 balls. Roll each ball into very thin 9-inch square on floured cloth-covered board. Cut into 3-inch squares. (Dough can be rerolled.) Place squares on ungreased baking sheet. Bake until crisp and golden, 8 to 10 minutes. Serve with spreads.   ABOUT 6 DOZEN WAFERS.

*If using self-rising flour, omit baking soda and salt.

DEVILED HAM SPREAD

Mix 1 can (4¼ ounces) deviled ham, 1 package (3 ounces) cream cheese, softened, 1 tablespoon mayonnaise or salad dressing and 1 teaspoon finely chopped green onion. Refrigerate until serving time.

HONEY SPREAD

Beat 1 package (3 ounces) cream cheese, softened, and 2 tablespoons honey until thoroughly blended.

SESAME SPREAD

Mix ½ cup butter or margarine, softened, and 2 tablespoons toasted sesame seed.

Shape dough into 6 balls; roll each into thin 9-inch square.

Cut into 3-inch squares and place on baking sheet; bake.

Index